MW01029949

PRAISE FOR *THE END OF TWO ILLUSIONS*

"This book should have been written a long time ago. It is the first bold and incisive deconstruction of the greatest fabricated binary of this century: 'Islam and the West.' This old Orientalist and destructive juxtaposition has survived until today and provided the moral justification for the brutal American assaults on Afghanistan and Iraq. This book offers a different genealogy for the emergence of this constructed binary, positioned one against the other in a poisonous, and artificial, relationship. Hamid Dabashi forcefully challenges this dangerous concept of 'Islam and the West,' offering an alternative de-racialized and humane perspective—visions of the past and future that will be essential for all who are embroiled and affected by this insidious and violent construct. Scholars and the wider audience will find in this book an accessible, honest, and very readable critique of a notion that impacts the lives of so many of us in this century."

ILAN PAPPÉ, Professor of History and Director of the European Centre for Palestine Studies, University of Exeter

"'Islam and the West' is a gnoseological invention (not a 'representation') cast in the binary logic undergirding the idea of Western Civilization. Dabashi's convincing and powerful argument is the call to extricate ourselves from this and all binary illusions that shatter thinking in order to manage subjective and intersubjective relations."

WALTER D. MIGNOLO, author of *The Politics of Decolonial Investigations*

"Dabashi, with all the erudition of a distinguished scholar, takes on and demolishes a fiction that has long been accepted as truth: that something called the 'West' and 'Islam' actually exist. This book both pushes back against mainstream and right-wing authors and takes on scholarly work that falls into the trap of creating an essentialized West. It then draws on millennia of history to expose the limitations of the 'Islam and the West' framework. This brilliant book is an important intervention at this historical moment when the empire of capital has assumed new forms to legitimate itself."

DEEPA KUMAR, Professor of Media Studies at Rutgers University and author of *Islamophobia and the Politics of Empire: 20 Years after 9/11*

The End of Two Illusions

ISLAM AFTER THE WEST

Hamid Dabashi

 UNIVERSITY OF CALIFORNIA PRESS

University of California Press
Oakland, California

© 2022 by Hamid Dabashi

Library of Congress Cataloging-in-Publication Data

Names: Dabashi, Hamid, 1951– author.
Title: The end of two illusions : Islam after the West / Hamid Dabashi.
Description: Oakland, California : University of California Press, [2022] |
    Includes bibliographical references and index.
Identifiers: LCCN 2021046891 (print) | LCCN 2021046892 (ebook) |
    ISBN 9780520376922 (cloth) | ISBN 9780520376939 (paperback) |
    ISBN 9780520976320 (epub)
Subjects: LCSH: Islam—History. | Islam and world politics. | East and West.
Classification: LCC DS37.7 .D33 2022 (print) | LCC DS37.7 (ebook) |
    DDC 297.2/72—dc23/eng/20211104
LC record available at https://lccn.loc.gov/2021046891
LC ebook record available at https://lccn.loc.gov/2021046892

31 30 29 28 27 26 25 24 23 22
10 9 8 7 6 5 4 3 2 1

For YASIR SULEIMAN
In Friendship and with Gratitude

Mirror, Mirror on the wall, who's the fairest of them all?

—*SNOW WHITE AND THE SEVEN DWARFS* (1937)

Contents

Acknowledgments

This book has been in the making for quite a long time. At least since the events of 9/11 in 2001 I have been thinking, reading, and writing on the subject matter of this book. But even before 9/11 I cannot even remember a time when this bizarre binary opposition presumed between "Islam and the West" had not given me an occasion to pause and wonder. Islam is a religion, of which I have been a student all my adult life; the West is a geographical designation, where I have lived and studied and taught for much of my adult life. How could these two entities, apples and oranges, as it were, be placed next to each other? Their transfigurations into two allegorical designations are precisely where my thinking began to take shape. The writing of this book is the final result of that thinking.

Naomi Schneider, executive editor at University of California Press, has been instrumental in seeing this book to fruition. Without her enduring commitment, professional steadfastness, and sustained encouragements, I would have been lost in the labyrinth of thinking this book through. Two anonymous reviewers have taken time to offer me detailed and constructive comments on an earlier draft. I am grateful to them. My research assistant, Toga Mohamed Badran, has been definitive to my research with her uncanny ability to locate obscure books and articles for me. She has a magic touch in her inroads into the back alleys of the internet.

Gil Hochberg, the chair of my department at Columbia, has been graciously accommodating with my writing habits. She is a blessing as our fearless leader! Joseph Massad is my closest friend, colleague, and interlocutor on the Columbia campus. His proximity and friendship to me is the last solace after we both lost Edward Said and Magda al-Nowaihi. Massad's exquisite text, *Islam in Liberalism* (2017), has been as crucial for my deliberations in this book as Edward Said's iconic *Orientalism* (1978). Their pioneering work forms the premises of my own.

My young colleague at Barnard College, Atefeh Akbari Shahmirzadi, has been a source of kindness and reassurances at these dire times. I cherish her friendship. Over the last few years, I have been increasingly blessed with the friendship of my other distinguished colleague, Ali Mirsepassi. I treasure his friendship and wise counsel. Mahmoud Omidsalar is the singular source of my peace of mind and scholarly confidence. He and I come from a deep tradition of textual hermeneutics that has very few traces left on North American campuses. Even when I am not texting or calling him to chat about sources, I am talking to him in my mind about critical editions. I deeply admire him and am blessed with his enduring friendship. Ismail Nashef, the distinguished Palestinian scholar of social sciences and humanities, has been another consistent source of inspiration for me. The bold, bright, and magnificent Ramin Bahrani, the dazzling filmmaker of uncommon brilliance, who began as my student and emerged as a dear close friend, adds a daily dose of grace and care in my life. Because of the COVID pandemic and other pressing conditions of our lives, I do not see these friends as much as I wish. But they are the shining stars sparkling in my darkest nights.

Abr-o Bad-o Mah-o Khorshid-o Falak (the Cloud, the Wind, the Moon, the Sun, and the Firmament), as the inimitable Sa'di says in a poem, have been at work to enable me to sit and bask in moments of peace and write this book. Thank you, friends!

Hamid Dabashi
New York
Spring 2021

Introduction
The Future of Two Illusions

A whole world riding upon an illusion—
Upon an illusion their war and their peace,
Upon an illusion their pride and their shame—
RUMI, *Masnavi* (1258–1273)

In mid-November 2019, as the prospect of an impeachment inquiry was haunting Donald Trump's presidency, of which he was later acquitted in the US Senate, yet another scandalous story broke out. The Southern Poverty Law Center, a highly reliable and widely respected civil rights and anti-racist stronghold, broke the news that Stephen Miller, a Trump White House speechwriter and trusted adviser to the US president, had been the author of hundreds of emails to the editors of *Breitbart News*, a white supremacist organ, exposing the man's obsession with immigration from Latin America and Muslim-majority countries into the United States. He did not like the idea. "An analysis of more than 900 emails from Miller to editors at Breitbart News," as Jamelle Bouie of the *New York Times* put it, citing the report, "shows Miller's single-minded focus on nonwhite immigration and his immersion in an online ecosystem of virulent, unapologetic racism. The Miller of these emails isn't just an immigration restrictionist, he's an ideological white nationalist."[1]

Mr. Miller was quite a powerful figure in Trump's White House, as Jamelle Bouie put it:

> The first travel ban, rolled out within days of President Trump's inauguration? That was Miller. Family separation at the border? That was Miller too. The relentless effort to limit asylum, deport protected migrants and block refugees from entering the country? Also Miller. The president's January address from the Oval Office, in which he spun gruesome tales of immigrant crime and violence ("In California, an Air Force veteran was raped, murdered and beaten to death with a hammer by an illegal alien with a long criminal history")? Stephen Miller.[2]

Among the revelations of this investigation was also the discovery of "a September 2015 email, in which Miller encouraged McHugh [his contact at the racist venue] "to show 'the parallels' between Pope Francis's pro-refugee statements and 'The Camp of the Saints,'" a 1973 novel by the French author Jean Raspail. In the book, an influx of Indian refugees—described as subhuman and led by a feces-eating demagogue—storm France, killing, stealing, and rampaging until they've completely occupied the country. Other migrants follow and eventually overrun Western Europe, turning white Europeans into a subject class.

Whence this animus, wherefor this hatred, to what purpose this xenophobia that is deeply rooted in an almost inexplicable fear of foreigners in general, and Muslims in particular?

Fear of Foreigners

In the actual report of the Southern Poverty Law Center, "Stephen Miller's Affinity for White Nationalism Revealed in Leaked Emails," we read in far more details about Miller's hatred of all sorts of non-white immigrants, chief among them Muslims.[3] Miller himself is from a family that recently immigrated from Belarus. How is it that he has forgotten or repressed his own immigrant background and so viscerally hates other immigrants, especially if they are Muslim? Boasting of his contacts with Pamela Geller, a notorious Islamophobe, Miller writes to his like-minded comrades: "I suggested Pamela Gellar [sic] do this to illustrate the absurdity of the Left's theory that you can't do anything which violates the tenets of fundamentalist Islam. What is more important to the Left: their 'gay rights' agenda, or appeasing Islamist immigrants?"

The story of Stephen Miller and his visceral hatred of Muslims and other immigrants while sitting right in the White House was neither unique nor limited to the United States. Anti-Muslim hatred and violent extremism targeting Muslims had been on the rise throughout Europe, the United States, Australia, and New Zealand for decades. With Stephen Miller that hatred had officially entered the highest elected office of the United States government. But the Trump administration was tapping into a much more powerful repertoire of Islamophobia that traveled from one end of the political spectrum to the other. From the Oklahoma bombing of 1995 to the mass murder in Norway in 2011, both committed by white supremacist terrorists, Muslims were first to be blamed before any solid facts were known. Both liberal and conservative venues were quick to blame Muslims for any act of public violence, to the point that the term *terrorist* has become synonymous with Islam and being a Muslim. I have already written about the systematic manner in which Muslims have become the very metaphors for hatred, fanaticism, and violence.[4] Other caring and competent scholars like Peter Gottschalk and Gabriel Greenberg in their *Islamophobia: Making Muslims the Enemy* (2007), Deepa Kumar in her *Islamophobia and the Politics of Empire* (2012), Khaled A. Beydoun in his *American*

Islamophobia: Understanding the Roots and Rise of Fear (2018), and Peter Morey, Amina Yaqin, and Alaya Forte in their edited volume, *Contesting Islamophobia* (2019) have written extensively on the fertile ground of hatred and prejudice targeting Muslim communities living in the United States or Europe. Whence this hatred, wherefore this bizarre fixation with making Muslims, just for the accident of being Muslims, the enemy of reason, sanity, and civilization?

Underlying all such antipathy is the unexamined presumption of an innate hostility between "Islam" and "the West"—two vast abstractions with frightening powers of persuasion. The constitution of this binary is predicated on a false but powerful presumption perhaps most effectively articulated by Samuel Huntington in his idea of the "clash of civilizations."[5] This presumed opposition between "Islam" and "the West" corresponds to a particular period of globalized capital when its innate and debilitating contradictions are in need of a fictive center and a global periphery cast as culturally inferior to "the West"—ready for abuse, plunder, and domination. Islam, as the inferior of these two ends, was systematically cast as a deranged culture destined to be ruled by white Christians. At this point, however, we need to overcome this binary. The simple fact is we have transcended it; the condition of empire is no longer bipolar but entirely amorphous. Yet a false consciousness, rooted in the nineteenth-century concept of Europe as the epicenter of civilization, continues to rely on its authenticity, especially after 9/11, which is given outsized importance at the expense of far more immediate, mundane, and political reasons. The works of Huntington, together with those of Francis Fukuyama, Bernard Lewis, and Alan Bloom, demonstrate a collective fear of losing the stronghold of white Christian supremacy. The power of this false consciousness is politically manufactured and was intensified after the election of Donald Trump. But the fact is the patterns of migration around the world are rendering these fictive frontiers between "the West" and "the

Rest" entirely obsolete, and thus Islamophobia provides a fodder for the vacuous but dangerous ideologies of white supremacy.

The objective of Islamophobic leaders in the United States and Europe, as well as Australia and New Zealand, is to end all Muslim migration to their lands. With the outbreak of COVID-19, Islamophobia has exposed its deeper xenophobic roots. "Muslim immigration is tied directly to Islamic terror": that is the mantra of leading Islamophobes like Pamela Geller and Stephen Miller.[6] It is precisely the fear and loathing embedded in that phrase that is in dire need of dismantling. But how exactly is that dismantling to be done?

Ghosts of Terrors Past

The Arab and Muslim identity of the assailants in the attacks against the United States on 9/11 and the subsequent US military campaigns against Afghanistan in the fall 2001 and Iraq in the spring of 2003, followed by an open-ended "war on terrorism," once again gave new life to the tired cliché of hostility between "Islam" and "the West." The underlying assumption was that this war represented yet another example of the irreconcilable differences between two civilizations: between the European Enlightenment and Islamic fundamentalism. Professional warmongers (Samuel Huntington) and born-again Orientalists (Bernard Lewis) who have built careers on this flawed assumption went on a rampage, solidifying the illusion of irreconcilable and transcendental hostility. This assumption is wrong; this binary opposition is fictitious, and a very recent colonial invention; as such, it has wreaked havoc in modern history. It has now exhausted its destructive course. This book is a nail in its coffin.

What I propose in this book may seem entirely counterintuitive. Precisely at a time when the whole world testifies to a *rise* in Islamic militancy, I propose the *end* of Islamism as one of the most potent political ideologies of the last two hundred years. And exactly at a moment when there is a militant crescendo in defense of "Western civilization," I suggest the final collapse of that colonial fabrication. What today is referred to with iconic certitude as 9/11 was the cataclysmic culmination of a colonially construed binary opposition between "Islam" and "the West." The planes that were crashed into the twin towers of the World Trade Center also collapsed the twin towers of "Islam" and "the West" as a representation of enduring hostility.

The US campaign against Iraq and the military operation in Afghanistan that immediately preceded and then accompanied it, as well as the illusory battle against terrorism, are not wars targeted against Muslims as Muslims. They are ideological wars against an abstraction code-named "Islam" launched from the premise of an even more vacuous abstraction called "the West." Many Muslim countries are effectively in the camp of the United States. Pakistan, Kuwait, UAE, Egypt, Bahrain, and Saudi Arabia are its military bases of operation. Jordan provides active and Turkey opportunistic support to US military campaigns. It is true that the populations of these Muslim countries overwhelmingly oppose such aggressions against their fellow Muslims, yet their unelected officials are completely incorporated into the US imperial project. Not even all Muslims oppose the US invasion of Iraq, as the active collaboration of the Muslim Kurdish population of Iraq with the invading army clearly testifies. This is a battle of abstractions with a deeply rooted material basis and benefits to it.

To understand the rising contours of the US empire—the geopolitics of its operation and the formative forces of its hegemony—it is imperative to begin to cultivate an accurate conception of the war against Iraq, of the previous wars in Afghanistan and Kuwait, and of the potential future wars in Iran, perhaps also with North Korea or even Russia and China. But no such accurate conception of the cumulative effects of these real and potential wars will emerge unless and until we discard the clichés and the assumption of a modern-day crusade against Islam, which is still predominant in both camps and predicated on a presumed binary opposition between "Islam" and "the West." This battle of abstractions has assumed a life of its own, overriding the far more urgent tasks the world faces. We need to dismantle, theorize, and overcome the delusional predicates of this battle.

The increasingly globalized migrations of labor, the amorphous nature of the capital it engenders, and the predatory militarism with which US imperialism is seeking to control and dominate these processes are entirely color-blind and faithless. The presence of Colin Powel and Condoleezza Rice among George W. Bush's top advisers and the inclusion of mercenary functionaries like Fouad Ajami, Zalmay Khalilzad, and Kanan Makiya among his less illustrious entourage bespeak more than just the equal-opportunity credentials of the Republican president who took Affirmative Action to the US Supreme Court. The emerging silhouette of the US empire needs a very careful reading, and there is no time to waste on outmoded clichés and superseded concepts. Now more than ever it is imperative to understand when and how the illusion of this binary opposition between "Islam" and "the West" emerged, and how and why it has now reached its last gasp of air. Then we can clear the air and move on to decipher and diagnose the real catastrophe we face: the rise of a predatory empire whose terms of hegemony are yet to be uttered and read.

My principal argument in this book is that the binary opposition "Islam and the West" is a very recent historical construct, born of a particular colonial project, and that with its political function concluded it is now entirely obsolete—having vacated the space it once occupied for a yet-to-be articulated set of alternatively dangerous configurations. To demonstrate this argument, I will first offer a perspective on Islam prior to its fateful encounter with European colonial modernity. Here I will begin with the charismatic tension that is constitutional to this faith in its historical conception and origin. I will then give an account of the composition of its premodern intellectual and discursive proclivities, before I demonstrate how with the rise of capitalist modernity it was transformed into a singular and exclusive site of ideological resistance to colonialism and thus lost the diversified texture of its multifaceted heritage, as it was mutated by Muslim ideologues into the mirror image of the paramount power they faced, which they called "the West."

Using this premise, I will then proceed to do a similar act of historical archeology, this time to provide the genealogy of what today we call "the West," and give an outline of the discursive process by which the historical emergence of capitalist modernity was narrated into the categorical conception of "the West." Here I will demonstrate how "the West" was constituted as a viable civilizational category covering and disguising the economic relation of power between globalized capital and abused labor. "The West" is a very recent conceptual invention, not earlier than the European bourgeois revolution, the concomitant emergence of the New Class, the collapse of dynastic and ecclesiastical orders, and the active formation of European national economies, polities, and cultures—all of which were brought under the generic rubric of "the West" and contrapuntally contrasted with the rest of humanity, now divided by mercenary Orientalists into various non-Western (Chinese, Indian, or Islamic) civilizations.

Once I historicize and locate "Islam" and "the West," I will then turn to the opposition that historically emerged between them. Here I will first give a detailed account of how both classical Orientalism and neo-Orientalism have been instrumental in fabricating, perpetuating, and authenticating this binary opposition; I will also demonstrate that when Orientalism was exposed as a colonial project—by

Edward Said in his magisterial achievement *Orientalism*—it was in fact paradoxically further ossified, fetishized, rarified, and consolidated. The cross-categorization of "Islam and the West" thus survived Said's intervention, first and foremost because the material basis of its continued validity persisted; second because Orientalists like Bernard Lewis and company dropped all pretensions to scholarship and went for an all-out assault, documenting the continued illusion of Manichean opposition of "Islam and the West"; and third because Said, due to his own invested interest in Enlightenment humanism, fell short of fully exposing the barbarity that European capitalist modernity has perpetrated upon the world. The dialectical fetishization of "Islam and the West"—not just "Islam" and "the West" but "Islam and the West" as a unit—survived the work of Said and his followers and continued undetected as the single most potent falsifying binary of our time. My contention in this book is not just that "the West" is a potent illusion, a subterfuge for the brutalities of capitalist modernity, but that anything it touches it turns into an illusion, rarifying it and gutting it of all historical complexity.

The power of the binary that persisted through Said's insights was picked up by subsequent seminal works such as Abdul R. JanMohamed's *Manichean Aesthetics: The Politics of Literature in Colonial Africa* (1983), as well as in the essays collected in Paul Gifford and Tessa Hauswedell's edited volume, *Europe and Its Others: Essays on Interperception and Identity* (2010), based on the proceedings of a conference held at St. Andrews University in 2007. More poignantly, in his brilliant essay "The Fetish of 'the West' in Postcolonial Theory," Neil Lazarus rightly took the whole postcolonial project coagulating around the concept of "the West" to task:

One of the anchors of the postcolonialist critique, latent in the very term "Eurocentrism," has been the fetish of "Europe" or "the West." ... The concept of "the West" as it is used in postcolonial theory, I want to argue, has no coherent or credible referent. It is an ideological category masquerading as a geographic one, just as—in the context of modern Orientalist discourse—"Islam" is an ideological category masquerading as a religious one.[7]

Most these studies have been preoccupied, and correctly so, with the false binaries produced by and through the dominant colonial thinking that these thinkers have sought to articulate and map out. Predicated on my much earlier work, in my own most recent books, such as *The Arab Spring: The End of Postcolonialism* (2012), *Can Non-Europeans Think?* (2015), *Europe and Its Shadows: Coloniality after Empire* (2019), and *The Emperor Is Naked: On the Inevitable Demise of the Nation-State* (2020), I have extended these arguments to the brink of detecting emancipatory avenues out of the cul-de-sac of such inherited binaries. It is this latter state that is my point of departure in this book, to no longer be reactive and plaintive about such binaries but to be proactive and altogether overcome them. This is where my argument of the epistemic exhaustion of "Islam and the West" as two confounding illusions finds its potent relevance. I make this argument not based on just epistemological grounds, but entirely on the material fact of a stage of capitalist postmodernity that has devoured its own ideological foregrounding and metaphoric repertoires. Critical thinkers like Lazarus have rightly underlined the fetishized commodity that calls itself "the West" and correctly criticized those postcolonial theorists who have further contributed to this fetishization. Here in this book, however, I examine the contagious disposition of that fetishized commodity, by virtue of its ideological hegemony, when it pairs itself with "the Rest" or "the East" or more specifically "Islam." It is this pairing that is of immediate interest to me in this book. The transmutation of Islam into a metaphor is the by-product of the fetishized commodity that calls itself "the West."

While appreciative of much that post-Saidian postcolonialists have done, Lazarus rightly points out:

> It seems to me that the way in which "Europe" has been conceptualized by the "provincializers" fatally undermines the efficacy of their critique. For in their hypostatization of "modernity" and "the West"—their dematerialization of capitalism, their misrecognition of its world-historical significance, their construal of it in civilizational terms, as "modernity"—these theorists ... seem to me to render the structurality of the global system either arbitrary or unintelligible.[8]

But what Lazarus disregards, and I underline, is that the fetishization of "the West" did not begin with Said or his followers. It began with "the West" itself—with the ideologues of its own capitalist modernity. Neither Oswald Spengler's *The Decline of the West* (1918) nor Niall Ferguson's *Civilization: The West and the Rest* (2012) nor countless other similar titles in between these two samples are exactly the highlights of postcolonial thinking! Said was not a Marxist and had no such claims either. He was a literary critic through and through, with ingrained liberal proclivities dominant on North American campuses, of which he was an illustrious product. His problem was to take the self-fetishization of "the West" on face value and set upon himself the task of mapping out the contours of its catalytic effect, and he did that task marvelously, but never turning to the material foregrounding of this "Western" self-fetishization as its most potent ideological commodity. This was not his project. It is my project in this book—exposing "the West" itself as the fetishized ideological commodity, an illusion that turned anything it touched into a fetishized commodity too, in this case what it called "Islam." Said clearly and repeatedly saw "the West" as a myth, but he never thought of unearthing the commodified fetishism at the roots of that myth. I do. People and their dominant cultures do not just invent things. Things are invented in their collective consciousness or sub-consciousness for a material reason—in this case, the fetishized com-modification of relations of production and domination. It was the ideologues of "the West" itself, not Said and his followers, who fell into this trap of the false assumption of a "Western" center for the operation of capital and its colonial peripheries. The factual relation of power and production had implicated a fictitious center-periphery binary that Said never cared to dismantle. I do—and once we do that, a globalized pattern of the abuse of labor by capital emerges that is identical in its central European theater as it is at its falsely periph-eralized domains in Asia, Africa, and Latin America. The result is the collapse of the center-periphery binary altogether. Colonialism, as I always tell my students at Columbia, is not something that hap-pens "over there," and capital something that is accumulated "over here." Colonialism is something that happens here, there, and every-where. Sweatshops in a Manhattan garment industry neighborhood are as abusive of cheap labor as they are in Guatemala or Honduras. The beneficiaries of the capital are as much in New York, London, and Paris as they are in Cairo, Buenos Aires, or Delhi. Capitalism works like a quilt, not a solar system. Said was after exposing the relation of knowledge production between a fictious center and its equally fictious periphery. He did not invent that fiction. He took it for granted—and critically dismantled its aura of authenticity. With-out Said's work I would not be able to expose the very fictitious dis-position of that binary, which was rooted in the material interests of the transnational capital (not "the West"), and at the heavy cost of transnational labor (not the "Rest").

"The West" was the single most potent, the single most fetishized, ideological by-product of capitalist modernity. The Marxist idea of fetishized commodity was encapsulated in the very delusion of "the West," its crowning ideological achievement. The ideological commodification of "Islam," when placed right next to this commodified "West," was not the work of Orientalists alone. Muslim ideologues themselves, from Jamal al-Din al-Afghani, through Muhammad Abduh, down to Ali Shari'ati, were integral to this project, as I map out in detail in my *Theology of Discontent* (1993). Neither Said nor any of his followers were even slightly interested in this contrapuntal (Said's own term) commodification of "Islamic Ideology"—fixated as they have been, and rightly so, with the "Western" side of the dangerous delusion. I have been and I remain as much concerned with this commodification of "Islam" by the colonized minds of Muslims themselves as I am with the "West," and thus my simultaneous attention to the commodified binary of "Islam and the West."

It is crucial here to recall Marx's original theorization of commodity fetishism:

A commodity appears, at first sight, a very trivial thing, and easily understood. Its analysis shows that it is, in reality, a very queer thing, abounding in metaphysical subtleties and theological niceties. So far as it is a value in use, there is nothing mysterious about it, whether we consider it from the point of view that by its properties it is capable of satisfying human wants, or from the point that those properties are the product of human labor. It is as clear as noonday, that man, by his industry, changes the forms of the materials furnished by Nature, in such a way as to make them useful to him. The form of wood, for instance, is altered, by making a table out of it. Yet, for all that, the table continues to be that common, everyday thing, wood. But, as soon as it steps forth as a commodity, it is changed into something transcendent. It not only stands with its feet on the ground, but, in relation to all other commodities, it stands on its head, and evolves out of its wooden brain grotesque ideas, far more wonderful than "table turning" ever was.[9]

This is precisely what has happened to "the West" too, as the most powerful ideological commodity, sustaining the course of commodity fetishization as Marx originally formulated it. "The West" too at first sight appears a very trivial thing, and "easily understood." It is from Marx in fact that I have learned that the analysis of "the West" "shows that it is, in reality, a very queer thing, abounding in metaphysical subtleties and theological niceties." It is in precisely Marxist terms that we can see the origin of "the West" as a metaphysical and theological proposition—that when Marx was theorizing "religion" he was in fact theorizing "the West," unbeknownst to himself. As a fetishized totem, "the West" fetishizes everything else it touches, guts it out of its historical complexities and by the power of its hegemony turns it into an illusion too.

Said himself and his epoch-making book *Orientalism* should not be fetishized either. This seminal text must be placed in its own proper context. It is imperative to keep in mind that long before the publication of Said's book in 1978, the colonial and epistemological problems of Orientalism, of the relation between power and knowledge, had been raised from within specific disciplines, such as by Anouar Abdel-Malek in his *Orientalism in Crisis* (1963) and by Talal Assad in his *Anthropology and Colonial Encounter* (1973), as well as even earlier by Raymond Schwab in his *Oriental Renaissance* (1950).[10] An even longer philosophical and sociological lineage that extends from Nietzsche to Gramsci, Max Scheler, Karl Mannheim, George Herbert Mead, and Michel Foucault, among others, has exposed the roots of the way people have produced knowledge to twist uncomfortable facts to comforting fictions. Long after Said, too, certain liberal and even left branches of Arab and Islamic studies continued with the thematic explorations of Orientalism and the mystique of Islam in the European context. In his *Europe and the Mystique of Islam* (1988) Maxime Rodinson historicized the rise of Orientalism as a discipline against the background of earlier encounters and interfaces. Particularly important in this book is what Rodinson called "theologocentricism in scholarship," as he sought to rescue the field of Islamic studies from the bondage of Orientalism, and yet still remained rooted in his own critique in that Eurocentric imagination. In the collection of essays that Albert Hourani gathered in his *Islam in European Thought* (1991), he gave his perspective as a professor of history at Oxford of how a sustained course of imagining "Islam" had formed what he called, in a bit of Arabism, *Silsila*, at the root of Orientalism. Ivan Kelmar's *Early Orientalism: Imagined Islam and the Notion of Sublime Power* (2012) was an equally important attempt at distinguishing between what he called the "soft Orientalism" of Bishop Lowth and the "hard Orientalism" of Hegel, through which Kelmar sought to give a deeper theological explanation for the idea of "Oriental despotism" as a primarily Western Christian theological issue. By the time Bernard Cohn published his *Colonialism and Its Forms of Knowledge: The British in India* (1996), we had already evidence of the expansion of the issue far beyond Islamic domains. Even before Cohen, Enrique Dussel in his *Liberation Philosophy* (1972) and Y. V. Mudimbe in his magisterial book *The Invention of Africa* (1988) had revolutionized the epistemological revolt against the colonial disposition of Orientalism. I could not have brought my Marxist historiography to bear on the global circulation of knowledge and power in my own *Persophilia: Persian Culture on the Global Scene* (2015) were it not for these pathbreaking and pioneering works. In other words, a Marxist historiography can remain solid in its historical materialism but still learn from the spectrum of postcolonial theories without falling into the trap of their (perhaps inadvertent) cross-essentialism, which was only the reactive conjugation of the essentialism that had crafted the illusion of "the West" much earlier.

That brings us to the future (which is the present) of these twin illusions—in where and what they have now concluded as their

outdated case. At the dawn of globalization, Islam has lost its interlocutor: the illusion of "the West" has exhausted its instrumental
use value and is now only of an archival interest. With the commencement of the spiral crescendo of migratory labor and refugees mutating into globalized capital, that binary opposition that
once categorically separated the colonial from the capital is no longer valid or operative—nor is any illusory cultural or civilizational
divide that was presumed to accompany it. A shapeless, graceless,
monstrous barbarity is now assuming the militant posture of a global
empire—with racist dinosaurs like Stephen Miller hallucinating putting a stop to this force of history. The amorphous capital that this
empire seeks to serve is too atrocious to submit to any given hegemony. The specifics of any hegemony are not clear to this empire,
nor are the signs of the emerging modes of resistance to it. The articulation of the fury of that empire and the terms of resisting it are a
whole different story I should tell at some other time. For now it is
crucial to keep a record of our vanishing history of the present, sustain a vivid memory for our future forgetfulness, witness the return
of the imperially repressed, and zero in on places and loci where the
twain of "the West and the Rest" have already met and dismantled
each other—where the cross-section of race, gender, and nationality
are forcing the false binary to expose and dispense with each other.

The Power of Ideology/The Ideology of Power

Let me now take a quick look at the marketplace of ideas where the
twin nemeses of "Islam" and "the West" have been much drama-
tized. Over the last quarter of a century, in a succession of bestsellers, ranging from Francis Fukuyama's *The End of History and the
Last Man* (1993) to Samuel Huntington's *The Clash of Civilizations
and the Remaking of World Order* (1998) to Bernard Lewis's *What
Went Wrong? The Clash between Islam and Modernity in the Middle*

East (2002), just to name a few of the most popular titles, the civilizational opposition presumed between "Islam" and "the West" has assumed intensified and ominous proportions. Even in perhaps the most sober and level-headed among these sorts of highly popular books, a volume on the emergence of Islamist movements, *Jihad: The Trail of Political Islam* (2002), the French political scientist Gilles Kepel has joined this argument and (disregarding a whole slew of colonial and imperial circumstances) has given a full account of the serious upsurge of militant uprisings in much of the Muslim-majority world as an indication of the cosmic battle between "Islam" and "the West" or "Islam" and "modernity." This particular episteme has been used and abused, milked and mutilated ad absurdum. It has become something of a refrain that "Islam" is in existential opposition to "modernity" and thus to "the West."

In this series of highly influential and popular bestsellers, Islam is first placed in the immediate vicinity of "the West," and then a quintessential malady is detected in it, right before a genealogy of its political degeneration is diagnosed. In Gilles Kepel's estimation, for example, representing a wide spectrum of sentiments in Europe and the United States, the principal purpose of these Islamist movements is toward the establishment of "a global Islamic state based solely on a strict interpretation of the Koran." I believe that such assumptions, and indeed the generic sentiments that they represent, are wrong. In such analysis "the West" is an innocent bystander, minding its own business, when suddenly erupts this insane "Islam" targeting its venom against it. These are flawed arguments. "Islam and the West" are just one unit. They must be considered together, as two sides of the same outdated coin. In this book I wish to argue how the crescendo of Islamist movements over the last two hundred years, first, is a recent phenomenon and, second, has in fact come to an end and that we are at the commencement of an entirely different phase in the social history of Muslims and their collective faith. This is so because the Manichean duet of "Islam and the West" has exhausted its epistemic conjugations. It has run out of mischiefs to do. Under the thick and disorienting smokescreen of relentless contemporary events, *longue durée* historical epochs have been effectively camouflaged under mostly journalistic analysis. In contrast to what is now prevalent in the field, in this book I intend to see and show through that smokescreen a far more balanced historical narrative. To gainsay the rising crescendo of such common and widespread suppositions, as I intend to do, is to navigate through a critical gateway leading toward a much more enduring insight into the changing historical circumstances of our age, applicable as much to "Islam" as to "the West" that has thus identified it by identifying itself.

I therefore write this book as a principal argument against this succession of US and European bestsellers for long defining the terms of our understanding and engagements, taking their flawed argument to task. Trying to reach a wider audience, they have systematically misinformed. Representing a wider range of similar sentiments, Gilles Kepel's book traces the rise of Islamist political movements in the late twentieth century, beginning with the success of the Islamic Revolution in Iran in the 1970s, continuing with the mobilization of Islamist movements in Afghanistan against the Soviets in the 1980s, and concluding with his assessment of the most recent, and more violent, manifestations of the phenomenon at the threshold of the twenty-first century. I believe such decidedly short and selective time spans are historically flawed, analytically limited, and as such theoretically misguided and misleading. "Islam and the West" are not two different phenomena. They are coterminous, both the outcome of an identical colonial condition, in need of a postcolonial critique—simultaneously.

In this book I will therefore place the current state of Islamism in a much larger frame of reference, in the global context of its categorical opposition posited against "the West," and with a concluding argument that the historical uses and abuses of that binary opposition of "Islam and the West" have had a politically productive history (for better or for worse) but have now categorically exhausted their analytical credence and even usefulness—and that we are historically at the threshold of a new phase in Islamic social history, with the categorical imperative "the West" having imploded unto itself, and thus can no longer place its doppelgänger "Islam" as its legitimate interlocutor.[11] In the current dominant discourse, both "Islam" and "the West" are talking to dead interlocutors. My objective is to liberate these exhausted master tropes and let them rest in peace, so the changing realities of the world that includes but has surpassed these two depleted master tropes can begin to reveal themselves.

I also write this book as a corrective lens to Edward Said's pioneering and justly celebrated *Orientalism* (1979). I take a few steps before and then a few steps beyond Said and try to historicize his classical argument, which for him began as a Foucauldian question of the relation between knowledge and power, was then transformed into a literary problem of representation, and then taken to a political hotspot and applied to the modes of knowledge production at the service of colonialism. My argument is that the absolute metaphor of "the West" that was so central even to Said's critique of Orientalism is of a very recent vintage and has now imploded and no longer exists, while "Islam," a principal focal point of Orientalist knowledge production, has, a fortiori, lost the historic interlocutor it had found in the course of the Muslim encounter with European colonial modernity. The world, as a result, is at the cusp of a new global reconfiguration of its emerging metaphors—into which that of "Islam and the West" has now dissolved. The current resurgence of the contradiction posited between "Islam" and "the West," I conclude, is a ruse political posture hiding a much more potent geopolitics of power.

This is a principal argument of my book, markedly different than all others in the same vein.

In direct reaction to the tragic events of September 11, 2001, the extended arguments of Samuel Huntington, Bernard Lewis, and Gilles Kepel in their respective books represent a rising concern about the nature and function of a militant Islamism that not just during the last quarter century but in fact over the last two hundred years has marked the passage of Muslim societies toward a critical encounter with European colonial modernity—a fact that all hasty analyses categorically share. Against the grain of these books, I wish to offer a decidedly historical, and not a mythic and symbolic, reading of Islam in world history, instead of offering yet another reductionist reading of the events of 9/11. Any assessment of the rise of militant Islamism must be in a frame of reference that does not picture Islamic societies in a historical vacuum. My reading of similar issues that these leading observers have raised is more dialectical and located between "Islam" and "the West," rather than endemic to "Islam" as such, more global to an imaginative geography that entails "Islam and the West" than local to Islamic societies held and observed in fetishized abstractions. "Islam and the West" is one coterminous unit of analysis, not two.

It is impossible to exaggerate the significance of dismantling this false opposition in our current political circumstances—with the rapid rise of Islamophobia on both sides of the Atlantic and the emergence of Muslims as the external and internal other of "the West." Given the critical urgency of the issues I raise in this book and their references to the political headlines of our daily news, it is imperative that this encounter with the combined perceptions of "Islam and the West" reaches a critical mass of the educated public. I believe it is imperative for us to shift the level of civic discourse about the prolonged assumption of a hostile relationship between two abstractions ("Islam" and "the West")—now concretely enunciated at the roots of the most violent military and militant acts in our contemporary history. Politicians, pundits, journalists, and far more importantly the public at large will need categorically to reconsider this false binary. This will not happen unless and until scholars with a long-standing record of informed interpretations of Islamic intellectual and political history write in a lucid language accessible to a much larger (informed, educated, and concerned) audience than the ones they ordinarily address on university campuses. I intend to write this book in a fairly simple, jargon-free, and accessible language, without the slightest compromise in simplifying the necessarily complicated issues at the roots of the matter.

The audience that I intend, envision, and anticipate to reach with this book is, as a result, precisely the audience that has made books such as Fukuyama's *The End of History and the Last Man*, Samuel Huntington's *The Clash of Civilizations and the Remaking of World Order*, Bernard Lewis's *What Went Wrong?*, and Gilles Kepel's *The War for Muslim Minds: Islam and the West* such huge international bestsellers.

The Map of Memory

I therefore write this book with the urgent need to recollect and to retrain our historical memory. Facts abound, documentations and exquisite scholarship into ancient history are plentiful, and yet they have failed to dislodge unexamined assumptions about false allegories dividing the world today. We need to go back to the earliest literary, philosophical, and historical evidence of our global history to retrieve a reading of our contemporary realities rooted in facts and evidence, informing an alternative vision of how we arrived at this point in our tumultuous history.

Let me point to some historical landmarks. When Xenophon (ca. 430–354 BC) wrote his *Cyropaedia*, Cyrus the Great (600–530 BC)

was already a classical imperial figure. The Persian Empire had dominated classical antiquity in political might the way Greek philosophy,
literature, and political thought had mapped the moral imaginary
of the Athenian city-state. But by the time Cyrus the Great had conquered the civilized world and Xenophon had written his classical
text immortalizing him in his mirror for future princes, the ancient
world was already replete with the memories of its own antiquity.
There was neither "Islam" anywhere in sight nor indeed its doppelgänger "the West." What happened between then and now? It is
imperative for us to locate the specific imperial context in which
"Islam and the West" came to be and abort any false extension of it
into worlds where the concepts could not possibly belong.

Look at the ancient map of contemporary "Middle East"—before
it was even called "the Middle East" (a very recent piece of colonial
geography): During the Old Babylonian civilization at the time of
Hammurabi (2000–1600 BC), down to the Assyrian Empire (1200–
612 BC), the Babylonian Empire (612–539 BC), and ultimately to the
Babylonian Captivity (586–539 BC) when the world had an entirely
different map. The beginning of the internecine warfare in the region
may be traced back to classical antiquity, at the time of the Persian
Wars with the Greeks during the Achaemenid Empire (550–330 BC).
This hostility was not between any East or West as we understand
them today, however, but between a massive global empire and one
of its small neighbors. Consider the two seminal works of Aeschylus's *Persians* (472 BC) and Xenophon's *Cyropaedia* (370 BC). Yes,
Greeks and Persians were sporadically at war and met on many bat-
tlefields. But their differences were not in the realm of metaphysical assumptions about some fundamental or archetypal hostilities.
Aeschylus's *Persians* is written from a deep sense of empathy with
the Persians, while Xenophon's *Cyropaedia* offers the model of the
Persian emperor as a mirror for future princes, used by Alexander
the Great in the course of his world conquests. That world of affinity

and proximity is worlds apart from the presumed hostilities we see today projected backward onto world history.

Many of the key events in ancient history inform us of much different and far more flexible geographies than a simplistic "East versus West" would or could warrant. The Persian Wars (490–480 BC), and the age of Pericles come to an end with the rise of Alexander the Great (336–323 BC), the Macedonian conqueror who created a vast empire connecting Greek, Persian, and Egyptian domains, polities, and political cultures into an integrated pluralism that redefined generations and dynasties to come. Today Alexander's conquests are falsely taken as a point of contestation between "the West and the East." It was no such thing. It is important to keep in mind that before Alexander's conquests much of world events were centered on Mesopotamia, with the conquest of Babylon by Cyrus the Great and the return of Jews to Palestine (539 BC) matching in the western part of the Achaemenid Empire their conquest of the Indus Valley (530 BC), and Cambyses II's conquest of Egypt and his campaign to Nubia (525–522 BC) marking the advance of Darius into Africa and his linking the Nile and the Red Sea by a canal (52 BC). "The West" has neither a presence nor any reference in this world. Darius I's invasion of Greece (492 BC), the subsequent Battle of Marathon (490 BC), and the Battle of Salamis with Xerxes I (480 BC), now entirely ahistorically read as the hostile encounter between "East and West," must also all be seen in that categorically different regional and global context, informed by regional geopolitics. It is important to keep in mind that in this era Thebes sided with Persia during Xerxes's invasion of Greece (480 BC), as in fact later Sparta too allied itself with Persia (412 BC). Therefore, before Alexander finally defeats Darius III in 333 BC we have a much more complicated geopolitics of the region than an "East versus West" paradigm would warrant. The same is true about the biblical opposition between the Israelites and the Assyrians. During the Punic War (264–202 BC), and as Rome conquered the Mediterranean world (201–31 BC), the selfsame geopolitics were at work. By the time Vergil wrote his *Aeneid* (19 BC), he offered a potent ideological force for the rise of the Roman Empire (31–476), while in the aftermath of Alexander's conquests the Macedonian conqueror was turned into a widely popular figure in Persianate sources as the Hellenistic heritage of his generals continued in the form of the Seleucid Empire, a fusion of Mediterranean and inland cultures as far east as India. None of these were any indications of a "West versus East" encounter, and reading them back to any such effect is a serious epistemic violence on their history. We must retrieve the vastly different emotive universes, political alliances, cultural exchanges, and pliable geographies in order to cultivate an entirely different historiography than the one we have inherited and that now over the last century has culminated in this dangerous fiction of "Islam and the West" as a particularly potent version of "the West and the Rest."

With the establishment of the Byzantine Empire (330–1453) the very idea of "Europe" (still in the making) was divided by strong sectarian terms between an Eastern Orthodoxy and the Roman Catholic Church. This was an internal division within Christianity that included what today we find in the eastern territories of the Levant. The Early Middle Ages (476–1000) ushered in the so-called "Dark Ages" in Western Europe (500–750), which now coincided with the birth and subsequent rise of Prophet Muhammad in Arabia and the tiresome Byzantine-Sassanid wars (602–628) leading to the collapse of the Sassanids under the onslaught of the Arab conquest and the subsequent rise of Muslim empires on one side and the consolidation of the Carolingians and the Holy Roman Empire (750–850) on the other. As the center of gravity in the Muslim-majority world eventually shifted from the west in Baghdad to Khorasan in the east under the Seljuqids, "Europe" (still nowhere near its future imperial self-consciousness) plunged into a self-destructive period and was in no position to posit an alterity for the triumphalist Islam and Muslims. The later hostile encounter between Christian Europe and the Muslim-majority world needs to be seen in this context. From the First Crusade (1096–1099) to the Fourth Crusade (1201–1204) and the Sack of Constantinople (1204), to the Hundred Years' War (1337–1453), to the Great Famine (1315–1317) and Black Death (1347–1352), these cataclysmic events dismantled the very assumption of a European identity or alterity. The very idea of "Europe" was still very much in flux, at a time when the center of the Muslim-majority world had moved east to Transoxiana. The twain simply did not exist, let alone meet.

The life and career of Prophet Muhammad (570–632) begins as a modest event in Arabia but eventually expands into the formation of the Umayyad dynasty (661–750) and soon after that the Abbasid empire (750–1258). As early as 668, the First Siege of Constantinople, lasting for about seven years, ends with a humiliating defeat for the Umayyads. By 717, the Second Siege of Constantinople also ended in a decisive defeat for Muslims. The fall of Constantinople and the subsequent collapse of the Byzantine Empire and the rise of the Ottomans, which followed a fifty-three-day siege that began on 6 April 1453, was a turning point in the history of Anatolia. But here again, vast territories linking Europe and Asia came together at the epicenter of that magnificent city. In many ways the Ottoman Empire replicated the Byzantines and before them all the way back to the Seleucids. The fact that the Ottomans were Muslims, the Byzantines Christians, and the Seleucids Hellenistic had only tangential impact on the cosmopolitan culture of their respective capitals and empires. Jews, Christians, and Muslims lived in this city and the multiple empires it celebrated. The binary of "Islam and the West" was alien within all these contexts. The followers of these three so-called world religions—Judaism, Christianity, and Islam—were integral to multiple Mediterranean cultures both successively and simultaneously. The assumption that Judaism and Christianity (let alone that fictitious construct called "Judeo-Christian heritage") are "Western" and stand opposite to Islam is constitutionally flawed and entirely ahistorical.[12]

The conquest of Spain (711), which eventually led to the Battle of Tours/Poitier (732), has been read as a confrontation between "Islam and the West." It was no such thing. By 711, Muslim commander Tariq ibn Ziyad had in the context of regional rivalries crossed the strait separating the two continents of Africa and Europe at the head of a small army and commenced the first phase of the Muslim conquest of Spain. He landed at Gibraltar at the invitation of heirs of the late Visigoth King Witica (Witiza) who had asked Ibn Ziyad to help him get rid of his internal rivals. Ibn Ziyad used the occasion to form a North African inroad into Spain. By 718 the entire Iberian Peninsula was under Muslim rule. By 732, in the famous Battle of Tours, Charles Martel halted any further Muslim conquest beyond Spain. But still, by June 827, Muslims conquered Sicily. The Arab conquest of Sicily was aided by Euphemius, a Byzantine naval commander rebelling against the emperor. In each and every one of such military encounters between Muslims and non-Muslims there were multiple Mediterranean military forces engaging in rival conquests, thereby mapping entirely different geopolitics of the region than "Islam versus the West." With the passage of time, the ideological foregrounding of such military encounters became more colorful and pronounced than they had been at the time of the regional conflicts that had occasioned them. The very words we use today in describing these events—*Muslims*, *Europe*, etc.—are now completely tainted by the much later colonial coloring of history. The way we use the word *Europe* today is far more ideologically loaded than the word *Afranj* at the time of such events.

Much of the Muslim world's attention was drawn eastward and inward during a period of vast imperial expansions. The Umayyads gave way to the Abbasids and local dynasties began to emerge to the east and west of imperial Baghdad, with the Samanids (819–999), the Ghaznavids (977–1186), and the Seljuqids (1037–1194) to the east and the Almoravids (1040–1147), the Almohad (1121–1269), the Aghlabids (800–909), and the Umayyads of Spain (661–750) popping up in the west. Baghdad was the Arab intellectual and Muslim moral epicenter of these empires, with Spain and the Greater Khorasan, situated in the northeast of Persia, as the two bookends of the Muslim world. With the eventual rise of the Mongols (1206–1368) a vast Eurasian domain was brought under the rule of a colossal empire that eventually yielded to the last three Muslim empires that came after the Timurids (1370–1507), successors to the Ilkhanids: the Mughals (1526–1857), the Safavids (1501–1736), and the Ottomans (1299–1922), just before their fateful encounter with European imperialisms, the British and the French in particular competing with the Russians to their east. Between the rise of Islam in the mid-seventh century and the last three Muslim empires of the Mughals, the Safavids, and the Ottomans, the single most important empire, holding much of the civilized world together, was the Mongols, whose political apparatus was held together by Genghis Khan's code of law, the Yassa (not the Qur'an), with Persian (not Arabic) as the courtly language of their royal historiography. All of these crucial historic realities are categorically erased when ahistorically we perpetrate the thick ideological rubric and the rude epistemic violence of "Islam and the West" backward upon them. During these long and formative periods "the West" as a conceptual category, a civilizational assumption, did not even exist to posit an alterity to "Islam," which was itself not yet fetishized into a monolithic abstraction. In this false formulation, "Islam" becomes a monolithic entity, as Arabs, Iranians, Turks, Indians, Central Asians, and others are all wrapped up together; their political and intellectual histories are collapsed upon each other, their inner conflicts and alternative solidarities with Jewish, Christian, or Mediterranean communities camouflaged. "Islam" was as much integral to "the West," if we are even to use these generic terms, as "the West" was to "Islam," and both of them were dissolved into more immediate and urgent historical realities.

The rise of "Islam and the West" as a de-formative and dangerous binary happens entirely in the fateful encounter of the last Muslim empires and the encroaching global domination of European empires, which takes us from the sixteenth to the twentieth century. Such was the ideological nomenclature of an imperial encounter: a self-narrative that kept feeding on itself from both sides of the divide. But, again, the divide was not true. It was and remains a false consciousness. It is long overdue that we dispense with these two misbegotten twins.

From One to Two Illusions

I borrow the title of this book, *The End of Two Illusions*, from the classic text of Sigmund Freud, *The Future of an Illusion* (*Die Zukunft einer Illusion*, 1927). But I do more than just borrow and expand that title from one to two twin illusions. As I propose the opposition posited between "Islam" and "the West" to be an illusion, both of them together, we first need to know what we mean by the term *illusion*. In *The Future of an Illusion*, Freud tells us what exactly he means by this term. So let us hear it from the master himself:

> When I say that these things are all illusions, I must define the meaning of the word. . . . An illusion is not the same thing as an error; nor is it necessarily an error. . . . One may describe as an illusion the assertion made by certain nationalists that the Indo-Germanic race is the only one capable of civilization. . . . What is characteristic of illusions is that they are derived from human wishes. . . . Thus we call a belief

an illusion when a wish-fulfilment is a prominent factor in its motivation, and in doing so we disregard its relations to reality, just as the illusion itself sets no store by verification.[13]

This is a truly seminal passage in a key text of Freud and definitive to my task in this book. Using this definition of *illusion*, I expand it from Freud's application to "religion" to the very idea of "the West," which having assumed metaphysical proportions fits perfectly with his conception of the term. As Freud says specifically, "One may describe as an illusion the assertion made by certain nationalists that the Indo-Germanic race is the only one capable of civilization." He of course had the rising ideology of the Nazis in mind. It is precisely that illusion that is at the root of the term "the West" too, where "the Indo-German race" has deluded itself into thinking it is a race and that it is exclusively bestowed with the gift of civilization. From this premise I then proceed to argue that the illusory power of this "West" is at the root of its hegemony, and thus any other "civilization" or entity it perforce encounters turns that too into an illusion. So the "Islam" we see facing the mirror of the illusion "the West" also has been turned into an abstract illusion, robbed of its historical vicissitudes, complexities, and conflicting realities. "Islam and the West" are two sides of the same illusory concoction, which fits perfectly with Freud's definition of the term.

"The West" thus becomes a secular religion with capitalist modernity as its liturgical substance, the ideology of its imperial conquests, the emblem of its white supremacy and civilizing mission, with "Islam" as its chief nemesis. "The West" is that Freudian example of the "Indo-Germanic race" turning itself into the metaphysical paradigm of a cult of conquerors.

"What is characteristic of illusions," as Freud says, "is that they are derived from human wishes. . . . Thus we call a belief an illusion when a wish-fulfilment is a prominent factor in its motivation, and in doing so we disregard its relations to reality, just as the illusion itself sets no store by verification." That is in fact a textbook definition of "the West," a wish-fulfillment, an attempt to cover up defiant realities, disregard them, and cast them into a false ideological consciousness that covers up the truth with illusion. This particular illusion they call "the West" is a false ideological camouflage seeking to center the world in a fictive field termed "Europe," thereby morally, imaginatively, and materially subjugating the world at large to its self-raising, other-lowering hegemonies. "The illusion itself," as Freud says, "sets no store by verification," for it does not exist except as an ideology of conquest and control. Anything else this "West" touches—Islam, Asia, Africa, Latin America—it turns into illusory constructs as well, bereft and robbed of their historical realities.

I would further add that here by *religion* Freud meant specifically Western Christianity, the version of Christianity that at least since the time of the Holy Roman Empire had placed itself squarely at the service of empire building and subsequently of colonial conquests, as perhaps best evident in the classical text of Bartolomé de las Casas, *A Short Account of the Destruction of the Indies* (1542), when the conquest of the Americas was done specifically in Christian terms. With this reading of Freud, I therefore propose in the dual construction of "Islam and the West" that the corrosive forces of not one but in fact two illusions are at work, and that here the primary illusion, by virtue of its power and hegemony, is in fact "the West," being the most powerful chimera that turned anything it touched into an illusion too. This is what I mean by "Islam and the West: The Future of Two Illusions."

Bataille de Poitiers en Octobre 732

The mounted warrior towers over the epicenter of the picture, with his raised right hand holding a triumphant axe, balancing on the

FIGURE 1. Charles de Steuben, *Bataille de Poitiers en Octobre 732* (1837). Oil on canvas. Palace of Versailles, Versailles, France.

white horse, with its long neck and golden mane, charging into the enemy. The heroic warrior is facing an eternity beyond the battlefield. From the watchful heaven to the tumultuous earth, all is subservient to his iron will and courageous embrace. Facing him is the defeat of his bearded opponent, defiant but overpowered, decidedly humbled in the encounter. Destiny is in the balance. A mother is holding her child between the two warriors. The future is at stake. Other combatants fill the front of the powerful drama. Deep in the background the battle rages apace. The warriors to the left of the scene are defending, those on the right are invading. The battle is fierce, the landscape resplendent with the will of the divinity.

Charles de Steuben's *Bataille de Poitiers en Octobre 732* depicts a triumphant Charles Martel (ca. 688–741) battling Abd al-Rahman Al Ghafiqi (died 732) at the Battle of Poitiers, also known as the Battle of Tours. Remembering and immortalizing the battle, Baron Charles Auguste Guillaume Steuben (1788–1856) was a French painter and lithographer of German origin who was active during the Napoleonic era. The time was ripe, the patron generous, the occasion not to be missed—the "European history" needed to invent a primogeniture for itself. The future of this "Europe" was awaiting, in the making. Steuben's romantic brush strokes reveal his association with the poet Friedrich Schiller (1759–1805), who was a family friend. He had come to Paris where he studied at the prestigious École Nationale Supérieure des Beaux-Arts, studying with the masters. He is now scarcely remembered for much other than this increasingly iconic allegory of a battle romanticized long after its haphazard origins.

The Battle of Poitiers in October 732, which Steuben here dramatizes, has now been blown completely out of all proportions as a clash between "Islam" and "the West," or even barbarity versus civilization. The actual encounter was in fact one among many other similar events initiated from Spain, which itself had "fallen" to Muslims and was then reclaimed from them, and yet heaven and earth were not shattered in either case. The Battle of Poitiers was indeed a victory for the Franks and a defeat for Abd al-Rahman—but it had no serious consequence in either of the two sides. Thanks to much ahistorical militaristic romance, however, and accompanying delusional historiography, today it is remembered as one of the most fateful events in European (and therefore world) history. Led by Charles Martel, grandfather of Charlemagne, the Franks defeated the Arab army headed by Abd al-Rahman, the ruler of Al-Andalus, who was killed in the battle. Generations of subsequent European historians and other public figures, however, have given their flights of fancy free reign and established this battle as the most important, the most vital confrontation ever. Yes, this was a battle between Christians and Muslims, but no, it was not the battle between "Islam" and "the West." That phantasmagoric invention has now come to haunt humanity on both sides of the delusional divide.

Soon after this entirely insignificant battle, the Abbasids came to power and their capital Baghdad became the epicenter of Islamic civilization. Neither for "the West" nor for "Islam"—two abstractions that had not even existed in juxtaposition against each other—did this battle mean much. Christian sources, which have always sarcastically referred to Muslims as "Saracens," "Agarens," "Mahometans," and so on, were entirely oblivious to such facts. Muslims have, of course returned the compliment, and considered the Europeans barbarian brutes. The initial account of the Battle of Poitiers can be found in the so-called Mozarabic Chronicle of 754.[14] Viewing it from that perspective, we can see how with the passage of time the systematic invention of "the West" has taken place.[15] Here we surely see the account of a military encounter between the two armies of Abd al-Rahman and the Franks. The text however was mostly unknown and obscure until its discovery in the sixteenth century. The Mozarabic Chronicle does indeed refer to "Europeans" but not in the sense that we understand the term today. The term *European* was entirely ambiguous at this point, compared with the term *Christian*, celebrating this victory.

Later European historians, however, were delighted to pick up on this term *European* in the Mozarabic Chronicle and run with it. With the rise of Charlemagne (748–814), the term was christened, as it were. But throughout the Middle Ages the Battle of Poitiers was never thought of as a turning point in anything particular. Some even thought a victory for Muslims would have been a welcome introduction of sciences and the arts.[16] It was left for Voltaire (1694–1778) and Edward Gibbon (1737–1794) to think of the Battle of Poitiers in grandiloquent terms of Europe becoming potentially Muslim or put under the "yoke of the Koran," as Gibbon put it. He dreaded that the

Qur'an would be taught at Oxford. Well, the Qur'an is today taught throughout European and US universities—and the earth has not stopped spinning around or circling the sun.

As Alessandro Barbero reports, in subsequent generations, especially from the nineteenth century forward, prominent European thinkers took turns celebrating the Battle of Poitiers in ever more highfalutin terms, among them the famous French historian Jean Charles Léonard de Sismondi (1773–1842) and the French doyen of Romanticism François-René de Chateaubriand (1768–1848).[17] This is post-French Revolution, and the agility of the merging French bourgeoisie is busy manufacturing a history of chivalry for itself. All of these fanfares come to a crescendo with the British historian Edward Shepherd Creasy (1812–1878), whose book *The Fifteen Decisive Battles of the World: From Marathon to Waterloo* (1851) prominently features the Battle of Poitiers.[18] Again, the obscure battle is being reimagined for the British imperial heritage. From there we get to the US president Theodore Roosevelt, who in his book *Fear God and Take Your Own Part* (1916) invoked the memory of the Battle of Poitiers and cited Charles Martel as his great champion.[19] From there it is only a short distance to the retired US Army lieutenant colonel and former member of the US House of Representatives Allen West (born 1961) who in 2011, again as Alessandro Barbero reports, defended the US invasion of Iraq by citing Charles Martel in the Battle of Tours. Among his illustrious deeds while serving in Iraq is the torture and fake execution of an Iraqi inmate. It is not accidental that in every imperial, colonial, and militaristic turn in Euro-American history Charles Martel and his Battle of Poitiers pop up as sanctified talismans of militaristic rituals.

That brings us down to the current moment when "Charles Martel has become an enduring icon of fascist and far-right movements, in France and other Western states." This according to an investigative piece by Iskander Rehman, "The Sword and the

Swastika: How a Medieval Warlord Became a Fascist Icon," in which we read:

A notorious division of French volunteers to the Nazi SS was named the Division Charlemagne after the great Carolingian Emperor and grandson of Charles Martel. In the years following France's bitter war in Algeria, a far-right group—the Cercle Charles Martel—conducted a string of terror attacks against Algerians and citizens of North African descent in France. More recently, the founder of the French Front National party, Jean-Marie Le Pen, reacted to the Charlie Hebdo killings by proudly claiming "Je suis Charlie Martel," in defiance of the more republican and inclusive slogan "Je suis Charlie." "Je suis Charlie Martel" has since become one of the rallying cries of French far-right activists.[20]

Thus in every atrocity of French fascist, colonial, and racist adventurism, Charles Martel and his Battle of Poitiers have served the most notorious forces laying a white supremacist claim on the continent and its colonial possessions and racist practices. By this time Charles Martel and the Battle of Poitiers have become iconic features of a secular/sacred pantheon of fascistic imagination. But the appeal of Charles Martel to European fascists is not limited to France or the French:

This sinister historical crush extends far beyond France. Anders Breivik, the Norwegian neo-Nazi who slaughtered 77 people in 2011, claimed in his online rants to have "identified" with the figure of Charles Martel. In the United States, a group called the Charles Martel Society funds the publication of a pseudo-intellectual and deeply racist journal, *The Occidental Quarterly*. Charles de Steuben's famous 19th-century painting of the Battle of Poitiers flashes through one of Richard Spencer's slickly edited "alt-right" videos, providing a brief and jarring backdrop to a long stream of nativist gobbledygook.[21]

Charles de Steuben's Battle of Poitiers painting is the most famous illustration of the illusion of "Islam and the West" appearing as two eternal Manichean adversaries: light versus darkness, truth verses falsehood, good versus evil. Neo-Nazi mass murderers are invoking Charles Martel, as do the most notorious racist and Islamophobic projects in the United States. As Iskander Rehman puts it:

> Right wing extremism's longstanding obsession with Charles Martel stems from three major preconceptions. The first is that the battle of Poitiers was truly decisive; the second is that it represented a civilizational triumph of Christendom over Islam, and the third is that Martel's victory provides proof of the innate martial superiority of the West over what Edward Creasy famously termed "the Semitic peoples" in his classic and racially tinged study of the conflict.[22]

Iskander Rehman then proceeds to dismantle these three false assumptions, but he leaves unanswered the more basic question of whence and wherefore such fabrications appear and limits himself to warning that the far-right "reading of western civilization's variegated past is crude, intellectually stunted, and most often erroneous."[23] The point, however, is to see when and how this "Western civilization" was cast as the alterity of all other civilizations, "Islam" in particular. Today we are living the future of these two dangerous illusions. Ahistorical and immaterial, these two opposing metaphors are entirely apathetic about the lived experiences of billions of human beings—Muslim, Jews, Christians, or otherwise—who in fact populate the defiant facts camouflaged by these two false and falsifying illusions. The "Islam" of this "Islam and the West" has scarcely anything to do with the common faith of some 1.5 billion human beings who consider themselves Muslims. The "West" of this "Islam and the West" has even less to do with the lived experiences of a plurality of cultures and convictions of even more millions of people forced into the illusion of "the West."

Two Falsifying Mirrors

If this is how the false binary was set up, then how did the mirage finally undo itself?

In *The Future of an Illusion* Freud examined religion as evidence of a false consciousness. That pioneering study enables more, even divergent, modes of thinking, not just "religion" being considered an illusion, but any given religion being falsely paired with another abstraction is cast into existential negation. Our task today is not to consider Islam or any other religion—Judaism, Hinduism, Christianity—as a false consciousness or an illusion, but to consider the falsifying circumstances when these religions are cast against even more abstract constructs that thus disfigure the worldly realities of people who believe in and adhere to these religions. In this book my concern is not with Islam as the religion of millions of human beings who consider themselves Muslims, but with "Islam" as falsely paired and systematically distorted against the grain of an even more vacuous abstraction called "the West." The belief in "the West" is even more metaphysical and unworldly than any true believer ever thought of Islam or any other faith. The real illusion is this "West." By disengaging these two falsifying sides of the binary my objective is to liberate both sides so we can begin to see ourselves in the light of much more urgent, much more immediate, and much more compelling realities.

The actual components of "Islam and the West," now turned into eternal antinomies, have not always even existed let alone been at war with each other. What exactly is "Islam," where exactly is "the West" when they are placed so ominously next to each other? The historical origins of these terms have now lost their formative normativity. We need to ask these questions anew. How can a religion of more than 1.5 billion people spread over five continents and developed over fourteen hundred years be considered one solid thing set at odds with an imaginative geography only recently invented and called "the West"? Today "the West" is no longer a geography; it is a set of imaginary normative mores, a constellation of a colonizing idea, a set of supremacist sentiments, a space of vaguely interrelated cultural convictions and imperatives presumed to be somewhere between Western Europe and North America, with an extension into Australia and New Zealand and a stopover in Israel and, until the end of apartheid, in South Africa. "The West" is in fact more than anything else a metaphor, an allegory, for European colonialism and all its settler colonies. The very supposition of "the West," however, has become something of a "religious" conviction especially when we place it next to Islam. Islam and Muslims in fact are spatially forced to retreat into an ulterior space outside themselves when placed next to this "West."

Can our contemporary binary opposition so fiercely and falsely presumed between "Islam" and "the West" have any room for actual historical figures who lived through a different moral and normative geography and had a wide circle of influences in the Mediterranean domain now glossed over by the cliché-ridden opposition paramount in our radical contemporaneity? When and where did these two oddities, "Islam" and "the West," thus uncompromisingly placed next to each other, become such intensely hostile alterities—their identities so utterly contingent on their being the other's doppelgänger? When and how did "Islam and the West" emerge as an irreconcilable binary opposition? Have Muslims and Westerners, thus coded, always been fighting each other? Is "Islam and the West" a subterfuge for "Islam and Christianity" perhaps? If so, when did "the West" replace "Christendom"? What about those Christians who are Arabs and deeply influenced by Islam? What about Jews who are Arabs? How do we deal with these inconvenient facts that crowd and confuse our comfortable presumptions? Is this a religious conflict? Or does "the West" stand for a larger civilizational domain that is now deemed at odds with and in danger from Islam as the representative of another civilizational domain? Can we reset the history to a point where these two concepts and the realities they presumably represent need not be posited as so hostile to each other? And if so, how? Does the word *civilization* itself posit a conceptual subterfuge for "the West" and its alterities?

These and scores of other similar or related questions today override the factual evidence of daily mayhem that extends from the Arab and Muslim world to Europe, the United States, and beyond. The flood of refugees and migrant laborers crossing dangerous seas to reach safety in Europe, the United States, or Australia have triggered hatred and anger and given rise to dangerous xenophobic sentiments agitating the political cultures of liberal democracies. The election of Donald Trump in the United States, the Brexit debacle in Europe, the rise of neo-Nazi groups in Europe and the United States, and countless cases of proto-fascist partisanship triggering classical anti-Semitism and Islamophobia are the clearest signs of this danger. The rise of white supremacist nationalism in Europe, North America, New Zealand, Australia, and beyond have created existential crises around the globe. Fear and loathing are poisonous and damaging to the very soul of solidarity and survival that must inform our urgent task of facing environmental calamities. Lifting this air of suspicion and mistrust, of unexamined "civilizational" divides and unexamined differences, and showing the horizons of a different global map of our historical circumstances are my main objectives in writing this book.

The Fading Memories of the Present

How can we retrace the origin of this hostility and place it in a much larger, much longer, historical continuum and frame of reference? The two metaphors corresponding to two vastly differentiated sets of realities have now evolved on two different but adjacent tracks, never even remembering the time when they did not exist. The shrinking imaginative geography of the world, I contend, has no room any longer for the illusion of such manufactured binaries that never existed in the first place. These two Janus faces have long since exhausted and effaced themselves. To detail my argument, I will follow a careful historical narrative to show both how the disparate notions of "Islam" and "the West" emerged fairly recently as two coherent but entirely lopsided civilizational categories and how upon that concocted coherence their presumed hostilities were then aggressively cast upon their prehistory, even though they did not actually exist. Equally important, I will show why these two inimical and mutually exclusive tropes have emerged and then fed on each other's demise. This presumed hostility is an extremely narrow interpretation of history, cherry-picking selective facts and disregarding any concern for factual evidence beyond the warfare that habitually informed and animated them. My objective is to re-historicize the focus on military encounters and broaden it by including cultural, intellectual, and other significant and ignored locations and circumstances of encounter. A shift between military history, philosophy, and literary and cultural encounters will frame the manufactured history of this hostility in any number of alternative narratives, all based on historical facts now all but forgotten. The emphasis, however, will be on the contemporary hostilities that have drawn a thick curtain over that much richer and more enabling history.

From mass murderers to prominent scholars, all are feeding on this fictive divide. Forget about the Norwegian mass murderer

Anders Behring Breivik, and consider this example: A prominent European historian, Niall Ferguson, recently published a book he called *Civilization: The West and the Rest* (2012). Its very title and its sustained arguments typify the perceived divide now categorically presumed between these two opposite realms and thus furthers the notion of "the West" being at odds—being the civilizational other—of everything else in human history. So much credence is given today to the myth of the clash between "Islam" and "the West," indeed a civilizational clash, that the enmity appears predetermined, a Manichean division between light and darkness, as if written into the DNA of people accidentally born on one or the other side of this fictive divide. That this whole dangerous fiction is historically flawed and very recently fabricated escapes neo-Nazis and university professors alike. The task is not to cherry-pick an alternative set of facts to negate this view. Rather, it is to retrieve the successive layers of historical consciousness that predates such presumed hostilities and is evident not just in specific incidents but in fact in the constellation of social formations that fundamentally challenge and historicize it. The recent fabrication of "Islam and the West" as binary opposites must be exposed for the sheer ideological vacuity it espouses.

But how are we to do so—how do we reconfigure the Mediterranean history beyond the fiction of "Islam and the West"? Let me cut to a crucial episode in Mediterranean history. The integrated world of Al-Ghazali, Averroes, Maimonides, and Aquinas, and what came before and what came after them, eventually gave way to that of Dante Alighieri (1265-1321). By the time Dante had composed his *Divine Comedy*, the civilizational confrontation between Islam and Christianity (not Islam and the West) had a markedly Levantine disposition going back to the Crusades, disregarding the factual evidence of a cosmopolitan reality evident in effectively all Mediterranean civilizations, from the Sassanids to the Romans to the Abbasids to the Ottomans. The local and regional history of the Crusades have now cast a long and ahistorical shadow over our present age. Forgotten is the scholarly proposition first made by Miguel Asín Palacios (1871–1944) in his 1919 text *La Escatología Musulmana en la Divina Comedia* proposing that Dante's *Divine Comedy* may have indeed been inspired by Muslim accounts of Prophet Muhammad's nocturnal journey to Heavens (Mi'raj). One need not necessarily agree with this speculative proposition in order to see the wider Mediterranean context of the Muslim/non-Muslim world in which Dante conceived his masterpiece and which was vastly different from the one we imagine it to be today. What Dante's negative view of Islam and Prophet Muhammad shows are in fact two things and not just one: that his European context was closely familiar with Islam and Muslims and that it is only his Christian anxieties and prejudices that cast that knowledge in a negative light. We therefore need to make a categorical distinction between, on the one hand, Christian animosities to both Islam and Judaism as a matter of doctrinal antagonism, and on the other hand, cultural contacts and contexts in which not just Islam and Christianity but in fact Judaism too came together to inform a larger "societal" frame of Mediterranean references. Oddly enough, in an age that prides itself as "secular" it is the Christian sensibilities of Dante that are now picked up as a sign of hostility between Islam and the West rather than the Mediterranean social and cultural context in which Dante's knowledge of Islam—including the very idea of Mi'raj (the Muslim Prophet's nocturnal journey to the Heavens)—at the heart of his masterpiece was possible.

These historical episodes will have to be drawn to their contemporary conclusions where and when a much richer and more pluralist conception of our cultural heritage is not just factual and possible but indeed evident and inevitable.

Al-Ghazali and His Contemporaries

Let us look at the figure of Al-Ghazali and his environs more closely. Four years into his prestigious position as a highly respected professor at Nezamiyeh University in Baghdad, Abu Hamid Mohammad Al-Ghazali (1058–1111) had a moral and intellectual crisis. Who was he? What was his task as a Muslim thinker? What did it all mean?[24] How does the life and thought of a Muslim philosopher some three centuries after the Battle of Poitiers figure in this presumed "Islam and the West" hostility?

By 1091, upon his arrival in Baghdad the future eminent Muslim philosopher was a thirty-three-year-old scholar and had come a long way through a straight map of the Islamic world that had brought him from his birthplace in Tus in Khorasan and from there to Gorgan and Nishapur, and finally to Isfahan in central Iran in search of his lifelong intellectual calling. In Isfahan, Al-Ghazali had met with the powerful Seljuq vizier Khawaja Nezam al-Molk al-Tusi (1018–1092) and had accepted his invitation to go to Baghdad to assume a highly coveted position in the multi-campus university the Saljuqid vizier had just established. But the position, prominent as it was, had not satisfied the restless, inquisitive Muslim philosopher for more than four years. He soon left Baghdad and commenced a decade-long wandering life (1095–1104) that centered around his visit to Jerusalem. Much of his intellectual achievements and the most important of his highly influential books date back to this decade, which, as fate would have it, coincided with the first Crusade (1096–1099).

What did it mean for Al-Ghazali to be a Muslim thinker at that time, and what does it mean today? The reality of who Al-Ghazali was then is drastically different from the preconceptions we today fathom about Muslim thinkers, and if we were to retrieve the historical circumstances of his life, we would see it rooted in a dynamic dialogue with thinkers across religions and regions that are today subjected to a deep and drastic civilizational divide. What Al-Ghazali did throughout his lifetime and for which we know and remember him is now almost completely lost in the thicket of the politics of remembrance of the European Crusades.

Because of the overwhelming Eurocentricity of the narrative, today we remember the Crusades in an entirely different way—in a way that thickly overshadows the memory of the historical Al-Ghazali. A towering Muslim philosopher tucked away somewhere in an apartment in that extraordinary cosmopolitan city living deep in contemplation is not the first thing that comes to our mind when we think of the Crusades, which is now a coded term for sectarian warfare and bloodshed between "Islam" and "the West." Much of what we understand today about the Crusades is in fact rooted in the work of the Scottish novelist Sir Walter Scott (1771–1832) and after him the French historian Joseph-Francois Michaud (1767–1839), both offering romantic and anachronistic perceptions of the Crusades as a normative origin of Western Christianity. We have all but forgotten about Al-Ghazali and his philosophical contemporaries in the heat of our misremembering the Crusades.

Al-Ghazali's case was no exception. It was the rule. This was the time of a different imaginative geography. Two of Al-Ghazali's seminal works, *Maqasid al-Falasifah* (*The Aims of the Philosophers*) and *Tohfat al-Falasifah* (*The Incoherence of the Philosophers*), become major points of references in the wider Mediterranean context far removed from his own immediate Muslim venues soon after they were written, ultimately influencing the thinking of the eminent Jewish philosopher Moses Maimonides (1135–1204), through the intermediary critical reflections of the Muslim philosopher Averroes (1126–1198), linking them both to the seminal Christian philosopher Saint Thomas Aquinas (1225–1274), through the intermediary function of his teacher Albertus Magnus (1200–1280). Today if we were to read the works of Al-Ghazali, Averroes, Maimonides, and Aquinas, we would be astonished by their common roots in Aristotle and almost identical endeavors to bring the Greek philosopher closer to their respective Muslim, Jewish, and Christian concerns. These iconic names and towering philosophical figures are signposts of an intellectual trajectory rooted in a far more integrated social context and speak of a common intellectual heritage indivisible into any religious denomination. The Mediterranean navigational routes and commercial interactions offer us a much more reliable frame of civilizational formations than the "religious" affiliations of these philosophers. The eminent French historian Fernand Braudel, in his seminal work *The Mediterranean and the Mediterranean World in the Age of Philip II* (1949), has thoroughly documented a far more accurate geographical domain in which Islam, Christianity, and Judaism were integral to a common seafaring, commercial domain with contingent culture interactions. The point here is not "the influence" of one philosopher over the other, but the tertiary space that philosophy had generated between any two denominational affiliations.

We must remember the case of these philosophers is the rule not the exception, speaking a *lingua franca* that was both commercially and intellectually foregrounded. Consider the fact that Maimonides wrote his seminal philosophical text, *Guide to the Perplexed*, in Judeo-Arabic. Why would he do that? The *Guide* was completed in 1190, translated into Hebrew in 1204, and eventually emerged as textual evidence of how its Jewish author drew freely from Jewish, Islamic, and Greek thinkers to give Judaism an enduring philosophical foundation. That foundation is as much Islamic as Jewish or Greek. Born in Cordoba and living much of his life in North Africa before he settled in Egypt, Maimonides was the product of a pluralist cosmopolitan culture in which Jewish, Christian, Islamic and Greek thinking came together for a happy, healthy, and productive rendezvous. His life and learning at a pivotal moment in Mediterranean history is a clear testimony against the presumption of an everlasting confrontation between Islam and the West as we are now led to believe.

How did it happen, and under what circumstances was it that this varied, rich, and integrated history of common moral and intellectual gatherings became so categorically bifurcated into two opposing camps? If we are to overcome this deadly confrontation and actively remember the succession of cosmopolitan realities whose suppression has resulted in placing "Islam" and "the West" against each other, we need to go back in history. It is necessary to start with the period long before the notion of "Islam versus the West" emerged, even before the very constituent terms of this binary existed. This historical prequel to "Islam and the West" will make clear that the opposition is not intrinsic and that "civilizational" thinking is endemic to all the diverse periods in human history. It will explain how this false dichotomy came to so perilously tower over our historical consciousness, and even perhaps our human destiny, for arguably today very few other conflicts threaten our very existence more than "Islam versus the West."

The Paths through the Ahistorical Confusion

How can we find our ways through this false binary? Upon what factual evidence can we hope to be delivered from it?

The geographical maps of interrelated histories where "Islam and the West" were part and parcel of a different global imaginary are now long since forgotten, and today an inaccurate and ahistorical conflation of Arabs and Muslims, and Muslims with the rest of the world, from Asia to Africa and Latin America, has emerged, against which the allegory of "the West" is narratively posited as a measure of truth. Muslims are not the only people at the receiving end of the global colonial project launched by Western Europe and later North America in the aftermath of the Industrial Revolution and the commencement of the European Age of modern empires. Asians, Africans, Latin Americans—they have all been subjects of European imperialism and colonialism. As a result, "the West" has come to be placed against everything and anything its ideologues wish to other and exoticize, dismiss and denigrate, overrule and dominate. But the shrinking universe humans now occupy, and its corresponding shrinking resources, can no longer accommodate such illusions.

We must begin to build on what has already been done to disengage "the West and the Rest." Perhaps the most serious attempts at explaining this duality between "Islam" and "the West," or more accurately "the West" and "the Rest," can be found in the pioneering works of the renowned literary critic Edward Said in his *Orientalism* (1978) and before him in the French cultural historian Raymond Schwab's *Oriental Renaissance* (1950). In his now classic work, Edward Said attributed the rise of this civilizational encounter to the ascendency of European colonialism and the concomitant cultural and academic knowledge production conducive to that relation of power. This colonial construct, he proposed, normatively sustained the political superiority of "the West" over "the Orient" it had "invented" to rule. "The Orient," in other words, was a politically modulated discursive construct, the civilizational other of "the West" there to fantasize, conquer, exploit, and civilize. Raymond Schwab, however, had an entirely different take. He considered the rise of European Orientalism as integral to the period in European intellectual history he termed "Oriental Renaissance," an eighteenth- to nineteenth-century movement that effectively augmented and expanded upon what in European historiography we call "Renaissance" proper. In a recent study, *Persophilia* (2015), I have offered a radically different perspective than both Said and Schwab, though obviously building on their respective insights. In this study, I propose that the European and, by extension, Eastern (India, China, Persia, more specifically) bourgeois public spheres were conducive to major social and intellectual movements that had global consequences. From the Enlightenment to Romanticism and even American Transcendentalism—I demonstrate—literary, poetic, and artistic elements from "the East" were instrumental in the making of the most transformative events in European and thus global history.

What dismantles "the West and the Rest" and brings it down upon itself is the intersectional space where race, gender, and class have crossed paths on a transnational public sphere. Let me first map the expanse of these transnational public and parapublic spaces. In my *Persophilia*, I have offered the idea of a *parapublic sphere* as a location in which in colonial contexts people have used ideas generated on the transnational public sphere to revolt against both domestic tyranny and foreign domination at the same time. My purpose in this has been to go beyond both Said and Schwab and to look at "Orientalism" as not just a site of cultural domination or exploitation, but in fact a concept definitive to the most consequential social and intellectual movements throughout the world. This is a far different perspective than giving Europeans the sole agential power and casting "Orientals" as a passive recipient without agency. It places Europe and non-Europe together as equals in the launching of movement with far-reaching global consequences. This dialectical reading of our condition of globality is a far more realistic understanding of the encounter among multiple cultures.

That was my first attempt at decoupling "the Orient" and "the Occident" as two adversarial sites prior to and subsequent to their colonial encounters, where through the articulation of a cross-cultural formation of a transnational public sphere I brought "the West" and "the Rest" together. With hindsight we can see how Edward Said's insights in his *Orientalism* were in fact very much animated by the Arab-Israeli conflict of the twentieth century placed in a larger European colonial context. Schwab's point of departure, on the other hand, was to complicate our understanding of the European Renaissance by bringing a non-European, Indian in particular, element into our consideration. While Said's insights considerably advanced our understanding of European colonialism, it embedded his *Orientalism* in a largely Arab-centric and perforce an ideological discourse. While Schwab's insights deeply complicated our reading of the social and intellectual history of European Renaissance, it categorically disregarded the transnational public sphere on which such cultural developments had global consequences.

To understand the deeper roots of the active components of that transnational public sphere we must recognize that Muslims, and Arabs in particular, are relatively recent factors in the false equation of "the West and the Rest." We must therefore frame "Islam and the West" in a pre-Islamic and pre-Western context, as it were, in order to point the way to a post-Islamic and post-Western world that I believe has already dawned upon us and is rapidly spreading its claim on our contemporary history. My purpose here is threefold: to disentangle what I believe is a false fixation on "Islam and the West," to re-historicize this false binary, and to map out alternative trajectories of far more fluid historical cultures, an understanding of which is necessary in order to confront urgent global issues of environmental catastrophes and perilous human migrations without being bogged down by nervous preoccupation with invented divisions. Consider the fact that in his July 2017 visit to Poland, US President Donald Trump—who had just withdrawn from the Paris climate agreement and promised to ban Muslims from the United States and build a wall on the US-Mexico border—once again flagged the battle between "Islam" and the "West" as the hallmark of his presidency.[25] It is precisely such egregious uses of the false binary that compel us toward disassembling it.

The active articulation of this transnational public sphere is where we can see how the outdated false rivalry presumed between

"Islam" and "the West" has been the end result of a flawed narrative of European colonial conquest of the globe and the rise of militant ideologies of resistance ranging from Islamic to Christian liberation theologies. In both Muslim and Latin American colonial contexts such liberation theologies have now performed their historic tasks and have been dissolved into larger political cultures, most evident in the rise of Arab revolutions and massive anti-austerity and anti-corruption rallies across Europe and Latin America. Produced at the height of the colonial encounter between Europe and the Muslim world, the "Islam and the West" narrative soon began to assimilate itself backward into history. One can easily pick and choose certain scattered memories of the Muslim conquest of Spain or the Crusades or even the Greco-Roman encounters with Persian empires as evidence of such moral and cosmic battles. Edward Said's *Orientalism* perhaps inadvertently exacerbated that false binary. His justified critique of European colonialism, animated with his passionate defense of the Palestinian cause, partaking in the wounded pride of Arab nationalism, all came together to launch a critique of orientalism at the expense of seeing the larger and longer patterns of transnational public spheres where resistance to colonial imperial and tyrannical forces assumes much more diverse forms.

Later in this book I will devote more attention to the active formation of this transnational public sphere where "Islam and the West" collapses upon itself. Equally important, however, is to keep in mind how some of the best cases marking the formation of this transnational public sphere and therefore effectively dismantling this illusion are the extraordinary women in both Islamic and European contexts crossing such fictive frontiers and forming tertiary spaces beyond "Islam and the West." Consider the case of the Mughal Queen Nur Jahan (1577–1645), whose towering example makes a mockery of every cliché we know about a "Muslim woman." Of noble Iranian origin, she was the most powerful woman of her time in India, playing a crucial role in running the vast Mughal empire. We will have to expand the horizons of our vision of the world far beyond the distorting frame of "Islam and the West" to accommodate her character and culture. The same is true about Lady Mary Wortley Montagu (1689–1762), an English aristocrat whom today we remember for her poetry but even more importantly for her letters from her travels through the Ottoman Empire. As evident in *The Turkish Embassy Letters*, her critical reflections on a body of issues do not fall into "the West and the Rest" binary. Right next to these two aristocratic women we have the revolutionary figure of Tahereh Qorrat al-Ayn (1814–1852), who led a major contingency of the most radical uprising of the Babi movement against the Qajar dynasty in the middle of the nineteenth century in Iran. She is comparable with such later revolutionary figures as Rosa Luxemburg (1871–1919), although almost a century apart. Equally crucial is another major figure, Taj al-Saltaneh (1883–1936), a Qajar princess who has left behind a remarkable memoir about the fate of her homeland comparable to Mary Wollstonecraft's *A Vindication of the Rights of Woman* (1792). Place these figures next to Bibi Khanom Astarabadi (1858–1921), a pioneering women's rights activist comparable to Simone de Beauvoir and who is today considered an iconic figure in this cause, and you are witness to a scene far richer and complicated than "the West and the Rest" would allow us to see. If we then include the figure of Gertrude Bell (1868–1926), an English traveler, colonial officer, and archaeologist who explored, mapped, and excavated ancient sites, then we have a richer conception of why today we remember her for her translation of Hafez's lyrical poetry. Put together, these women defied the cliché bifurcation of "Islam and the West" and in their lived experiences crossed the thick imaginative wall of "the East and the West" and in their very lives proved it illusory and porous.

The presence and significance of these women, from the highest echelons of the aristocracy to the most revolutionary, is evident on a transnational public sphere that we must then animate with the crucial functions of race and class that placed the workforces of nations alongside each other. I will devote the last three chapters of this book to these crucial issues of race, gender, and class and their intersectionality on the transnational para/public sphere. What cuts through the fake civilizational divides of "Islam and the West" is the fact of a *world system* in which the global circulation of labor, capital, raw materials, and markets generates and sustains cross-border similarities that are defiant of fake frontiers. In this transregional circulation of accumulated capital, abused labor, and raw material, where the beneficiaries and those disenfranchised by it remain the same, civilizational divides expose themselves to be utterly ludicrous.[26]

That brings us to the central question of race, which in the case of "Islam and the West" comes to a closure in the Black Muslims experiences in the United States and the revolutionary figure of Malcolm X. Born and raised and having come to political consciousness in "the West," the towering figure of Malcolm X and his revolutionary Islam completely dismantles the fake binary in one revolutionary experience. The figure of Malcolm X in and of itself exposes the embedded experiences of disenfranchised, ostracized, and marginalized pariahs of this "West" that the triumphant allegory has had to hide in order to paint itself with a white supremacist brush.

Race, gender, and class therefore animate the transnational public sphere into which any such fake civilizational divide fades and dissolves. In her classic essay "Demarginalizing the Intersection of Race and Sex: A Black Feminist Critique of Antidiscrimination Doctrine, Feminist Theory and Antiracist Politics" (1989), Kimberlé Crenshaw has introduced and theorized the space where race, gender, and class come to interact. Here is a crucial passage in her seminal essay:

Because the intersectional experience is greater than the sum of racism and sexism, any analysis that does not take intersectionality into account cannot sufficiently address the particular manner in which Black women are subordinated. Thus, for feminist theory and anti-racist policy discourse to embrace the experiences and concerns of Black women, the entire framework that has been used as a basis for translating "women's experience" or "the Black experience" into concrete policy demands must be rethought and recast.[27]

The theoretical logic of intersectionality plays out on the transnational disposition of the parapublic sphere where the races, genders, and classes of multiple colonial and postcolonial communities come together to map out an entirely different vision of the world than the delusional civilizational divide could lead us to fathom.

Illusions on Feeble Grounds

Let us one more time visit Freud's crucial insights into the way illusions work. He writes:

At this point one must expect to meet with an objection. "Well then, if even obdurate sceptics admit that the assertions of religion cannot be refuted by reason, why should I not believe in them, since they have so much on their side—tradition, the agreement of mankind, and all the consolations they offer?" Why not, indeed? Just as no one can be forced to believe, so no one can be forced to disbelieve. But do not let us be satisfied with deceiving ourselves that arguments like these take us along the road of correct thinking. If ever there was a case of a lame excuse, we have it here. Ignorance is ignorance; no right to believe anything can be derived from it. In other matters no sensible person will behave so irresponsibly or rest content with such feeble grounds for his opinions and for the line he takes.[28]

Everything Freud has theorized about "religion" as an *illusion* is even more applicable to the illusion that calls itself "the West." But illusions can indeed "be refuted by reason" when their durations have exhausted themselves and the world outside those illusions has overwhelmed them. The illusion of "the West" did indeed enjoy "so much on their side—tradition, the agreement of mankind, and all the consolations they offer"—for which reason it endured for long. But today Freud's diagnosis of illusions remains solidly applicable to the illusion of "the West" and all other illusions it has occasioned: "Ignorance is ignorance; no right to believe anything can be derived from it. In other matters no sensible person will behave so irresponsibly or rest content with such feeble grounds for his opinions and for the line he takes."

Let me now return to Charles de Steuben's *Bataille de Poitiers en Octobre 732* (see page 31). There is a remarkable visual and structural similarity between Charles de Steuben's 1837 painting and Picasso's *Guernica* (1937). The similarity is so striking it could not possibly be accidental. Picasso must have had Steuben's picture in mind when doing his *Guernica*. Consider the figure of the mother and her child in the middle of both pictures. Notice how in Steuben's picture the figure of Abd al-Rahman is raising a long sword extended behind him, that gesture and shape are transfigured in Picasso's picture to bring a lantern into the distraught gathering instead of a sword. See how the head of Charles's horse is severed in Picasso's painting and reversed. The rest of Steuben's painting, too, is all there in Picasso's but rendered in cubist disfiguration. Consider also the dates of the two works. They are exactly one century apart, from 1837 to 1937. What has happened in the span of this century? Picasso's masterpiece of anti-war, anti-fascist art is the sublime representation of a world no longer under the illusion of any civilizational category or bifurcation as allegorized in Steuben's painting. Europe has awoken from its self-delusions and false consciousness. "The West" here is

FIGURE 2. Pablo Picasso, *Guernica* (1937). Oil on canvas, 137.4 in. × 305.5 in. Museo Reina Sofía, Madrid, Spain.

doing to itself what it had claimed "Islam" was perpetrating against it. Here, beyond any "Islam and the West," humanity is dismembered to its constituent limbs and forces of fear and violence, ready for a painful reconfiguration of truth beyond civilizational fictions.

Between Charles de Steuben's *Bataille de Poitiers en Octobre 732* and Pablo Picasso's *Guernica* is the dangerous zone where the illusion of "the West" turns inward and against itself, and this introverted turn of the dangerous illusion entails the horrors of the European Holocaust, when the central racist trope of "the West" begins to devour itself.

The Road Ahead

Following this introduction in which I have offered some details of the primary point and purpose of this book, the rest of my arguments will unfold in three interrelated parts. First, I give an account of how as two incongruent categories Islam and the West were placed into the corrosive binary of "Islam and the West"; second, I explain how the two parts of this illusory nexus ultimately self-imploded; and third, I show how and where the factual evidence that overcomes the false consciousness has materialized and set us free. At the beginning of each chapter that follows I will place you at the forefront of the argument that I will offer to move through these three parts to my conclusion: that "Islam and the West" has been a an illusion that has caused much moral, imaginative, and material terror upon this earth; that the false binary was a fetishized by-product of capitalist modernity that ideologically needed, demanded, and exacted a fictional center for itself and a demonized, colonized, and ravaged periphery for others; that the delusional pairing has now ultimately self-imploded; and that the transnational public sphere upon which issues of race, class, gender, and nationality have been mapped out has occasioned a liberating plain of possibilities for postcolonial agency that once and for all overcomes the very condition of coloniality that had occasioned the chimeric alchemy of "Islam and the West."

Civilizational boundaries have collapsed, cultural configurations are in a state of flux, national identities have dissolved into their alterities, continental divides have become porous and permeable by the force of massive labor and refugee migrations. Atomized individuals, solitary labor migrants, desperate refuges, widespread refugee camps, and a systematic rise of reactionary white supremacy have all come together to make a mockery of the very assumption of such civilizational divides as "Islam and the West." This book is therefore both the scene of an autopsy and the site of a pathological examination, an obituary in anticipation of a liberating rebirth.

I   *The Colonial Catalyst*

1   *Islam in the World*

By the declining day,
Lo! mankind is in a state of loss,
Save those who believe and do good works, and exhort one another to truth
and exhort one another to endurance.

THE QUR'AN, 103: 1–3

"The struggle of Muslims with and for modernity is taking place, not just in Cairo, Tehran and Islamabad, but also among Muslims living in the West."[1] The most serious attempt at understanding the current crisis the world over, even by the most seasoned commentator in the most respected news outlets, presumes a Manichean distinction between "Islam" and the "West." Even Muslims who live in this "West" are not of "the West." Muslims, by virtue of being born Muslim, are just incapable of being modern, being Westerners—that is, being capable of leading a modest, decent, quiet life anywhere in the world. This is an existential crisis for Muslims, and of course for "the West." It is a proverbial catch-22. That irresoluble riddle, that paralyzing paradox, is the epistemic foregrounding of everything the world today understands by the binary formulation "Islam and West."

My central thesis so far has been very simple: The "Islam" that we see in the enthralling articulation of "Islam and the West" is the invention of that very "West" itself. Eurocentric modernity has systematically sought to cross-authenticate itself (in order to naturalize and immortalize the power of capital it thus fetishizes) by inventing outdated and inferior civilizations: Islamic, Indian, Chinese, African, and so on. They are all there to nourish and centralize the insatiable appetite of "the West" morally, imaginatively, materially. Muslim and non-Muslim critical thinkers have hitherto responded in kind, and by criticizing this very "West" they have in fact cross-authenticated it—made the metaphor even stronger than before they began criticizing (or alternatively praising) it. It does not make any difference if we say "the West" is God's gift to humanity or "the West" is evil. In both cases we are fetishizing a normative abstraction. I have therefore used aspects of both Freud's notion of religion as an "illusion" and Marx's idea of "false consciousness" to propose that these two seminal European thinkers were in fact theorizing the illusion and false consciousness of "the West" as the single most important metaphysical underpinning of their own time—an illusion far stronger and pervasive than any other "religion"—that Marx and Freud were in fact self-theorizing their own historical consciousness in "the West." The "Islam" that this "West" has invented as its inferior Other, or that Muslims have reversed as superior to this "West," is markedly different from the lived experiences of Muslims across lands and times.

If this "Islam" of "Islam and the West" is as illusory as "the West" itself, as I propose here, then the obvious question is what was Islam before it was coupled with the false consciousness of "the West." To answer that question, in this first chapter my task is to articulate a vision of Islam as a real lived experience before the illusion of "the West" descended upon and began to eat into its varied realities. Islam is a fourteen-hundred-year-old reality, while "Islam and the West" is a very recent commodity, the product of the fetishism of capitalist modernity that had reached its colonial outposts. How did Muslims experience Islam before this fateful encounter?

At this point in history, it would be utterly futile to say that Islam is not *this*, but Islam is *that*. Instead, I must put forward an "idea" of Islam, a way of reading Islam as a dynamic proposition that accounts for its historical effervescence and worldly presence. The point is not that the Islam of the "Islam and the West" is bad and I am going to introduce to you a good Islam. Rather, I must put forward for your consideration an idea of Islam beyond good and evil, an Islam of the lived experiences of Muslims. I therefore need to provide *a perspective* on Islam prior to its fateful encounter with European colonial modernity, the moment and the occasion when "Islam and the West" came to be. To do so, I begin with the charismatic tension that is constitutional to Islam in its very historical conception and origin—for it is absolutely imperative for us to remember and recognize Islam not as the "other" of "the West" but as the constellation of doctrines and sentiments emanating from its own central charismatic moment. I will therefore offer a deeper historical account of the composition of Islamic moral and intellectual disposition and discursive proclivities prior to the arrival of European capitalist modernity. I will then turn to demonstrate how with the rise of this Eurocentric modernity Islam was transformed into a singular and exclusive site of ideological resistance to colonialism, not simply by Orientalists but by Muslims themselves, and thus it lost the diversified texture of its multifaceted heritage. It was mutated by Muslim ideologues into the mirror image of the paramount power they faced, which they called "the West." This is the moment when Islam becomes Islamism.

The thematic mutation of Islam from its own historical complexities to its colonial and postcolonial disposition is rarely, if ever, the subject of discussion by scholars who attend to the predicament of Muslims in colonial modernity. But this is a particularly critical issue, for which my scholarly work in the fields of both modern and medieval intellectual history qualifies my project. It is imperative for us to think of Islam in Islamic terms, as it were, before we can see how it fared in its encounter with the imperial allegory of "the West."

Islam's turn from its multifaceted fullness into a site of ideological resistance to European colonialism was a gradual mutation. We need to know how this gradual mutation was performed in combative conversations with the abstract assumption of the colonial entity calling itself "the West" as the principal interlocutor of Muslim ideologues. What Islam was before it entered this binary—that it was a prophetic mission, predicated on a charismatic character and built through a succession of empires and their governing scholastic and humanistic modes of knowledge productions and the intellectual reactions they inevitably provoke—is now all but forgotten except for recondite scholarship and its limited readership. We need to remember these episodes in order to put what we know of Islam today in a much deeper historical context. We need to remember how from the charismatic memory of Prophet Muhammad eventually multiple discourses of truth and authenticity emerged—how Islamic law laid a claim on the *nomocentric* disposition of the Qur'anic revelation, while Islamic philosophy cultivated a *logocentric* take on truth, as Islamic mysticism eventually offered Muslims a *homocentric* option. From India to North Africa, Muslim lands became the polylocal domain of multiple readings of Islam, while successive imperial formations, from the Abbasids through the Ottomans, crafted the cosmopolitan context of life and fortune for multiple nations under their imperial domains. Islam was multilingual and polylocal, and thus it spoke with multiple commanding discourses. Islam was confident, curious, self-universalizing. Under the abiding power of European imperialism, however, all that confidence disappeared and Muslims themselves, more than any Orientalist could ever do, trapped

Islam in a monolithic site of resistance to the foreign invaders and occupiers.²

Muslims in History

The historical experiences of Muslims over the last two hundred years have been constitutionally different from that of the preceding twelve hundred years—that is to say, with the rise of colonial modernity in the late eighteenth century Muslims throughout the world were systematically forced to transform their ancestral faith from a rich and multifaceted metaphysical and cultural experience into a site of inflexible ideological resistance to colonialism. In order to demonstrate the nature and function, causes and consequences, of this transformation, we need to recall the outline of a reading of Islamic history that is constitutional to its doctrinal disposition and endemic to its epistemic discourses and institutional character. What we today call Islam is overwhelmingly colored by its recent— roughly the last two hundred years—aggressive mutation into a site of political contestation against European colonialism. In order to see the particulars of this transmutation in terms domestic to its encounter with colonial modernity, it is imperative to have a picture of its premodern history. Although the term *pre-modern* is itself too broad to capture the rise and vicissitudes of a world religion, still it does convey the cultural composition of that faith before its encounter with colonial modernity late in the eighteenth century. The point here is not to give a sweeping account of the cultural panorama of a world religion, but to suggest the theoretical disposition of its doctrinal character—*before* colonial modernity, code-named "the West," made its appearance.

At its very core, as evident in the moment of its initial historical unfolding early in the seventh century, Islam is *a religion of protest*. It has historically emerged as the collective faith of the outcast and the downtrodden, of the forbidden and the denied—and as such, it spoke the truth of dispossession to the power of possession, until it came to power itself and thus negated itself. In that paradox dwells the historical longevity of Islam. Born in 570, Prophet Muhammad began to receive what he believed to be systematic Divine messages in 610. His first converts, after the members of his immediate family and circle of friends, were the poor of Mecca, the outcasts of its tribal aristocracy, outsiders to its commercial elite. Between 610 and 617, the Prophet had gathered enough supporters to pose a threat to the Meccan establishment and was thus forced to send a group of his converts to Abyssinia under the protection of its Christian king. Between 617 and 622, Muhammad continued to gather more supporters among the poor Meccans, much to the anger and hostility of those who held power and influence. By 622, the Meccans plotted to murder the Prophet, and he escaped from certain death to Yathrib (later to be named *Madinat al-Nabi*, or City of the Prophet) to intervene in tribal hostilities between two rival clans. At his triumphant arrival in Medina in 622, he divided his supporters into two revolutionary categories—those who abandoned Mecca and emigrated with him to Medina (the Muhajirun), and those who helped them establish a Muslim community in Medina (the Ansar). By way of this revolutionary pact, Arab tribal affiliations were momentarily abrogated in favor of an Islamic revolutionary community—formed around the charismatic character of the Prophet and his Divine revelations.[3]

The revolutionary character of Islam as a religion of protest continued well into its Medinan period, between the migrations of the Prophet from Mecca to Medina in 622 (the commencement of the Islamic calendar) to his death in 632.[4] In the span of these ten years, Muhammad launched a succession of guerilla attacks against the Meccan commercial and political establishment, disrupting their lucrative caravans moving between Syria and Yemen, blocking the

principal trade route of the Meccan business elite, and then strategically retreating to the Medinan fortresses. More poor and disenfranchised Arabs and non-Arabs were attracted to Muhammad's
rebellious cause, charismatic character, Divine revelations, and
increasingly universal message of freedom and salvation. A brotherhood of bandits and rebels, renegades and revolutionaries, came
together from the tribal vassals of the two major empires of the
period—the Sassanids to the east and the Byzantines to the west.
By the time Muhammad defeated the Meccan commercial elite,
returned to Mecca triumphantly, destroyed the idols of the pagan
Arabs in Ka'bah in 630, and then died in peace in 632, he had established a solid political community to guarantee the historical continuity of his divine message. His was no religion of *turn the other
cheek*, nor did he wait for *an eye* to be taken to take *an eye* in exchange.
His was a successful revolutionary movement, divinely inspired,
peopled by the poor, fired by a revelatory imagination. And soon
after his death, it spread east and west like a brushfire. Islam was a
religion of protest from its very historical origin, and in the fabric of
its doctrinal principles.[5]

At the center of this revolutionary rise of Islam is Prophet
Muhammad's charismatic character, for he is believed by Muslims to
be the recipient (according to Islamic doctrines) of a Divine revelation. The charismatic authority of the Prophet of Islam was and has
remained constitutional to its revolutionary character and definitive
to its institutional formation.[6] Prophet Muhammad's charismatic
authority was predicated on the Qur'anic doctrinal position that in
His Infinite Justice and Benevolence, God Almighty, the Qur'anic
Allah, does not leave humanity at large to its own flawed devices but
periodically sends Divine emissaries to put them on the right path.
From Adam, through Abraham, Moses, Jesus, and finally Muhammad, God has sent prophets with a clear message (in the form of a
revelation, or *wahy*) as to what humanity needs to do to stay on the

Right Path (the Qur'anic *al-Sirat al-Mustaqim*) and achieve salvation. There is a dialectical correspondence between the prophetic necessity of *risalah* (Divine emissary) and the revelatory language of *wahy* (Divine revelation)—between Prophet Muhammad's revolutionary charisma and the spontaneous revelations of the Holy Qur'an—that cross-references and mutually authenticates both.[7] The charismatic character of the Prophet and the revelatory nature of the Qur'an thus form a creative nucleus that critically disturbs the status quo of its receiving culture and subjects it to major metaphysical sublation.[8]

Already evident in the course of Muhammad's prophetic career, the nature of his revolutionary character, and the very text of the Qur'an were signs and suggestions of an emerging charismatic paradox, a doctrinal contradiction, a creative tension that at once pulls its insurrectionary energy together and yet pushes its claim to structural stability apart—defines and destructs its metaphysical claim to legitimacy at one and the same time. Between 610 and 622, Prophet Muhammad is in a thoroughly defiant and rebellious posture, denouncing both Arab paganism and the Meccan commercial establishment. Between 622 and 632, however, he commenced the groundwork of establishing a state apparatus, the political infrastructure of a world religious community. The two episodes of his prophetic career—one iconoclastic and rebellious, the other institutional and state building—at once negate and yet dialectically constitute his prophetic mission. This paradoxical disposition of Muhammad's prophetic career is best evident in the text of the Qur'an itself, which is categorically divided into (the shorter) Meccan and (the longer) Medinan chapters—the former largely revolutionary, insurrectionary, transgressive, and iconoclastic; the latter regulative, inhibitive, forbidding, and legislative: One a *declaration of independence* from patrimonial tribalism; the other a divinely inspired *constitution*.

This charismatic paradox remains central to the doctrinal disposition of Islam throughout its history—giving it a revolutionary character when it is in its insurrectionary posture (reminiscent of the
Meccan chapters of the Qur'an and the rebellious memory of the
Prophet), and yet a repressive and tyrannical temperament when it
is in a position of power (evocative of the Medinan chapters of the
Qur'an and the Prophet's period of state formation and institution
building). Thus it gives rise to its own antithesis by reverting back to
its own revolutionary vision of itself. The history of Islam is the history of a cyclical pendulum oscillating between its insurrectionary
Meccan pose and its repressive Medinan memory. This predisposi-
tion is internal to the Islamic revelatory remembrance of its historical experiences—at once the central cause of its political instability
and the secret reason for its historical endurance. All historical acts
of what Max Weber called the "routinization of charisma" have been
transitory and impermanent in Islam.[9] They have been temporally
and temporarily successful in establishing modes of legitimate
authority but have always been susceptible to active revolutionary
insurrection, occasioned by material causes for popular uprising and
triggered by the unresolved—and irresolvable—charismatic paradox
at the heart of the Islamic revelation.

The World after Muhammad

No charismatic outburst explodes in a vacuum—it always disturbs
and disrupts an already operative social and moral order. The rise
of Prophet Muhammad's charismatic mission and revolutionary
movement early in the seventh century was expressed against the
pre-Islamic Arab oligarchic patrimonialism—divided into and operative within a network of tribal affiliations.[10] The pre-Islamic Arab
patrimonialism, what in his classic typology Weber would call a traditional pattern of authority, put up a stiff resistance to the rise and

ascendancy of the Prophet's charismatic movement.[11] The defeat of the Meccan commercial elite was also the defeat of Arab paganism—or what the Qur'an dismissed as the period of Jahiliyyah ("Ignorance"). The Prophet of Islam occasionally had to make concessions to pre-Islamic practices by way of a political maneuver, such as when (disappointed with the Jewish tribes of Medina refusing to acknowledge him as a biblical prophet) he changed the direction of Muslim prayer from Jerusalem to Mecca. A more controversial example would be the case of the so-called Satanic Verses, in which the prophet first acknowledged and then rescinded the inclusion of a number of pagan idols among the Islamic deities.[12] The clash between his charismatic authority, representing the new revelatory religion, and the Meccan commercial establishment, representing Arab paganism, continued unabated almost to the end of the Prophet's life, and this battle between charisma (rebellion) and tradition (law) remains definitive to the rest of Islamic history.

The confrontation between the pre-Islamic *traditional* and the legacy of the Muhammadan *charismatic* modes of authority continued almost immediately after the death of the prophet in 632 and during the course of the so-called *crisis of succession*.[13] The crisis (and the clash that it harbored) generated a central paradigm of *creative conflict* within the Islamic institutional and doctrinal discourses. From this creative conflict between *two* constitutionally different modes of authority *three* paradigmatic patterns of legitimacy emerged in the immediate aftermath of the Prophet's death: What would later be called the Sunnite, the Shi'ite, and the Kharijite branches of Islam were varied forms that that creative conflict between the Muhammadan charismatic and the Arab *patrimonial* modes of authority assumed. The result of this early so-called sectarian conflict was the generation of a doctrinally polyfocal texture to Islam—none of these sectarian branches having a complete control over Muslims' revolutionary disposition. It is critical to keep in mind that in this paradigmatic sense, the Sunnite, Shi'ite, and Kharijite versions of a resolution to the crisis of succession (covering the more irresoluble charismatic paradox), were normatively operative throughout Islamic history and applicable to *all* Muslims—that is to say, while Muslims were nominally divided into Sunni, Shi'i, and Kharijite communities, there was a more subtextual operation to these paradigmatics of legitimacy that did not discriminate between one group of Muslims and another. While *Sunni Islam* sought permanent pillars of legitimate authority in the dual institutions of Caliphate and the Ulama, *Shi'i Islam* sought to perpetuate the charismatic moment of the Prophetic presence in the figures of its infallible Imams, and *Kharijite Islam* opted for an anarchic populism (or radical democracy) that refused enduring legitimacy to any leader beyond immediate insurrectionary causes.[14] In short, I offer what is usually read as the "sectarian" conflicts within Islam as its enduring modalities of political culture centered around the charismatic figure of the Prophet.

The charismatic paradox at the heart of the Islamic historical and doctrinal experiences was not limited to such so-called "sectarian" conflicts. Soon after the consolidation of the text of the Qur'an under Caliph Uthman (caliph, 644-656) and the subsequent institutionalization of Islamic law, the emergence of Islamic philosophy, and the rise of Islamic mysticism, a yet further (equally consequential) creative conflict emerged in Islamic intellectual history. The dialectic energy of this conflict was entirely predicated on the destabilizing vibrations of the selfsame charismatic paradox constitutional to what might be called a prophetic paraphrastic in Islamic intellectual history—whereby the initial revelatory experience of the Prophet is paraphrased in intellectual terms. While what would gradually emerge as Islamic law (*Shari'ah*) opted for a nomocentric reading of the prophetic experience, the effervescent rise of Islamic philosophy (*Falsafah*) would opt for a logocentric reading of the selfsame phenomenon—both of which movements were soon to be challenged by a homocentric proclivity in Islamic mysticism (*Tasawwuf*). The result was the simultaneous generation of an epistemically polyvocal texture to Islamic intellectual disposition that would not allow any one particular intellectual disposition to claim the entirety of its prophetic legacy.[15] While the nomocentric tendencies of Islamic law insisted that the purpose of the prophetic revelations was *to do* what God had commanded, the logocentric proclivity of Islamic philosophy insisted that the purpose was *to know* God and his worldly creation—both of which presumptions were soon to be challenged by the homocentric insistence of Islamic mysticism that aggressively mutated the metaphysical fear of God—in either juridical or philosophical terms—into a theo-erotic love of God because it insisted the prophetic mission was for man *to retrieve* its Edenic image of God. The creative conflict among these three epistemic formations disallowed any enduring sense of "orthodoxy" to be valid at any point in Islamic history. Any orthodoxy was basically a politically successful heterodoxy waiting to be overruled.

That was not the entirety of the Islamic story before its encounter with European colonial modernity. The doctrinal polyfocality of Islam and its epistemic polyvocality was then expanded geographically far beyond the Arabian birthplace of its origin and thus gradually gave birth to a culturally polylocal world religion that extended from one end of Africa to the other end of Asia, and from the southern shores of Europe to the northern banks of Pacifica. As Arabs, Persians, and Turks joined Kurds, Afghans, and Turkmans; Eastern Europeans, Central Asians, and South Asians; Chinese, Indonesians, and Malaysians; Africans, African Americans, and then North and Latin Americans came together in Islam and went away to their homelands, a huge tapestry of colors, cultures, and ethnicities, languages, races, and nations—domestic to their own communal terms or later colonially fabricated and presumed—defined and divided a world religion impossible to be imperially dominated by one meta-narrative or another. Muslims were Muslims far more by their differences than by their similarities.

Doctrinally polyfocal, epistemically polyvocal, and culturally polylocal, Islam has witnessed a global history impossible to narrate in any solitary language in any moment of its history. All these normative variables in the making of the moral imagination of a Muslim person were entirely limited to the religious dimensions of the Islamic cultural universe. When we name "Islam" as a designated term for a vast cultural universe, we also include active references to its literary worlds that grew to spectacular fruition entirely independent of these moral and intellectual developments. The subject of literary humanism is an entirely different universe of imagination that came to create a moral universe quite independent of, albeit adjacent to, Islamic intellectual history.[16] On the premise of the moral diversity of Islam as a world religion, successive Islamic empires were built—from the Umayyads and the Abbasids in the seventh to the thirteenth centuries, through the Seljuqid and the Fatimids during the European Middle Ages, down to the Ottomans, the Safavids, and the Mughals in the fourteenth through the nineteenth and the twentieth centuries. This material expansionism of Islam occasioned and embraced a literary humanism that in the reach and globality of its appeal rivaled the Qur'anic transmutation of Islam in doctrinal directions. Religion (*din*) and literary humanism (*adab*) developed simultaneously and divided the sensibilities of a cultured Muslim. Such a "religion" was no "illusion," for it was never limited to any set of fixed doctrinal dogmas that any believer had to hold immutable.

At the peak of its social and intellectual history before its encounter with "the West," Islam was a multifaceted culture that spoke philosophically with philosophers, theologically with theologians, juridically with jurists, mystically with mystics, and imperially with world conquerors. In languages and discourses, institutions and narratives, Islam was at one and the same time culturally polylocal, epistemically polyvocal, and doctrinally polyfocal. All these narrative variations on the revelatory language of the Qur'an were quite independent of the multilingual and multicultural literary humanism that emerged in Arabic, Persian, Turkish, and Urdu, the four principal languages of Muslim people. The moral universe of a medieval Muslim had contemplative texture to it and a conjectural dexterity. Nothing was stable except the urge to override dogma. Every dogmatic wall was an invitation to a debate. A vast topography of normative choices and speculative dispositions painted the horizon of a Muslim mind and moral universe in which Muslims lived, all against the background of the poetic potency of a literary imagination that boastfully placed the word of the poet in man right next to the Word of the Eternal from God. All "illusions" of any otherworldly divinity had dissipated into the mundane dispositions of being-a-Muslim-in-this-world.

But din/religion and adab/literary humanism were not the totality of a Muslim's universe. A vast plethora of sciences—from mathematics and medicine to geography and astrophysics—also engaged a Muslim's cultural imagination. The science of geography was elevated to an unprecedented level, as was groundbreaking reflection on the philosophy of history. The science of linguistics emerged from Qur'anic hermeneutics but was soon connected to prosody and poetics. From the same scientific interest in mathematics grew a systematic musicology. From medicine grew pharmacology and botany, from mathematics trigonometry and algebra. These were mostly Muslim scientists who developed these sciences—their scientific universe adjacent to any act of faith they might confess. There were Jews among these Muslim scientists and there were Christians, Zoroastrians, and agnostics. Their science was not independent of their faith, it was rooted in it, however far from the root of revelation their reasoning might have grown. This universe, from revelatory roots to flowering reasons, was no illusion. Add to the scientific universe of a medieval Muslim the colorful expanse of Islamic art and architecture and we begin to have a fuller view of what it meant to be a Muslim before colonial modernity that called itself "the West" arrived on the scene.

When Islam Became an Abstraction

It is critical not to confuse a full vision of the moral and intellectual universe of a Muslim with a nostalgic and flawed conception of such bizarre concoctions as "true Islam" or "traditional Islam" that have plagued contemporary encounters with colonial modernity. Like all other world religions, Islam has had a tumultuous and, on many occasions, murderous history. Since the earliest stages of the Islamic encounter with European modernity, constitutionally flawed and fallacious ideas about a fictitious golden age in Islamic history have been constructed in contrast to "the evils of modernity." Predicated on the fabricated binary opposition between "Islam and the West," a pure and serene fantasy began to emerge about a period in Islamic history in which things were not corrupted by "the West," which is thus assumed (first) to have an autonomous reality and (second) to be corrupt and corrupting. These are figments of a disturbed imagination—disturbed by the vagaries of colonial modernity.[17]

What I am suggesting here is quite the opposite. Islam (as have all other world religions) has had a long and tumultuous history—and since Muslims themselves (not the colonialists and Orientalists) have been principally responsible for the negation of the multifaceted reality of their own historical experiences, Islamic history is at once enriched and enraged by multiplicities of visions and claims to its moral veracity and material relevance. My principal point here is to show the dialectical diversity at the center of Islamic historical experience—a multiplicity of visions (at once intellectually fertile and politically tumultuous, but always morally multifaceted) that Muslims systematically lost by a willful act of collective amnesia when confronted with the colonially mediated "modernity." Critique of this colonial modernity via a recollection of the tumultuous history of Islam is vastly different from a blind hatred of "modernity" in the name of a fictitious "pure Islam." There is no such thing as "pure Islam." Islam has always been defined by a diversity of claims, even mutually exclusive claims on it. That paradoxical diversity is Islam.

The task at hand is not to replace the illusory "Islam" of "Islam and the West" with the fictitious Islam of "pure Islam." The task is to retrieve the dialectical tensions within the Islamic moral and intellectual imagination in order to decouple it from the illusion of "Islam and the West" and, we might add, distinguish it from the equally fictitious Islam of "pure Islam" of latter-day Muslim gurus in "the West." Islam is a religious reality, a *totality* contingent on an *infinity*.[18] It has always changed in its essence and attributes through creative conversations with its varied historical interlocutors. Like all other shades of reality, Islam is narrated into a culture that is constitutionally conversational, deliberately dialogical in its texture and disposition, and it has always become the reflective image of its principal interpolator. At the dawn of its history some fourteen hundred years ago, when it emerged in hostile conversation with Arab patrimonialism, it turned out to reflect the timbre of its tribal origin in its first dynastic manifestation: the Umayyads (661-750). As it began to lay an imperial claim on every domain of knowledge during the Abbasid period (750-1258), and its site of self-reflection assumed the combined effects of the Greek, the Persian, the Indian, and the Chinese philosophical and wisdom literature, Islam became philosophical and contemplative. When the reflective mirror of its self-awareness became the Jewish and Christian theologies and jurisprudence, Islam became theological and juridical in kind. When that persistent questioner changed and assumed the guise of Christian, Manichean, and Buddhist monasticism, Islam became mystical and gave birth to Sufism. When the Roman and the Persian Empires were its defeated enemies, Islam became a conquering power. When the Abbasid dynasty became the civilizational custodian of the best that the Byzantine and the Sassanid dynasties had delivered to it, Islam radically mutated from its tribal origin and became learned, cultivated, urbane, and cosmopolitan. First in Arabic and Persian, and subsequently in Turkish and Urdu, it gave rise to some of the most magnificent shades of literary humanism in history. The same was true in its art and architecture. Islam was (and is) a claim to truth, its evident totality always modified by its transcendental claims on infinity. No other claim to truth or beauty or vision could come its way without Muslims turning around and mirroring their own reading of truth in the light of that new vision. Islam has been dialectical from the dawn of its history to the end of its moral imagination when faced with the consequences of predatory capital that knows no limit, that spins on every turn of events its own version of truth, a truth that serves its (always momentarily) best interest.

The Hegemony of a Fetishized Abstraction

Islam thus became an abstraction when Muslims, facing the onslaught of European imperialism, robbed themselves of the dialectical logic of their own heritage in exchange for a flatfooted Islamism to help them put up a futile resistance. The only difference between the encounters of the past and this last fateful interface with "the West" is that all those were engaged from a position of power and authority and this from a position of weakness and defeated triumphalism. The more Muslim lands and minds were conquered and dominated by "the West," the more triumphalist the abstraction of "Islam" vis-à-vis "the West" became. Here it is also crucial to remember that historically the rising Muslim empires faced two imperial nemeses (not just one): the Sassanids (224–651) and the Byzantines (395–1453). Muslim armies defeated them both, pushing back against the Byzantines and eventually conquering and absorbing the Sassanid domains and using their imperial blueprint as the model for their own imperial domination. The Byzantine Empire survived the early rise of Muslim empires only to succumb to the Ottomans in 1453. From the Abbasids' takeover of the Sassanids in the eighth century to the Ottoman takeover of the Byzantines in the fifteenth, both modeling themselves on an Islamic (Sassanid) imperial design, the inner dynamics of two imperial models—Persian and Roman—created a political dynamic rarely matched in human history. The synergy of these two imperial conflations in the succession of imperial dynasties that followed gave Muslims of multiple generations a sense of political triumphalism that could never come to terms with European cultural hegemony, code-named "the West." The collapse of this historical memory into "Islam" as an abstract by-product of "the West" was a consequence of systematic Islamic collective amnesia.

All of these internal dynamics of Islam, from its antiquity to its encounter with colonial modernity, was of course utterly foreign to both Freud and Marx in their reflections on "religion" as an "illusion," a false consciousness, the opium of the masses. Therefore, it was a total abstraction. Here is the context in which Marx considered "religion" to be "the opium of the people."

Religious suffering is, at one and the same time, the expression of real suffering and a protest against real suffering. Religion is the sigh of the oppressed creature, the heart of a heartless world, and the soul of soulless conditions. It is the opium of the people. The abolition of religion as the illusory happiness of the people is the demand for their real happiness. To call on them to give up their illusions about their condition is to call on them to give up a condition that requires illusions. The criticism of religion is, therefore, in embryo, the criticism of that vale of tears of which religion is the halo.[19]

What exactly is this "religious suffering" as opposed to, or as a protest against, "real suffering"? Marx's conception of "religion" is almost entirely Christian, its doctrine of redemptive suffering of Christ. As such, it has very little resemblance to other world religions, such as Islam, Judaism, Buddhism, or Hinduism. Muslims for example did not just sit there and sigh as oppressed creatures, and their collective beliefs were never the soul of soulless conditions. When their conditions were soulless and dire, they picked up arms and went after their tormentors. They never turned the other cheek, nor did they ever think the meek will inherit the earth. If anything, their faith has made Muslims hyperactive rather than sedated, oppressed, and awaiting real happiness. But by the time Marx speaks of "illusory happiness" we know for a fact he is really talking about Christianity and its coded identity under capitalist modernity, "the West." Marx wishes to dispense with this illusion of vacuous happiness in the interest of real happiness. The only way to read that prospect is precisely the Marxist proposition of dispensing with the false consciousness that is now pronouncedly called "the West." This illusion, this false consciousness, this ideology of the dominant class, is what prevented the working class from becoming conscious of its dire circumstances while partaking in the bourgeois ideal of being part of "Western civilization." That ideal did not remain stationary in its own domain in "the West." It went around the globe and made all the other visions of humanity that it touched mere illusions, chief among them "Islam."

2 "The West"
Groundwork for the Metaphysics of an Illusion

The Negroes of Africa have by nature no feeling that rises above the trifling . . .
even though among the whites some continually rise aloft from the lowest
rabble and through superior gifts earn respect in the world. So fundamental
is the difference between these two races of man, and it appears to be as great
in regard to mental capacities as in color.

IMMANUEL KANT, *Observations on the Feeling*
of the Beautiful and Sublime (1764)

As I began working on this chapter in mid-March 2020, the news of a coronavirus pandemic wreaking havoc around the globe had just reached the East and West Coasts of the United States. In one of his first reactions to the pandemic, US President Donald Trump referred to COVID-19 as "a foreign virus." He went on to remark, "This is the most aggressive and comprehensive effort to confront a foreign virus in modern history. I am confident that by . . . continuing to take these tough measures we will significantly reduce the threat to our citizens and we will ultimately and expeditiously defeat this virus."[1]

[78]

By the end of those two sentences, it was no longer clear whether President Trump was talking about a virus or about foreigners, or perhaps about foreigners as viruses. As Nükhet Varlik, a professor of history at Rutgers University in Newark, New Jersey, and at the University of South Carolina, told CNN in response to this presidential remark: "Jewish populations were accused of deliberately poisoning the wells and causing the plague. We know examples of this from many places in Europe. As rumors spread, Jews were killed, buried alive and burned at the stake. And they weren't the only group erroneously blamed for causing the disease." Who were the other enemies other than Jews? Nükhet Varlik specifies: "European accounts talk about plague as 'Oriental Plague.' . . . They look at the Ottoman Empire as the origin of the plague."

In all such narratives, in between Jews as the internal enemy and Muslims as the external enemy, stands "the West," solitary, innocent, and vulnerable, the epicenter of a fictive geography whose chief custodians were the white men holding their citadel against all enemies, "foreign and domestic." Furthest from Donald Trump's mind, of course, was any historical or philosophical underpinning of his xenophobia. But our task is precisely to uncover such roots in order to overcome them.

Historically, we know the manufacturing of "the West" was predicated on a Hegelian philosophy of history that was teleological to the core. It begins the prehistory of "the West" in Indian and Chinese civilizations, and with the Persian Empire prepares to come forward to the Greeks, the Romans, and all the way down to Hegel's own homeland. If we remember that the Sassanids (224–651) were the contemporaries of the Romans, we see how in the Hegelian schematization "the Persians" had become merely a trope, as in fact the entirety of world history is channeled to zoom in on "the West" as its historical *Geist* (spirit) in the making, its promise delivered.[2] The memory of the Persian Empire, from the Achaemenids to the

Sassanids as the main alterities to the Greeks and the Romans, is here totally repressed by "the West," and in effect "Islam" is turned into the summation of an eternal enemy. But if the Sassanids were brought in, an imperial triangulation would emerge that would dismantle the binary of "Islam and the West." Byzantium was the Eastern part of the Roman Empire, and this "East-West" within "the West" itself generated a duality that affiliated Byzantium effectively with the Sassanids. When both these empires collapsed to successive Muslim empires, "Islam" as a coded term consolidated all these easternmost anxieties. The invention of "the West" was therefore tantamount to an articulation of a metaphysical entity, a "religion," the way Freud describes the illusion—though unbeknownst to himself he was describing the illusion of "the West" as the most potent metaphysical foregrounding of European modernity.

We therefore need a similar act of historical archeology, parallel to what I did in the previous chapter with Islam, but this time providing the genealogy of what today we call "the West," giving an outline of the discursive trajectory through which the rise of capitalist modernity was narrated into the categorical conception of "the West" as its towering metaphor. Just as I provided a perspective, a plausible vantage point, on Islam and how it has unfolded in history, we also need a similar reading of the illusion of "the West," and how in the course of capitalist modernity it emerged as the touchstone of a fetishized ideology. This comparatist perspective will enable us to see how "the West" was constituted as a viable civilizational category covering and disguising the economic relation of power between capital and labor, fetishizing the commodification of ideologies with a certain metaphysical authenticity, originality, and inevitability. Predicated on a very long European history, when neither "the West" nor indeed even "Europe" carried the metaphoric meaning they do today, "Islam and the West" began its journey as a very recent civilizational invention, one no earlier than the European bourgeois revolution, its concomitant emergence of the New Class, the collapse of European dynastic structures and Christian ecclesiastical orders, and the active formation of European national economies, national polities, and perforce national cultures—all of which were brought under the generic rubric of "Western civilization," or "the West" for short, contrapuntally contrasted with such Orientalized civilizations as the Chinese, the Indian, or the Islamic. "Western civilization" to all these "other" civilizations was like a mature man compared to an indigent child, as the self-confidence of the European bourgeois culture at once cannibalized and infantilized other cultures.

With a view toward our contemporary history, I therefore propose a critical account of how, against a much richer and more diversified history, "the West" emerged in the immediate aftermath of the French and the Industrial revolutions, the collapse of the dynastic and ecclesiastical orders as the organizing forces of "European" cultures, and the replacement of the idea of "Christendom" by its functional Enlightenment equivalent: "Western civilization." The succession of European empires (the Spanish, the British, and the French in particular) and their mode of knowledge and power production ultimately reaches the Protestant Reformation, and after that the French Revolution, the Industrial Revolution, and eventually globalized capitalism and its colonial consequences, among which is the manufacturing of the concept of "the West" and all its antitheses: "the East," "the Orient," "Islam." This globalizing capitalist modernity needed and invented a metaphysics of its morals. "The West" was the talisman of that metaphysics.

The Invention of "the West"

The manufactured Manicheanism of "Islam and the West" inevitably conceals complex and unruly realities that are thus homogenized and codified so that they might be ruled better. The vibrant exchanges of goods and products, as well as ideas and sentiments, between merchants and traders as well as philosophers, poets, scientists, religious thinkers, and so on, were evident in the classical period and up to the Renaissance in both the imperial and the emerging bourgeois public spheres, whose geographies have never been reducible to any such binary as "Islam and the West." Here the point is not merely to mark the accidental "influences" of one or two thinkers on each other, but to show the structural spaces around the Mediterranean basin where navigational routes from Asia and Africa were directly linked to Europe before it was "Europe" in the sense of the cultural unity and continuity we are led to accept today. Here we can see how both Christianity and Islam are in fact staged historical takes on Judaism, where their scriptural similarities and cross-references speak of not just unitary originals but shared experiences. Here we can see how the emergence of Islamic law, theology, philosophy, and mysticism were in fact integral to their counterparts in Judaism and Christianity—not just by dint of the common "Abrahamic tradition" but also by the shared historical, geographical, and cultural experiences around the Mediterranean basin. These exchanges and formations of common heritage were not limited to "religious" experiences, but were equally evident in philosophy, mysticism, poetry, and the arts and sciences. The shared cosmopolitan spaces of this Mediterranean world are where the binary of "Islam and the West" will have no way of inserting itself. If we look at major cities like Baghdad, Cairo, Jerusalem, Damascus, Istanbul, and Cordoba, we see that the lived experiences of Muslims and non-Muslims were predicated on urban topographies made of alternative tapestries of truth and identity.

Here it is crucial to remember how the formation of "the West," short for "Western civilization," was coterminous with the catastrophic mutation of Islam into "Islamic Ideology" as one of the most potent sites of political contestation against colonialism, almost the same way Latin American Christianity turned into "liberation theology" to oppose and end tyranny. While "the West" was the code name for a metaphysics of domination and exploitation, "Islamic ideology" and "liberation theology" were sites of contestation against it. In this context, "the West" was a categorical invention coined and made current with the advent of Enlightenment modernity. The very denominational divide of "civilization" is itself an Enlightenment creation for very specific reasons and objectives. Neither the aristocratic dynasties that the Enlightenment destroyed nor the ecclesiastical orders of feudalism and scholasticism it discredited thought in terms of or strove to enact civilizational standards. From Hegel's philosophy of history to Goethe's conception of "Weltliterature" to Herder's idea of "World History" to Kant's groundbreaking metaphysics of morals, the conceptual categories of civilizational thinking were coined and set in motion at the commencement of capitalist modernity. From the dawn of civilizational thinking in Kant, Hegel, and Herder to the wake of instrumental rationalism in Max Weber, the collapse of what had not yet given birth to the very idea of Europe as a cultural contingency announced the supra-tribal formation of "Western civilization." Islamic, African, Chinese, and Indian "civilizations" were simultaneous abstractions invented and narrated by an army of mercenary Orientalists to authenticate and corroborate, via negation of those others, their own "Western civilization." As a categorical invention, "Islamic civilization" was mapped out by Orientalists (at the service of colonialism) to corroborate the Enlightenment invention of "Western civilization." But Muslims were Muslims. They led a moderately civilized and occasionally barbaric life long before mercenary Orientalists conceived them into a category that would negationally verify an equally empty invention of "Western civilization." Take the mirror of Islamic (or Chinese, or Indian) civilization away from the face of

Western civilization and there will remain nothing to call "Western civilization." It is an illusion, and it needs the illusions of other civilizations to fabricate the assumption of a reality for itself. This is the core of my argument in this book.

It is crucial to remember that the premodern configuration of power in medieval Europe had established the aristocratic houses and ecclesiastical churches as the bipolar centers of social order, corresponding with a dynastic historiography (aristocratic) claiming Christendom (ecclesiastical) as its universal frame of reference. At the dawn of the emergence of capitalist modernity, the aristocratic and ecclesiastical nuclei of power gradually gave way to the rising bourgeoisie, and as a result the dynastic historiography yielded to conceptions of "national cultures," while Christendom simultaneously yielded to the corresponding contraption of "Western civilization," with the rising Enlightenment philosophers replacing the clerical class as intellectuals organic to the new social order. The idea of "Western civilization" at the commencement of capitalist modernity was to the European "national cultures" what Christendom was to dynastic histories during the medieval period. As the rising bourgeoisie replaced in power and prestige both the aristocratic houses and the ecclesiastical orders, the conceptual legitimacy of dynastic histories and Christendom was lost to that of European "national cultures" and their enframing and emplotment in "Western civilization." Because of its anxiety of class legitimacy, and because it could not genealogically compete either with the aristocratic dynasties or with the ecclesiastical orders, the rising new class of the bourgeoisie was intuitively drawn to such universal and universalizing abstractions as "national cultures" and "universal civilizations."[3]

There has been a division of labor in the nature and function of national cultures and their civilizational context. While national cultures corresponded to national economies and polities as the operative unit of the working of labor and capital, their constructed civilizational context targeted the colonial consequences of the selfsame operation. European national cultures were the domestic expressions of the national economic units of working capital, while the simultaneous construction of "Western civilization" identified and distinguished the constellation of these national capitals and cultures from their "overseas" colonial consequences. The European national cultures were the ideological insignia separating the European national economies and polities as the currencies of cultural exchange-value, while the very idea of "Western civilization" was to distinguish the accrued totality of those cultures and economies from their colonial extensions. It is not accidental that practically the entire scholarly apparatus of civilizational studies of non-Western civilizations was the handiwork of Orientalism as the intelligence arm of colonialism. Islamic, Indian, or Chinese "civilizations"—in plural and contrapuntal conversation with their European blueprint—were concocted, crafted, documented, textualized, and narrated from scattered bodies of alternating evidence by successive armies of European Orientalists, who were in effect cross-authenticating the simultaneous construction of "Western civilization." As the idea of "Western civilization" was being crafted by thinkers from Hegel to Herder, far less illustrious but far more numerous Orientalists were mirroring its civilizational others as "Oriental civilizations" in general, and Islamic, Indian, and Chinese in particular. As the colonial territories were mined to extract the raw material of a massive productive machinery switchboard in European capitals, the same exploitations were at work on the historical memories of colonized societies to serve the ideological foregrounding of "Western civilization." Practically all these civilizational mirrors were constructed to raise "Western civilization" as the normative achievement of world history and lower all others as its subnormal antecedents.

How Immanuel Kant Made "the Western" Subject Universal

The invention of "the West" was always contingent on the metaphysical underpinning of a "European" knowing subject. The philosophical constitution of an autonomous European subject, omniscient and omnipotent, and as such made fully universal, was the principal achievement, and the chief historical agency, by which the critical and creative domain of "Western civilization" was charted—and no philosopher was more instrumental in the articulation of that European subject than Immanuel Kant (1724–1804). Born in Königsberg, Kant's early exposure to his parents' ascetic piety became definitive to the fabric of his moral philosophy. In 1740, Kant entered the University of Königsberg at the age of sixteen, graduated in 1746, and in 1755, at age thirty-one, found a regular teaching position as privatdozent at the same university. By this time, he had earned the title of "der Schöne Magister" because of his social grace and teaching elegance. Kant died on 12 February 1804, having lost the complete use of his faculties—but not before his critical interpretation of the European subject as the principal agent of history.[4] The Kantian construction of the European subject is a pivotal point in the fetishization of "the West" as the engine of history. Although historically we can go back and forth from the Crusades to our own time as to the efficacy of this fetishized illusion, Kant's philosophical project, later historicized in Hegel's philosophy of history, remains at its epicenter.

Between 1781 and 1790, in his major three masterpieces—*The Critique of Pure Reason* (1781), *The Critique of Pure Practical Reason* (1788), and *The Critique of Judgment* (1790)—Immanuel Kant mapped out the details of a critical metaphysics of historical agency and moral autonomy for an unabashedly and exclusively European subject. The cumulative summation of these three works, with echoes and reverberations in his other writings, constitutes Kant's critical philosophy. Dedicated to Karl von Zedlitz, the minister of education under Frederick the Great, the enlightened monarch, *The Critique of Pure Reason* revolutionized the Platonic philosophy of the subject by locating the origin and destination of *reason* within the actual domains of the human faculties. This is by far the single most significant philosophical move of what was now solidly consolidated as "Western philosophy," at one and the same time claiming the Greek philosophical tradition all for itself while transcending it.

In his subsequent book, *Prolegomena to Any Future Metaphysic That Shall Lay Claim to Being a Science* (1783), Kant included an attempted reformulation of the difficult passages of *The Critique of Pure Reason* (1781). Five years later, in 1787, the second edition of *The Critique of Pure Reason* appeared, in which Kant revised even more difficult passages of his seminal text. The following year, he published *Critique of Practical Reason* and two years later, *Critique of Judgment*. The principal task of Kant in these seminal works was to articulate the foundation of a metaphysics that is self-referential, where "reason" is presumed to be independent. Such a prospect of a priori knowledge was presumed to be independent of lived experiences. To what extent could reason be a priori, or should it even be assumed to be capable of being a priori? In Kant, more than ever before, Europe was self-universalizing. The "Western" experience was made normative, and "non-Western" experience was an aberration: particular, local, exotic, incapable of being that of a knowing subject. Philosophy, the very ability to think, thus became coterminous with "the West." Kant's knowing subject was, ipso facto, European, "Western."

These ideas paved the way for Kant's moral philosophy, mapped out in his *Groundwork of the Metaphysics of Morals* (1785), soon to be followed by his *Religion within the Limits of Reason Alone* (1793), published during the reign of Frederick William II, whose minister, Johann Christoph von Wöllner, took exception to it and wrote to Kant admonishing him. Undeterred, Kant soon published *The*

Metaphysics of Morals (1797) on politics and law. The European Enlightenment, to which Kant's "What Is Enlightenment?" (1784) is a tribute, both enabled and disabled its own critiques. It is not until the rise of poststructuralism and postmodernism generations later that the Kantian constitution of the (European) subject is critically dismantled. But neither Kant nor the poststructuralists realized that was in effect constituting the colonizing subject as the only knowing subject. If we keep in mind that as Kant was writing these highfalutin philosophical tracts the neighboring British Empire, which he deeply admired, was conquering India, and the East India Company was robbing the Indians blind, we see that the result of his philosophy was the detailed invention of the European colonizer as subject and the simultaneous de-subjection of the non-European colonized.

Kant's moral philosophy was and remains decidedly European in its origin and purpose—a metaphysical cornerstone of "the West." It is important that we not read Kant's notorious passage on Africans quoted at the head of this chapter as merely a racist aside and rather recognize that racism was definitive to his philosophy.

> The Negroes of Africa have by nature no feeling that rises above the trifling. Mr. [David] Hume challenges anyone to cite a single example in which a Negro has shown talents, and asserts that among the hundreds of thousands of blacks who are transported elsewhere from their countries, although many of them have even been set free, still not a single one was ever found who presented anything great in art or science or any other praiseworthy quality, even though among the whites some continually rise aloft from the lowest rabble and through superior gifts earn respect in the world. So fundamental is the difference between these two races of man, and it appears to be as great in regard to mental capacities as in color.[5]

This is not Donald Trump talking about Mexicans. This is Immanuel Kant writing about a whole continent of people. This is not accidental racism to a European person. This racism is structural to Kant's moral philosophy. As soon as an Asian, African, or Latin American so much as stands up and utters a reasonable sentence, Kant's entire moral philosophy, and with it "Western civilization," collapses.

The fault lines and the metaphysical underpinning of Kant's critical constitution of pure, practical, and judgmental reasons are exclusively European and as such are central to any post-Westernism or post-Islamism that adheres to the false universal appeal of secular humanism at the heart of Enlightenment modernity. Working toward a critique of the Kantian constitution of the modern (European) subject, which simultaneously empowers the colonizer and dehumanizes the colonized, inevitably leads toward the exposure of the bourgeois basis of Kant's moralizing abstractions, his power-basing agency, and his instrumentalization of reason, which has in turn resulted in incessant production and consumption prepositional to the globalized operation of capital.

Kant's conception of the European subject is the foregrounding of a "Western" metaphysics, and as such it lacks any universal validity beyond the philosophical hegemony it imperially assumes. It is "European" because Kant is the very engineer of the idea of "Europe," before Hegel historicized and Nietzsche, in his own subversive way, in effect authenticated it. That metaphysics appears to be universal only in order to give it an aura of ahistorical validity. In its constitutionally European conception of the subject, along with a false claim to universality to place itself against the aristocratic and ecclesiastical claims to historical longevity, Kant's conception of the subject was a quintessential bourgeois project, and as such a colonizing subject. In enabling the European bourgeoisie to assert itself universally against nature and the planet, Kant in effect facilitated the instrumentalization of a reason compatible with the rising reason of capital to control and captivate the market. In thus theorizing a quintessentially colonizing subject, Kant crafted a colonizer and a colonized, subjecting the former and de-subjecting the latter. The Kantian subject is thus *not* critical in any epistemically enduring sense of the term and is entirely native to the history of the domestication of the subject in Christianity. Kant in effect de-Christianized the subject, but obviously, though apparently paradoxically, the extent of his de-subjection was limited to and by Christianity. Neither his subject nor the domain of its philosophical apparatus is critical in any enduring or universal sense. As such, it leaves no room for a built-in auto-critique. Kant rescues the passively compromised Christian subject only to unleash it upon the material world for his contemporary "Europeans."

The poststructural and postmodern critiques of the Kantian subject are ipso facto and a fortiori geared toward a critique of Kant and are epistemically post-Kantian. Kant's entire philosophical project, his critical philosophy, was geared toward an effective subjection of the European bourgeoisie in universal terms that enabled its global agency. This he achieved via constituting the European bourgeois subject in universal terms and then making it the global master of the non-European objective world. Kant achieved this end via two immediately related projects: first his critical and second his moral philosophies. Both "European" projects proceeded at the heavy cost of submitting the lived experiences of non-Europeans—thus branded—to the conquering will of "the West."

The philosophical constitution of the European (Kantian) knowing subject was the principal premise of the formation of the allegory of "Europe" and all the Others it needed to believe (in) itself. In its successive gestations, this dualism, mirroring the colonizing power of this very "Europe," was variously manifested in the formation of the Orient, thus making the Occident self-evident. My proposal to consider "Islam and the West" as the metaphysical vertebrae of this Manichean dualism might commence with any number of points of departure, from the Crusades to the Enlightenment to the transformation of the bourgeois public sphere (Habermas) in the nineteenth century—in each successive case reading history backward to authenticate itself. In any case, the Kantian philosophical project was coterminous with all such historical unfolding, as it universalized the European knowing subject and racialized all its others.

Philosophy of History, Geography of Conquest

Kant's decidedly Eurocentric metaphysics was soon augmented by Hegel's *Philosophy of History* (1837), where he establishes a teleological narrative of world history with the (European) State as its ultimate goal, Napoleon as the anticipated consequence of Alexander the Great, and thus implicitly Hegel himself as the consequence of Plato. Similarly, Nietzsche's idea of "We Europeans" throughout his oeuvre plays right into the hands of Kant's constitution of the European subject, though he was decidedly subversive to all such systematic philosophies. Freud's Oedipalization of the (European) subject would later create and constitute a mommy-daddy-baby triumvirate that is entirely modulating on the productivity of capital and the market. Marx's critique of capitalism therefore categorically buys into the Kantian colonial de-subjection and leads him to create and dismiss "Oriental despotism" and the "Asiatic mode of production," never realizing his own blind spot. Edward Said dismantles the discursive constitution of the Orient, but failing to see Orientalism as integral to Enlightenment modernity, he propagates its secular humanism. Simultaneously with Said, Gayatri Chakravorty Spivak critiques the white masculinist constitution of the subject and marks the de-subjection of the subaltern, but does so still entirely enamored of and limited by poststructuralist counternarratives, fearful of theorizing a subject from the postcolonial ground-zero up, her encounter with the white-masculinist theorists dominated by the terms of their engagements. More recently in his *Cosmopolitanism: Ethics in the World of Strangers* (2007), as well as in *The Lies That Bind: Rethinking Identity* (2018), Anthony Kwame Appiah has offered a detailed discussion of overcoming "the West and the Rest" at the root of Kantian metaphysics, but he does so from the abstract vacuity of a cosmopolitanism that remains decidedly rooted in European capitalist modernity, disregarding what in *The Darker Side of Western Modernity* (2012) Walter Mignolo has rightly identified as its darker purposes.[6] The same is true in Seyla Benhabib's *Another Cosmopolitanism* (2008), which dives into what she calls a civil society that is governed by "cosmopolitan norms of universal justice" without the slightest critical stance vis-à-vis the unjust foregrounding of that "universal justice." From Said to Benhabib, despite all their political differences, all these critical thinkers remain firmly rooted in the Hegelian philosophy of history and its Kantian metaphysics.

Against this Hegelian philosophy of history and the Kantian metaphysics that informed it, we need an actively critical project of resubjection. What would a resubjection of the postcolonial person look like in this context? Resubjection of the postcolonial person means moving the European bourgeois subject, hidden as it is behind the camera as spectator, and bringing it in front of the camera as spectacle and the gazed upon. But this is not by way of a vindictive, "the empire strikes back" kind of position. The whole apparatus of the Kantian subjection, and the kind of Enlightenment modernity it enabled, needs a collective critique beyond the vagaries of what is hurriedly dismissed as "poststructuralism," "postmodernism," or even "postcolonialism."

How exactly it is that an abstraction can categorically dominate a spectrum of historiography as vast as that of the last two hundred years without it being even once challenged as a viable concept is beyond comprehension. The term *the West* and the vast universe of imagination that term entails have dominated the historical imagination of the last two hundred years with such power and ferocity that not once has anyone put forward the simple fact that for all of recorded history (minus the last two hundred years), the term *the West* the way it has been turned into a metaphysical allegory has never existed, and the word *west* has meant nothing other than a geographical direction where the sun sets. How exactly the term *the West* came to signify what it today means has never been questioned, so powerful and domineering has it been over generations of historians all over the globe. Its philosophical foregrounding in the works of Kant and Hegel has positioned the term with metaphysical sanctity.

The result of this unquestioned centrality of the term is the aggressive centralization of thinking about civilization in the very fabric of historical imagination. So much so that when in the 1930s Arnold Toynbee and later in the century Marshall Hodgson and William McNeill were contemplating alternative narratives to national historiography, they proposed even grander narratives around civilizational divides, for example, classical antiquity around the Mediterranean, East Asian, Indian, and Islamic domains. The template of all such suggestions was of course "Western civilization" itself.[7]

Somewhere in the middle of the 1700s, the age of European imperial modernity asserts itself, defeating all its rivals in Asia, extending its dominions into Africa and Latin America. What happens in the middle of the 1700s is a *global* development in the making of "the industrial revolution," which means a massive increase in productivity whereby an increasingly smaller proportion of total populations was needed to be farmers and other food producers for communities to survive. A number of other critical factors were contingent on this crucial development. New sources of power were discovered or invented, infectious diseases were brought under control, life expectancy as a result increased, the infant mortality rate dropped, women were freed from lifetime bondage to childbearing and joined the labor force, and the momentum became even more acute. The Industrial Revolution was a global phenomenon, but its fictive center was presumed to be "the West." From cheap labor to raw material to expanded markets to the highly skilled labor force, all were global, but the cultural hegemony of "Europe" divided the world between the West and the Rest.

The assumption that the Industrial Revolution and all its material consequences took place in the western part of Europe, in "the West," is an untenable proposition contingent on the belief that the operation of capital was independent of its colonial consequences. The operation of capital and its colonial consequences were integral to each other. The colonial site was not accidental but integral to the operation of capital, and the necessary colonial extension of the capital was not limited to the horizontal (external) operation of capital. The operation of capital, as accumulated surplus value, was as much contingent on its external colonialism as it was on its internal abuse of labor. The operation of British capital was as much contingent on its colonial setup in India as it was in Ireland or Scotland. There is a structural similarity among Ireland, Scotland, and India, as there is a structural similarity among the beneficiaries of the operation of capital in England, Scotland, Ireland, and India. The idea and practice of national liberation movements is thus a fallacy because it creates a flawed unit of operation called "the nation," which lumps together the beneficiaries and those who are disenfranchised by the operation of the always already globalized capital. The same holds true for the assumption of imperialist "nations," such as England, France, or the United States. Imperialism is in the interest of capital and not in the interest of labor, whether that labor is in Washington, DC, or in Iraq. Saddam Hussein and the band of his generals were as much the beneficiaries of US imperialism as the CEOs of Enron. This globalized operation of capital makes a mockery of the assumption of civilizational divides between "East and West."

What today the so-called "globalization" has made clear is nothing other than the fact that the assumption of a Western European *center* to the initial operation of capital was categorically wrong. What today we call globalization reveals nothing other than the fallacious basis of a categorical assumption that capital was ideologically centered in Western Europe and then colonially extended to the rest of the world, and thus the process of so-called Westernization, or Western Imperialism. "Western Imperialism," again, is nothing other than the imperialism of capital over labor, labor both domestic to its national operation and global to its globalizing proclivity. There was never a center to the operation of capital. Ever. Capital was always global, from its very inception. It abused labor wherever it extended its control, whether at home or abroad. There was never a home for the capital and thus no abroad. Colonialism was not accidental to the operation of capital. It was integral to it. Nor was colonialism something that capital did "overseas." There was plenty of colonialism going on right in the very neighborhood of capital. Capital is homeless. "Colonialism" means nothing other than the abuse of labor by capital writ global. Capital is color-blind. It robs labor blind in whatever color, shape, gender, or ethnicity it comes in. There is no "West" to the operation of capital—or East, or South, or North. It colonizes (abuses) labor East, West, North, and South of its compass and calendar. Capital is amorphous, homeless, and global; its only logic is its own incessant accumulation, which means an incessant abuse of labor. "The West" was the grandest illusion of capital; it used "the West" to hide itself behind a civilizational façade.

The Industrial Revolution did not take place in a figment of imagination called "the West."[8] That figment of imagination, predicated on an imaginative geography of power, appropriated the Industrial Revolution into its self-territorialized fiction. So far as the Industrial

Revolution was a universal breakthrough in primarily agricultural societies, whereby new sources of power and energy led to overproduction and the resultant accumulation of surplus value, it was an entirely global development, with the colonial peripheries of the capital completely integral to its increasingly globalized operation. Within this fictive imagination, "the West" was a co-invention of the colonial world in precisely the same way that "the Third World" was a co-invention of "the West." What we are dealing with here is a dialectic of reciprocity originated in the centers of power and reflected back in the sites of domination by and in fact through resistance to it. Whether "the West" was obeyed or resisted, it was confirmed in its assumption of being "the West." The Orientalists serving the imperial hubris that codified itself as "the West" went on a global rampage, savagely robbing people of their local cultures and customs and forcefully narrating them into a passive discourse of obsequious subjugation to a world order in which "the West" came up first and the rest came next.

A particularly notorious term that has baffled the historians and generated a heap of "modernization" theories by other social scientists is *modern. Modern* means partaking in modernity, and modernity was a specific project immediately related to a widespread ideological movement called "the Enlightenment." The Enlightenment modernity was a universal ideology of the new class, the middle-class bourgeoisie that began a global takeover of power from its aristocratic and ecclesiastical antecedents. The bourgeois takeover of power was universal, while its particulars assumed local cultural colorings. The bourgeois appropriation of power and prestige in Europe was culturally different from its counterparts in Asia, Africa, or Latin America. The global and globalized bourgeoisie partook in the Enlightenment modernity wherever they were. Because it was shallow and rootless, the global bourgeoisie was particularly in need of a globalizing ideology with globalizing claims to abstract authenticity. Reason and Progress were the hallmarks of Enlightenment modernity over-anxious to give its clientele class a sense of universal mission and autonomy. Kant and Hegel, in articulating the assumption of Pure Reason and Historical Progress, were the twin prophets of Enlightenment modernity and as such the primary theorists of a globalized class that was about to conquer the world. The panoply of modernization theories addressed by American and British social scientists are unable to understand that modernity was a universal development at its very inception. The difference was between the beneficiaries of capitalist modernity and those disenfranchised by it, and this division was by no stretch of imagination across the national divides or civilizational boundaries, both of which were ways of dividing the world in capital and colonial terms to conquer it better.

In the course of this historical crescendo of capitalist modernity, navigational techniques had advanced enough to make the global traffic of raw material and labor a perfectly plausible proposition. What followed was the gradual formation of a trading-post empire, paving the way for territorial colonization, all geared toward the aggressive formation of a globalized economy. The Portuguese trading posts in India, Africa, Malaya, and China; or those of the Dutch in Jakarta, Ceylon, India, and Japan; or of the British in Bombay, Madras, and Calcutta, were all active networks of trading posts that would facilitate the formation of a transnational economy in which the national unit of economic production was of very little use. In this geography of domination, the Hegelian philosophy of history and Kant's metaphysics of bourgeois morality all came together to make "the West" the epicenter of our human condition.

Ruling Ideologies, Ruling Classes

The ideologically conditioned schematization of "Islam and the West" disregards and suppresses alternative histories that have existed and have cast their long shadows on the lived experiences of nations. Contingent on the centrality of "the West," all its alterities have come together to conceal those lived experiences. Let us recall another key passage in Marx's critique of "religion" to see the power of the illusion of "the West":

> Criticism has plucked the imaginary flowers on the chain not in order that man shall continue to bear that chain without fantasy or consolation, but so that he shall throw off the chain and pluck the living flower. The criticism of religion disillusions man, so that he will think, act, and fashion his reality like a man who has discarded his illusions and regained his senses, so that he will move around himself as his own true Sun. Religion is only the illusory Sun which revolves around man as long as he does not revolve around himself.[9]

What Marx says here about "religion" in general is far more applicable to the metaphysical underpinning of "the West," meaning the colonizing force of "Western Christianity," which has been "the imaginary flower" on the chain of European nations thinking themselves inheritors of a superior civilization, while the beneficiaries of that fiction have robbed them blind. In the same vein, the critique of "the West" disillusions "the European man," which Marx took for "Man," for humanity at large, facing the dismantling of his illusions and regaining his senses. "The West," we might thus paraphrase Marx, "is only the illusory Sun which revolves around man as long as he does not revolve around himself." But this illusion is not limited to "the West," for it extends into any binary it has manufactured to believe in itself and to ground its metaphysical authenticity. Marx continues:

> It is, therefore, the task of history, once the other-world of truth has vanished, to establish the truth of this world. It is the immediate

task of philosophy, which is in the service of history, to unmask self-estrangement in its unholy forms once the holy form of human self-estrangement has been unmasked. Thus, the criticism of Heaven turns into the criticism of Earth, the criticism of religion into the criticism of law, and the criticism of theology into the criticism of politics.[10]

Has the task of history already begun to establish the truth of this world beyond its habitual illusion of "the West and the Rest"? Are we tasked with the responsibility of unmasking this self-estrangement rooted in the metaphysical underpinning of "the West" that has turned its received theology upside down? Gramsci's theory of hegemony, predicated on Marx's insights, points toward the recognition that societies are not ruled by force alone, but also by ideas. The ruling classes come with their own ideologies—to convince themselves and others whom they rule that this is the philosophical truth of the world as they rule it. Gramsci's insights were rooted in the earlier insight of Marx that the ruling ideas have always been the ideas of the ruling class. From Kant and Hegel, we may have inherited the metaphysical underpinning of "the West," but in the equally powerful works of Marx, Freud, and Gramsci we can also read "the West" against itself and thus seek to liberate the world from its last grandest illusion.

Consider Gramsci's diagnosis of how and when and why hegemony works: In his *Prison Notebooks* while discussing the structure of political parties, Gramsci writes about social classes becoming "detached" from their traditional political parties, and how the state mobilizes its intellectual cadres to bring these classes back into its ideological domains. This he calls the crisis of "the ruling class's hegemony," at which point "a crisis of authority" is generated that is "precisely the crisis of hegemony, or the general crisis of the State."[11] This is how hegemony works for Gramsci in his European contexts. We need to adjust Gramsci's theory of hegemony to the global condition of capitalism beyond its Eurocentric limitations, where European colonialism embraces its much wider colonial holdings, and where this fetish of "the West" has acted precisely in talismanic, hegemonic terms. Friends and foes of this "West" are put in service of that hegemony. This is precisely the magical power of the commodified fetish that has historically called itself "the West."

We are not beyond that hegemony. We are dismantling it from its very center—exposing its futility, morbidity, outdated mendacity. By the time I was putting the finishing touches on this chapter, US President Donald Trump's major contribution to addressing the global pandemic of COVID-19 was to call it a "Chinese virus." According to news reports:

> The chairwoman of the Congressional Asian Pacific American caucus on Saturday said it is "dangerous" for President Donald Trump to continue referring to Covid-19 as the "Chinese virus" at a time when misinformation has led to racist and xenophobic attacks against Asian Americans or anyone in the US who looks East Asian.[12]

Whether for political expediency during an election year or just a typical racist slur, the fact of Donald Trump's identification of a global pandemic with an Asian country that itself has been a victim of the virus sustains the course of "the West and the Rest" right into the headlines of our daily lives.

3 *The West and the Rest*
Condition of Coloniality

In this book is attempted for the first time the venture of predetermining history, of following the still untravelled stages in the destiny of a Culture, and specifically of the only Culture of our time and on our planet which is actually in the phase of fulfillment—the West-European-American.

OSWALD SPENGLER, *The Decline of the West* (1918)

In an insightful essay on the French occupation of Morocco, Whitney Abernathy writes about

a new brand of French "Christianity" [that] was utilized to morally justify France's authority over the Moroccans. Uncovering the underlying moral rhetoric shared by Catholics and secularists in France after the Separation of 1905 elucidates why the notion of a "Christian France," though officially discredited by the French government, continued to be utilized in public discourse. The label "Christian" underlined the presumed superiority of French civilization, and in particular its sexual superiority, in comparison to the morally inferior Moroccan Muslims. Even though the imagined binary between Christianity and Islam was not a novelty to contemporaries, its continued use after 1905 suggests that "French Christianity" had begun to take on a more secular meaning in the early twentieth century. That is, the label "Christian" was employed in rhetoric regarding Morocco to highlight France's civilized and moral superiority over a religious inferior rather than to imply any type of collective, national religious devotion.[1]

This is a crucial and insightful observation for both what it shows and what it implies. The critical insight of Abernathy here is to see how in the colonial context of the French domination in Morocco Christianity becomes a conduit of "civilizational" conquest. Equally important is where we see the selfsame Christianity take on a more "secular" meaning. But what would that exactly mean? How exactly could a religion be secular? The answer is in the condition of coloniality where the religion of the dominant conquerors becomes the dominant ideology of conquest and brands itself as "secular." Here and elsewhere in the colonial context, Christianity has assumed the posture of "secularity," meaning it has become colonially convenient. It has in effect concealed itself under the camouflage of secularity, so that universalism and Christianity have become one and the same. It is right here that the civilizational superiority that Christianity as secularity has assumed calls itself "the West," and thus everything Marx and Freud have thought about "religion" is in effect about Western Christianity in its colonizing disguise, which has termed itself "the West."

With this chapter I am shifting gears, before moving into part 2 of the book, "Return of the Repressed," where I wish to demonstrate how the condition of coloniality has been the chief catalyst abstracting "Islam and the West" as a particularly potent manifestation of "the West and the Rest," where "the West" stands for secularized Christianity as the chief ideology of colonial conquest. This condition of coloniality is therefore at once a political and an epistemic proposition, for it is the *conditio sine qua non* of the sustained course of conceptual validity extended to such illusions as "Islam and the West." "Islam" was here produced as the supreme Other of "the West," which was the thinly disguised "Western Christianity." And Islam was there to corroborate and help "the West" conceal its Christian disposition while paradoxically, in fact, revealing it as other than Islam. This "Islam," as a specific aspect of "the Rest," was like raw material with which "the West" could feed its condition of primacy.

The ideological construction of "the West and the Rest" served to conceal the factual evidence of the trade and commerce that revealed a different truth about the European conquest and exploitations. The far more expansive and enabling interplay among neighboring and adjacent cultures eventually transformed during the European Enlightenment (particularly in reference to India, China, and Persia) and finally came to a crescendo during the rise of capitalist modernity, where the manufactured civilizational clash became a head-on collision. During the European Enlightenment, aspects of non-European cultures and civilizations (from China, India, and Persia in particular) were assimilated thoroughly into the making of the world historic period. But beginning with the globalized project of capitalist modernity, the self-universalizing "West" became the yardstick of truth against which all of its colonial shadows were measured. It is in this period that the binary opposition between "Islam" and "the West" finds its strongest economic and political roots and cultural effervescence.

"The West" was and remained an overwhelming illusion—a compelling fetish that has waged wars and harbored racist ideologies. "The West" devours all the historical richness and complexity of what it generically calls "the Rest," and then turns it into an equally vacuous illusion. "The West" is like the color "white" for white supremacists. It does not exist. It is an empty ideological hole— into which racist ideologues have deposited dangerous delusions.

There is no such color for human skin—unless one is suffering from some dermatological illness.[2] White supremacists first rob people of their humanity by calling them Black, Yellow, Red, or Brown—thus corroborating their own delusional color—and then start investing those colors with all sorts of diabolical attributes. The same is true with "the West"—as the fetishized ideological commodity that mystifies the operation of globalized capital and the colonized labor and raw material it systematically abuses. It is not just that Islam needs to be decoupled from the West, or the West from Islam; rather, the whole apotheotic pairing between "Islam" and "the West" needs to be dismantled and our histories and humanities liberated from its claws.

Coloniality: The Interlocutor

For the last two hundred years the ever-changing interlocutor of Islam became first European colonial modernity and then the combined forces of US and the Soviet imperialisms. In response, Islam gradually but consistently mutated into a singularly ideological site of political resistance to colonialism and imperialism. With the loss of its own imperial heritage—ranging from the Abbasids in the eighth to the Ottomans in the twentieth century—Islam also lost the moral dexterity of its creative imagination. Throughout their history, Muslims have been in a cosmopolitan conversation with the world around them. But following their fateful confrontation with European colonialism, Muslims gradually transmuted—almost imperceptibly to themselves—their own multifaceted religion into a single-minded contestation against the politics of colonial power. With the European ideological hegemony as its chief inspector, Islam gradually lost the cosmopolitan character of its own culture and became singularly passive and persistently reactionary. An inertly platitudinous faith on one side and a bitterly militant ideology on the other—on

one side a passive pandering to fate, on the other an aggressively suicidal zeal to alter it—replaced the rainbow of languages and ideas
that they violently suppressed and categorically dismantled.

From the late eighteenth to mid-twentieth century, European
colonialism was the principal catalyst of the most consequential
changes in the normative fabric and political dexterity of Islam as
a faith, radically triggering a self-degenerative agent in its moral
and intellectual imagination. The more Muslim intellectuals and
Islamic anticolonial movements engaged with Eurocentric colonial modernity, the more effectively the epistemic foundation of
Islamic intellectual history was corroded. Then it went from bad to
worse. The emergence of the United States and the Soviet Union
as two superpowers in the twentieth century gradually substituted
nineteenth-century European colonialism with their respective
imperialisms—and thus further intensified the constitutional transmutation of Islam into a site of political resistance to global domination. Muslims became capitalists in conversation with globalized
capitalism. Muslims became socialists in conversation with Soviet
socialism. Muslims became anticolonial revolutionaries in response
to imperialism and colonialism. All such responses were inevitable
and perhaps even logical. But in the process, Islam too transmuted,
from a robust intellectual heritage into a passive and reactionary
sounding board.

In addition to the imperial competition between the United
States and the Soviet Union, among which Muslims further divided
their attention and disintegrated their own social and intellectual
disposition, two other critical events helped in the aggressive transformation of Islam into a site of political contestation against colonialism: First, the creation of the state of Israel in 1948, and second,
the partition of the Indian subcontinent along the Hindu-Muslim
divide at the very same time. Halfway through the twentieth century,
the formation of the state of Israel—as first a white European, then a

white American, and now even a white Russian colonial settlement—on the broken back of the Palestinians further intensified the political radicalization of Islam. As European colonialism conditioned and US and Soviet imperialisms ossified the aggressive mutation of Islam into a singular site of political resistance, it was all but inevitable that the formation of a Jewish state could not but forecast the creation of an Islamic Republic, first in Pakistan in 1948 and then in Iran in 1979. It took some thirty years after the establishment of Israel as a Jewish state in 1948 for an Islamic Republic to emerge and consolidate itself in Iran in 1979—thirty years of aggressive transmutation of a worldly religion into an anti-imperialist liberation theology. Thus, Zionism and Islamism, as two opposing by-products of European colonial modernity, began to be pitted against each other, while at the very same time aggressively violating the moral and intellectual integrity of both Judaism and Islam.

So what today we call Islam is the ancestral faith of a people actively mutated into a singular site of ideological resistance to colonialism. Precisely the same colonial project that dispatched an army of mercenary Orientalists to craft and create an "Islam" (as well as an India, a China, etc., and altogether an Orient) as the civilizational Other of "the West" in order to authenticate an otherwise fabricated apparition also led Muslim revolutionaries to take the same set of sacred memories and turn it into a site of ideological resistance to colonialism. Orientalism and militant Islamism are thus the two sides of the same colonial coin: an ideology of domination vs. an ideology of resistance, between the two of them crushing the multifaceted memory of Islam in its precolonial history. In this remarkable act of historical dialectics, in which "Islam and the West" was made evident and its two components became dialogically entangled, Islam was transmuted by "the West" that it opposed, as "the West" was corroborated by the "Islam" it had invented to rule. The dialectic was richly rewarding for "the West," deeply calamitous for Islam.

Recasting the Global Politics of Space

"Islam" and "the West" thus emerged as the mirror images of each other. The colonial fabrication and confrontation of "Islam" and "the West" in turn revived and refabricated a medieval binary opposition domestic to Islamic jurisprudential imagination—Dar al-Islam vs. Dar al-Harb ("the Abode of Peace" vs. "the Abode of War"). This opposition between the abodes of war and peace was an almost exclusively juridical division. Because among its various meanings Islam also connotes peace, the territorial conquests under its cultural domain were identified under the general rubric of "the peaceful region," where no war was conducted, whereas "the abode of war" was where the Islamic imperial proclivities—always constitutional to its nascent character—were contested. The peculiar resuscitation of this old and outdated juridical bifurcation in Islamic jurisprudence was a strange Orientalist project that sought to replicate the presumed hostility between "Islam" and "the West" in terms domestic to Islamic culture. The identification, however, was patently a mismatch. The dual diversity construed between "Islam and the West" was critically current and potent, while that of Dar al-Islam and Dar al-Harb was markedly medieval and categorically juridical. Nevertheless, the dialectic of reciprocity engaged between the colonizers and the colonized—acted out between the European Orientalists and the Muslim ideologues—gave currency and credibility to both these sets of binary oppositions and ossified the assumption of an eternal hostility between two civilizational camps.

Islam and colonialism were thus materially and symbolically entangled in a corrosive conversation. Throughout the nineteenth and then the twentieth and now well into the twenty-first centuries, militant Islamism, as the rising banner of a nativist movement, joined nationalism and socialism as they collectively constituted the three most effective modes of resistance, first to European colonialism and then to the US and Soviet Cold War imperialisms. Socialist movements indulged in Soviet dreams of a just world and either took advantage of or were exploited by the Soviet Union. Islamist movements, meanwhile, remained closest to their grassroots, partook of both bourgeois nationalism and working socialism as two diametrically opposed modes of ideological resistance to imperialism, and fought the global domination of the Europeans, the United States, and the Soviets.

Socialism failed to deliver at its imperial peripheries, as it also miserably collapsed at its Soviet centers. Bourgeois nationalism resisted colonial domination, accepted its territorial logic of dividing the conquered in order to rule them, proceeded to give some colonially fabricated nations measures of self-determination, and left others—such as the Palestinians, the Kurds, the Uighurs, the Rohingyas, the Kashmiris—disastrously dispossessed. As two powerful ideological modes of mobilization, both nationalism and socialism were instrumental in creating a sustained political agency in much of the Muslim world—from Morocco to the Indian subcontinent, from Central Asia to South Pacific. Militant Islamism was at the same time equally instrumental and far more popularly based in its political mobilization against foreign domination. But whereas militant Islamism succeeded politically to craft a measure of moral agency to resist the complete colonization of the Muslim mind, it failed miserably to secure any meaningful measure of institutional endurance toward the making of a free and democratic society. Between Wahhabism and militant Shi'ism Muslims became the agents of their own exacerbated sectarianism under colonial duress.

The failure of democracy in much of the Muslim world is squarely rooted in the colonial context of its encounter with capitalist modernity. Muslims received the ideals and aspirations of Enlightenment modernity through the gun barrel of colonialism. The very Enlightenment ideals that were supposed to give them an enabling sense of universal emancipation and an embracing hope for democratic ideals in effect denied them any agency to do so. European modernity had a very long colonial shadow, and in the dark side of the Enlightenment everything was the carbon copy of its hopes and aspirations.[3] The result is that today the Islamic world from one end to another has not a single exemplary model of democratic representation. Muslims as a people have collectively failed to have a solitary model of democracy because democracy as a political ideal was integral to a modernity they received through the same colonial gun barrel that denied them agency while dividing them among their nationalist, socialist or Islamist sentiments—the first two borrowed from their colonizers, the third a nativist reaction to them. The whole plethora of pathological ponderings that bemoans the absence of democracy in Islamic societies but categorically disregards the colonial context of this malady provides the most scandalous case study of precisely the colonized mind that the colonial project has generated and sustained.

Colonizing the Muslim Mind

The making of a moderate or militant Islamism—as a primarily political project coterminous with colonial modernity and as such singularly responsible for transfiguring the multifaceted faith of a people into a singular site of ideological resistance to colonialism—was a sustained record of generations of Muslim ideologues aggressively unsheathing the political power of their religion out of the universe of its moral imagination in order to battle colonialism. They got more than they bargained for. The more belligerently they stripped their faith of its historical dexterity and moral imagination, the more paradoxically it became politically potent and intellectually bankrupt. The principal site of such encounters was invariably where European colonialism was paramount. The prominent Egyptian reformist Rifa'a al-Tahtawi (1801–1873) was one of the pioneering Muslim intellectuals who wedded his al-Azhar education to a European learning when Mohammed Ali (1769–1849; viceroy of Egypt, 1805–1848) appointed him at the head of a group of Egyptian students sent to Paris. In his writings and translations, al-Tahtawi tried to strike a balance between Islam and the promises of European modernity.[4] Al-Tahtawi is a pioneering figure in the active transmutation of his ancestral faith into a political apparatus that sought to accommodate the Enlightenment under colonial duress. Soon after him, Seyyed Jamal al-Din al-Afghani (1838–1897) was perhaps the most influential Muslim intellectual and activist of his time who responded systematically against the onslaught of colonialism. He traveled widely throughout the Muslim world and Europe, wrote extensively against corrupt Muslim leaders and their colonial masters, and was directly affiliated with revolutionary uprisings in Iran, Egypt, and Ottoman territories.[5] His vision of a unified Islamic front against colonialism forever changed and redefined Islam in response to the onslaught of colonial modernity. The combined efforts of al-Tahtawi and al-Afghani ushered in the inaugural phase of the aggressive ideologization of Islam—Islam made politically potent, intellectually monotonous.[6]

A close follower of al-Afghani, Muhammad Abduh (1849–1905) was forced into exile by the British and spent time in Beirut, Tripoli, and Paris. He returned to Egypt and began a writing career that would radically reformulate Islam into a political ideology capable of responding to the changing circumstances of the modern world. Abduh's version of Islam instrumentally rationalized the faith and made it responsive to the political needs of his world.[7] Abduh in fact believed that the Europeans had learned about the liberating ways of Islam during the Crusades, and that this was the cause of their modern ascendancy! Such ludicrous indices of Muslim ideologues having no clue what had actually happened in the course of colonial modernity became prototypical in much of the reformist Islam. Rashid Rida (1865–1935), who was a disciple of Abduh, in his journal *Al-Manar* sought to propagate the ideas of his teacher, particularly in lines compatible with the rising Egyptian and Arab nationalism. One public intellectual after another was digging a deeper grave for their historical heritage in a misguided attempt to confront an enemy they could not even define.

All these aggressive mutations of Islam into a site of resistance and confrontation with colonial modernity occurred at a critical time in the global domination of Europeans in the Islamic world. The British had occupied Egypt in 1882; the French, Tunisia in 1881; and the Italians, Tripoli in 1911. By 1917, the British were in Baghdad and Jerusalem. These colonial occupations occurred all at the time of Rashid Rida's political maturity. The call for Arab nationalism was in response to European colonialism and with a full metamorphosis of Islam into a potent ideology. Another student of Abduh, Ali Abd al-Raziq (1888–1966) was a product of this very environment. He too combined his al-Azhar and Oxford educations and redefined the political legitimacy of power following the final destruction of the Islamic caliphate in 1924. Ali Abd al-Raziq was the mature intellectual of the post-1948 period and the moral havoc that the establishment of the state of Israel wrought on his generation of Arab and Muslim thinkers. During his lifetime, Egypt changed from a monarchy, after the abdication of King Faruq in 1952, into a Republic in 1953. Abd al-Raziq witnessed the Iraqi revolution of 1958 and the Lebanese civil war of the same year, and he was also a witness to the catastrophic consequences of the Arab-Israeli war of 1967. Al-Raziq's concern with the nature of political legitimacy in Islam reflects the moral and intellectual anxiety of these events for a Muslim intellectual. His call for the destruction of the medieval political culture and the adaptation to new political principles was articulated with radical rereadings of Islamic doctrines and history. There is nothing in religion,

Abd al-Raziq concluded, that prohibits Muslims from rivaling other nations in all their modern sciences and social institutions. Thus the political power of the colonizers combined with the allure of Enlightenment modernity to turn the moral imagination and intellectual agility of Islam into a monolithic echo of Muslim political failures— and these Muslim ideologues were its harbingers, enabling Muslims to stand up to colonialism, but at the grave and irreparable cost of erasing their own intellectual memories.

When the League of Arab States was formed in 1945, it gave expression to the long-standing hope of Arab unity sought by many Arab public intellectuals. Amir Shakib-Arsalan (1869–1946), a Lebanese reformist, extended Abduh's ideas further into the Levant and wrote effectively of weaving Islam into the cause of Arab nationalism.[8] Islam is by its very nature, Shakib-Arsalan believed, against degenerate traditions. It is perfectly compatible with the mandates of a modern life, he thought. He lashed out against what he considered the backward custodians of the Islamic lore and sought to appropriate the Qur'an and the Prophetic wisdom for a renewed encounter with the predicament of colonial modernity. He was logical and persuasive, and he spent heavily from Islam to fortify an ideological fortress against "the West."

Not all Muslim intellectuals were unanimous in their conviction that Islam and nationalism were compatible. A contemporary of Shakib Arsalan, Sati' al-Husri (1880–1964), a Yemeni-Syrian reformer, had a universal conception of Arab unity in which Islam was not to have a critical centrality.[9] But even he considered Arab unity as a prerequisite of the far more inclusive Muslim unity. Abd al-Rahman al-Bazzaz (1913–1977), al-Husri's Iraqi contemporary, was to the contrary a firm believer that Arab solidarity had to be rooted in Islamic unity. All such hopes for either Arab or Muslim unity were of course illusions that never materialized. But they did transform Islam into a radically reactive ideology resisting the predicament of colonial modernity. As Arab nationalism and pan-Arab socialism began to take root in North Africa and Western Asia, Islam was put on the defensive to respond in kind, and thus both nationalism and socialism began to exert an exceptionally enduring catalytic effect on it, muting the very political language and multifaceted culture of a faith that had for centuries played the logocentricism of its philosophy against the nomocentricism of its law—balancing them both by the homocentricity of its mysticism.

As these public intellectuals were busy engaging their ancestral faith in a critical conversation with the consequences of European colonialism, the prolonged presence of the British in India was producing a similarly politicized Islamic response—violent and rebellious at times, pacifist and pensive at others. Sir Seyyed Ahmad Khan (1817–1898), for example, was smack in the middle of "the Mutiny" of 1857 but remained totally loyal to the British. Ahmad Khan's primary concern was the translation of his contemporary European texts in order to make them available to the rising Indian Muslim bourgeoisie in an attempt to mediate a dialogue between what was now actively designated as a binary opposition between "Islam" and "the West."[10] Ahmad Khan went so far as to establish what he called the Anglo-Muhammadan Oriental College at Aligarh in 1874 in order to educate a whole new breed of Muslim intellectuals, and then founded the Muhammadan Anglo-Oriental Education Conference in 1886 in order to institutionalize further the encounter with "European sciences." No enduring institution of civil liberties, civil society, or political participation was achieved by any of these developments. But they did constitute an Islamic discourse of resistance or accommodation to colonialism.

Soon after Sir Seyyed Ahmad Khan, Abu al-Ala al-Mawdudi (1903–1979) was adamant in his assessment of the constitutional contradictions between Islam and modernity, as best exemplified by the project of nation-building. Islam and nationalism, he thought, are diametrically opposed to each other. Al-Mawdudi's ideas were paramount among the population of the Indian subcontinent that came to constitute Pakistan.[11] While the Pakistani political elite were under the impression that Islam was a mere cultural context for a constitutional democracy, al-Mawdudi and his Jama'at-i Islami were busy demanding a thoroughly Islamic state, from its economic framework to its civil and legal administration. The 1956 Constitution of Pakistan was far more religious in its doctrinal foundation than the one drafted in 1958. But in 1963 the Islamic nature of the Republic was restored, until in 1973 Prime Minister Bhutto declared the state an Islamic Socialist Republic, to be further Islamicized by his successor, General Zia al-Haq. The catastrophe of the postcolonial partition of India into its Muslim and Hindu components not only did not diminish the horrors of interfaith barbarity but antagonized both Islam and Hinduism into radically politicized camps—both stripped of their respective moral imagination and creative conversations with history.

Those Indian Muslims who remained in India after the Partition had to reconfigure their faith in a way compatible with their living in a postcolonial, nominally secular state, notoriously prone to violent Hindu nationalism. One of the most eloquent and prolific Muslim scholars of the Indian subcontinent was S. Abid Husain (1896–1978), who as a professor of philosophy and literature at Jamia Millia Islamia University (1925–1956) and Aligarh Muslim University (1957–1960) wrote copiously on the fate of Muslims in modernity.[12] Husain sought to alleviate the perception of a sharp contrast between Islam and secularism in order to accommodate for nationalism as a secular ideology. Secularism, he believed, was not necessarily opposed to religion. Whereas Husain achieved his moderate conception of nationalism in a political vacuum and in abstraction, his fellow Indian Muslim scholar Mushir ul-Haq (b. 1933) was far more succinct in identifying what sort of nationalism is acceptable to a Muslim and what is contradictory to the faith. The result was further discord between Islam and an increasingly secularized world. The demoralized faith had offered the soul of its political potency to no effective social or institutional avail. Nationalism and socialism now threatened to steal Islam's constituency from under its feet.

Anticolonial movements against Holland and Britain in Indonesia and Malaysia resulted in similar responses. The colonial domination of these regions had in fact been instrumental in unifying their Muslim populations against foreign domination. In the Java wars of 1825–1830, Muslim clerics, in collaboration with Prince Dipanegara (1785–1855), a disaffected member of the aristocracy, led a peasant resistance movement against the Dutch. In the 1840s and 1850s a massive millenarian movement swept across the Banten region of Java with a populist revival of Islamic revolutionary sentiments against decades of Dutch colonial abuse of the Javanese nobility and peasantry alike. In 1912 in Java, Hajji Ahmad Dahlan (1868–1923) established Muhammadiya, a reformist religious establishment with a wide range of educational and social projects. By 1929 Muhammadiya had spread widely into remote villages with an elaborate pedagogical system that combined the study of Arabic and Dutch with an educational project that was part religious and part secular. Meanwhile a robust women's rights movement was associated with Muhammadiya, and its reformist agenda soon swept across a succession of social institutions.[13]

Simultaneous with these movements, a group of reformers known as Kaum Muda ("The Young Group"), sharing a pan-Islamic sentiment, began a sustained project of revising their religious laws along the lines of European modernity.[14] Numerous voluntary associations were formed to facilitate such conversations. Two prominent reformists, Shaykh Ahmad Khatib (1855–1916) and Shaykh Muhammad Tahir (1867–1957), who had studied in Mecca and had become familiar with Shaykh Muhammad Abduh's reformist ideas, returned to educate a new generation of Sumatran and Malayan scholars, intellectuals, and activists dedicated to updating their ancestral faith with political potency. Shaykh Muhammad Tahir established a newspaper, *Al-Imam*, in Singapore and began to propagate the cause of a reform in Islamic education, with its common motif being a return to the Qur'an and Prophetic traditions and an absolute conviction that a renewed covenant with these sacred sources was sufficient to enable Muslims to live a rich and fulfilling life as contemporary members of a vastly changing world. No such thing happened. Muslims remained as disaffected in Indonesia and Malaysia as elsewhere in the world, their religious faith and the metaphysics of their morals stripped of their enabling mysteries, exposed to both the corroding elements of instrumental reason and the madness of colonial power.

The more diligent public intellectuals, transitioning from the old Muslim world to the new by trying to oppose and end European colonialism, which they summoned under the rubric of "the West," dug the grave of their own deeply colonized minds. The stronger they contested "the West" the mightier the illusion assumed a reality sui generis. The more adamant they became that "Islam" was the answer, the more they recast their own ancestral faith as the mirror image of this very "West" they thought they were opposing. "The West" was a categorical trap—and Muslim intellectuals fell right into it.

The Role of the Rentier Intellectuals

Under colonial duress, Muslim public intellectuals were thus the principal agents of changing their own ancestral faith into an unrecognizable site of ideological contestation with what they categorically identified as "the West"—the self-designated code with which the hegemony of colonial modernity faced and stared down the world at large. Factual relation of power between colonial modernity and Islam eventually gave rise to fictive terms of opposition between European colonial ideologues and Muslim public intellectuals. At the threshold of the twenty-first century, and in the immediate aftermath of the cataclysmic events of 9/11, enough remnants of this binary supposition were resuscitated for us to see the psychopathological origin of its formulation, and the political potency of its appeal.

To see how this dialectic of generating and sustaining a fabricated hostility between "Islam and the West" has worked over the last two hundred years, we can take a look at our own time when a handful of US public strategists, feeding on the previous generation of Orientalists, began to bank on this projected binary opposition. It was a strategy predicated on a very intellectual universe that operated on the assumption that "Islam" was defeated and bitter, and thus Muslims were terrorizing "the West." The argument was very simple; it was also very lucrative. It fit the lowest and most common denominator of a frightened and mentally paralyzed public.

A few names in the immediate aftermath of 9/11 became instantly identified with the bellicose and violent reading of an already tense and terrorized condition. Bernard Lewis, Salman Rushdie, Thomas Friedman, Fouad Ajami, Michael Ignatieff, Farid Zakariya, Christopher Hitchens, and Dinesh D'Souza were chief among many others who each in his own way (they were mostly men, though Oriana Fallaci may be added to the list) was to join Samuel Huntington and posit the emerging geopolitics of the matter on an "Islam and the West" axis. These people are products of power—symptoms of a social disease that any bloated accumulation of power can generate in any society, in any culture, and at any point in history. It is crucial for us to look at these characters closely and examine the pathology they represent carefully. In them we can fairly accurately identify the original virus that infected the moral imagination of the generation that saw the political benefit of fabricating a center for colonial modernity and naming it "the West"—casting the rest of the world to its periphery. The disease is symptomatic of a much more pernicious purpose than Edward Said discovered and diagnosed in his magisterial achievement, *Orientalism*. He thought that these characters were merely serving the political interests at the center of that colonialism that had dispatched them to manufacture an Orient they could rule. But the disease is far more serious than that, and standing on the shoulders of Said, we can see further than he did. First, however, we need to take a closer look at our own contemporary creatures.

Much of the comments on the geopolitics of our predicament from the people named above of course amounted to nothing more than a bizarre kind of disinformation produced under duress, meant to wage war and generated by way of addressing such supercilious questions as "Why do they hate us?" or "What is wrong with them?" It perpetually cast in front of an "us" a "them" that, like wild animals, needed to be made to behave. This was no knowledge. This was a failed attempt at collective therapy for innocent bystanders at large, a demonstrably banal assessment of professional columnists, a foray into career opportunism for native informers looking for lucrative jobs, or dismal last calls for out-of-commission Orientalists. Out of ignorance, conceit, or charlatanism—it made no difference—the "Middle East specialists" responded by having "Islam" and "the Middle East" explain themselves. This was a public act of delusion, categorically wrong in the questions it raised and the foregone conclusions it served. "Islam and the West" was now the hobby horse of rentier intellectuals at the service of misinforming the ruling power.

In the middle of a frightful confusion, people were being taken for a ride, as were members of the US Congress, who were told by these mis-informers that US academics had failed to serve *their* empire, and that people with critical views of US foreign policy or Israeli colonial occupation of other people's lands ought to be silenced. When US soldiers—by and large from poor and disenfranchised families—came back home in body bags nobody asked people like Fouad Ajami or Kanaan Makiya, powerful native informers, what happened to those singing and dancing Iraqis and their flowers and baklavas that were supposed to welcome the US army into Baghdad. The native informers went about their business and disappeared into their suburban homes. In a just world criminal charges would have been brought against these people and whoever else encouraged the Bush administration to go to war against the specific mandates of the UN and the wishes of millions of people throughout the globe who in sub-freezing temperatures on 15 February 2003 poured into streets denouncing the pending war against Iraq. But ours is not a just world, nor does anyone hold these people responsible for their public encouragement of massive and terrorizing acts of violence. The rentier intellectuals were squarely at the service of the empire with their propagation of "Islam and the West."

In the absence of that justice, we are still in possession of critical judgment—and a particular text published by a senior member of these imperial secretariats in the immediate aftermath of 9/11 demands particular attention, because in it we can detect and examine the germs of a much more sinister disease. Bernard Lewis's *What Went Wrong? The Clash between Islam and Modernity in the Middle East* (2002), which first appeared as an article in the *Atlantic* (2002), began on the false premise that Muslims had fallen behind "the West," were envious of "the West," and therefore blamed "the West" for all its own shortcomings and backwardness. "The West" was free, Muslims were in bondage, and therefore "the West" had gone ahead and advanced while Muslims suffered in ignominy. The opening paragraph of Bernard Lewis in his *Atlantic* essay sums up his sentiments:

In the course of the twentieth century it became abundantly clear that things had gone badly wrong in the Middle East—and, indeed, in all the lands of Islam. Compared with Christendom, its rival for more than a millennium, the world of Islam had become poor, weak, and ignorant. The primacy and therefore the dominance of the West was clear for all to see, invading every aspect of the Muslim's public and even—more painfully—his private life.[15]

How could a man be so pathologically wrong in every sentence he uttered? What went wrong, indeed, with Bernard Lewis? Under the delusional spell of disgust for an entire people and their very presence in the world, Lewis never wrote a sentence in his long life that did not reek of hatred for Islam and Muslims. He is now dead, but the legacy of his long life is summed in one sentiment: "The West" was the best, "Islam" was the worst. What a terrifying legacy for a human being to leave behind!

Turning the Other Cheek

The condition of coloniality is amorphous but deeply historical. The moral and political bankruptcy of propaganda officers like Bernard Lewis is contingent on the far more massive discipline of knowledge production that was Orientalism, itself predicated on an even older history that a certain brand of Christianity (akin to Zionism, Islamism, and Hindu and Buddhist jingoism) has provided to earlier versions of colonialism—all of them predicated on the positing of a hostile and irreconcilable difference presumed between "Islam" and "the West." This particular case, however, is only one specific brand in a more universal binary opposition presumed between "the West" and "the Orient," which was effectively between "the West" and "the Rest." The emotive origin of Orientalism among Christian missionaries accompanying colonial officers is a matter of critical significance here.

In the classical history of colonialism, culminating in Christopher Columbus's voyages to the Americas, the colonial officers have slapped the natives in the face, as Christian missionaries were there to teach them how to turn the other cheek, in true correspondence with their Christian sympathy for the locals. Historically, European colonialism and Western Christianity have been constitutionally integral to and categorically subservient to each other: Colonialism serving Christianity by paving the way toward the global Christianization of the world, and Christianity serving colonialism by teaching the natives how to turn the other cheek. Though colonialism is constitutional to the operation of capital, because colonialism is nothing other than the geographical expansion of cheap labor and raw material supply for the insatiable appetite of capital, sub-serving colonialism is not constitutional to the message of Christianity. As the history of liberation theology in Latin America clearly indicates, Christianity can remember and reconstitute a revolutionary memory for itself and *not* give unto Caesar what is *not* Caesar's.

In the categorical symbiosis between colonialism and Western Christianity all the way back to Columbus's "discovery" of the Americas, a morally impoverished version of the Christian faith provided a sympathetic understanding of the natives, even as colonialism was robbing them of their dignity and wealth. Not all Christian missionaries were blatantly reckless and racist in their wanton disregard for Native American religious and cultural legacies. But their apathy toward Native Americans' suffering was matched by an even more sinister counterpart: sympathy and appreciation. Bartolomé de Las Casas's *Short Account of the Destruction of the Indies* (1542) is ordinarily cited for its advocating for the cause of the natives.[16] But precisely in its sympathetic attention to the natives, Las Casas's account stands as a landmark in harmony with—and not contrary to—the emerging re-modulation of classical into modern colonialism.

Las Casas's condemnation of the Spanish massacre of Native Americans and Spain's genocidal operations was meant not to advocate for an end to colonization but for a colonization that was more humane and productive. Both Bartolomé de Las Casas's *Short Account of the Destruction of the Indies* and its successor, the six-volume history of European colonies in the Indies and Americas *Philosophical and Political History of the Two Indies* (1770) by Abbé Guillaume Thomas François Raynal (1713–1796) and Denis Diderot (1713–1784), are in fact landmarks in the historical mutation of European colonialism from its initial theological justification by medieval Christianity to the European Enlightenment. Diderot, we should remember, was the editor of the *Encyclopédie*, the very organ of French Enlightenment. With the Enlightenment, colonialism became more "rational," and with that rationalism sympathy for the colonized natives replaced genocidal extermination, a practice that was neither economical nor beneficiary. And as classical (territorial) colonialism gave way to modern (capitalist) colonialism, so too did Christian missionaries yield and pass on their baton to Orientalists and anthropologists as the intelligence arm of colonialism.

Enlightenment modernity created cultures and manufactured civilizations with very specific purposes. Nationalized cultures succeeded dynastic histories, and civilizational boundaries replaced Christendom and Heathendom. The Islamic world, part and parcel of the Orientalized globe, was created, one among many, to authenticate the fabricated concoction called "the West." Enlightenment modernity needed the Islamic, the Chinese, the Indian, the African, and all other civilizations to corroborate and authenticate the empty abstraction at the center of the European bourgeois imagination code-named "the West." Mercenary Orientalists were dispatched to pick up precisely where the Christian missionaries had left off in subserving colonialism, to create and document these civilizational boundaries with passive sympathy to match the active hostility of colonial officers, marching on toward an aggressive integration into the globalizing effervescence of capital. "Islam and the West" was just the tip of this iceberg.

Why is it that this deadly combination—of active hostility by first the European colonial and now the US imperial powers and passive sympathy by academic (neo) Orientalists—continues? The reason is the unremitting operation of alienating capital, which was left completely out of consideration in the groundbreaking diagnosis of Orientalism by Edward Said. He saw and correctly diagnosed Orientalism as a discourse of colonial domination, which is of course what Orientalism also does. But Orientalism does something far more serious, fundamental, insidious, and critical to the operation of capital that Edward Said completely ignored. Orientalism is no mere discourse of colonial domination. Orientalism is a pernicious discourse of alienation. This is how it works: The mutation of classical (i.e., territorial) colonialism into modern, capitalist, and aterritorial colonialism corresponded with its counterpart mutation of medieval Christianity into positivist Orientalism. Orientals were not just told to turn the other cheek; they were told they were inferior beings if they refused. This was a historical development right in the bosom of European Enlightenment modernity. Classical colonialism was militaristic in disposition and represented the deranged dynastic proclivity for territorial expansion, while modern colonialism emerged from the heart of European capitalist modernity, the logic of its globalizing operation, and as such it represented the economic interests of the ruling bourgeoisie.[17]

Medieval Christianity, which in such figures as Bartolomé de Las Casas produced the first anthropological studies of the slaughtered natives, was represented by evangelizing missionaries fully at the service of their respective churches and their coteries of aristocracies. The new colonialism that was engendered and empowered by the rise of capitalist modernity required a whole new intelligence arm to serve it immediately and effectively without the medieval baggage of Christianity. Capitalist colonialism was rationalized colonialism, there to serve it correspondingly, and thus Orientalism became the rationalized "Christianity," as it were. Orientalism was the result of this ideological mutation at the service of accumulated capital. In its passive sympathy for the colonized, Orientalism in fact extended the constitutional hypocrisy of Enlightenment modernity (not *dialectic*, as Adorno and Horkheimer thought, but *hypocrisy*).[18] Immanuel Kant wanted to eat his cake and have it too—have the bourgeois subject posit a universal claim to agency and yet deny that claim to the colonized populations that put champagne and caviar on its table. In the massive body of detailed scholarship that it produced on the Oriental edges of its imagination, Orientalism continued with its fake sympathy toward the colonized that it had inherited from the Christian missionaries.

Where Is the Orient?

Orientalism crafted and othered "the Orient" but not just as a matter of discursive colonial domination and agential de-subjection. No. Orientalism engineered and othered the Orient (which was effectively the entirety of the colonized world) by hiding the fact that colonialism is nothing but the abuse of labor by capital writ global, that if you take the colonial out of the operation of capital, the center of capital modernity collapses like a sand castle. Orientalism was therefore something far more pernicious than a mere discourse of imperial domination of colonized nations. Orientalism was a discourse of alienation, aggressively distancing colonial labor from its accumulation into capital. What Marx thought constituted the nature and texture of capital, that in fact it is "the dominion of past, accumulated, materialized labor over immediate living labor that stamps the accumulated labor with the character of capital,"[19] was generically true in the global configuration of the relation between labor as un-accumulated capital and capital as accumulated labor. "The colonial" is nothing but geographically expanded and culturally diversified labor and raw material alienated from the commodity it produces and the capital it engenders, accumulates, and sustains. "The colonial" is a misnomer—a smokescreen, a subterfuge—for none other than abused labor and plundered raw material.

Orientalism is a distancing discourse, constitutionally alienating and categorically othering the colonial from the capital, catapulting it into an exotic, estranged, and alienated abode so that it would not recognize itself as the very labor that is accumulating in capital. Orientalism aided and abetted the global operation of capital by helping it disguise itself discursively under the camouflage code-named "the West," and then alienated, distanced, and estranged the labor that was constitutional to its formation and called it "the East," "the Orient," or more specifically "India, Islam, China, Africa, Latin America." Marx observed, "It is only the dominion of past accumulated labor over immediate giving labor that stamps the accumulated labor with the character of capital."[20] If we consider the fact that the domain of this dominion of dead over living labor—capital—is global in its very moment of inception, then the colonial site is constitutional to that whole operation. This pernicious function of Orientalism in facilitating the operation of capital escaped and remained completely hidden to Edward Said, and even before him to Karl Marx, who too partook in the discursive delusion of Orientalism. Without understanding Orientalism as the externalized, estranged, and exoticized alienation of labor from capital, this very alienation will remain incomprehensible to the presumed centers of its operation too.

Colonialism is the abuse of labor by capital writ global. The local abuse of labor by capital is colonialism at home. Having thus used "local" and "global" in binary and complementary senses, we immediately realize that in fact there is no exclusive domesticity or globality to the operation of capital as accumulated abused labor. Capital is always already global and domestic, simultaneously, from which we must conclude that in fact there is no center and thus no periphery to the operation of capital as accumulated abused labor, and that colonialism as a reality sui generis and independent of the operation of capital is a sham. In fact, capitalism from its very inception was a globalizing operation that infiltrated and gradually mutated the classical operation of colonialism as territorial expansion and made it integral to its exploitation of natural resources and abuse of labor. Ultimately, Marx was wrong in separating the treatment of colonialism from his reading of capital, for postulating such nonsensical categories as "Oriental despotism," and he did so because he too was a creature of Enlightenment modernity and could not have not shared its blinding constitution of the world in terms of national cultures and civilizational boundaries.

In the same way that the abused living labor is unaware that the reigning capital is none other than its own dead past by means of the forces of alienation and commodity fetishism, colonialism too is unaware that the equally reigning capital is none other than its own dead past by means of the false assumptions that race and ethnicity are the paramount causes of colonialism—and, even more significantly, by Orientalism having created a false consciousness for it by way of alienating it from recognizing the fruits of its own peripheralized labor in the heart of the centralizing capital. Capital disguised itself as "Western civilization," while globalized labor was camouflaged under the distancing guise of colonialism crafting an Orientalist discourse that traveled around the world and disguised its abused labor as "other civilizations."

Orientalism was not just a simple discourse of colonial domination creating an Oriental other to rule over. Far more insidiously, Orientalism was a discourse of alienation. It did not create the Orient just to be ruled by the Occident. It created the Orient in order to constitute a separate realm for the colonial and thus alienate it from its integral connectedness to capital. Just like Karl Marx, Edward Said did not see this because he too was particularly enamored by Enlightenment modernity and its global promise of a secular humanism.

"Capital," Marx believed, "presupposes wage-labor; wage-labor presupposes capital. They condition each other. Each brings the other into existence," to which Marx immediately adds, "Does a worker in a cotton factory produce only cotton goods? No. He produces capital. He produces values which serve anew to command his work and to create by means of its new values."[21] Labor, in short, produces the means of its own bondage and alienation. But that cotton factory is not just in Scotland, Lyon, or somewhere in Brussels. It is also in Bombay, Cairo, Mexico City, Johannesburg, and somewhere in Guatemala. The colonial is constitutional to the capital. We can very easily replace the word *proletariat* and read Marx as saying (paraphrasing): "Increase in capital, therefore, is increase of the colonial."[22] If we do that, we realize that the whole phenomenon of "globalization" is nothing but the lifting of the smokescreen that Orientalism had created and used to separate the abuse of labor by capital, casting one in London and calling it "Western Civilization" (capitalism) and the other in Bombay and calling it "The Orient" (colonialism). Both state-sponsored nationalism and anticolonial nationalism are effective mechanisms of the nationalization of political cultures under the suzerainty of the ruling states. All of these contribute to the Orientalist creation and constitution of the colonial site as hermetically and hermeneutically sealed reality unto itself, that has to either catch up with "the West" or resist "the West," but ends up in both cases authenticating and corroborating "the West." That is the cruel trap that for over two hundred years Orientalism had set for the natives—no matter if they accepted or rejected "the

West," celebrated or rebelled against it, they ended up corroborating it and thus getting further and further alienated from the fruit of their own labor.

State-sponsored nationalism positively and anticolonial nationalism negationally have corroborated the principal task of Orientalism in dividing the world between "the West" and "the Rest"—thus disguising the abused labor at the colonial site from the capital that it has generated and sustained in what Orientalism insidiously crafted and camouflaged in such binary terms as "Islam and the West." Orientalism as a system of knowledge production—bought and paid for by capitalist modernity for services rendered on its colonial sites—is the chief alienating discourse that first and foremost creates and constitutes "the Orient" via a negational project of validating and authenticating "the Occident." By separating "the Orient" and "the Occident," Orientalism sustains its epistemic origin in European Enlightenment modernity and its positivist agenda in assigning to national cultures and civilizational boundaries a claim to universal validity and authenticity. The project is quintessential to the designation and authentication of the politically peripheralized colonial universe as something categorically different from the ideologically centralized operation of capital. This in turn results in concealing the operation of the colonial as anything other than the abused labor distanced from the source of its abuse, the increasingly swelling capital.

Both state-sponsored and, its exact nemesis, anticolonial nationalisms paradoxically aided and abetted Orientalism in alienating the colonial from the capital, but so have such so-called "authentic" or "nativist" movements as Islamism or Hindu fundamentalism. Islamism, as one particularly poignant example, takes the idea of "the West" seriously and postulates itself against it. But, and here is the rub, the more Islamism opposes "the West," the more it authenticates and validates it, and in effect and in practice authenticates and validates itself. Take "the West" out of an Islamist discourse and it collapses on its face. Take "the Orient" out of "Orientalism" and it joins Islamism on the same ground. For this reason, Bernard Lewis was the closest ideological ally as well as the staunchest political enemy of Islamic fundamentalism, because any kind of radical Islamist movement in effect corroborates Bernard Lewis's monumental role in narrating and documenting one of the deadliest inventions of the colonizing imagination.

While both state-sponsored and anticolonial nationalisms take the idea of national polity and national cultures seriously, Islamism takes the idea of "Western civilization" too seriously. So while the former authenticates the capital invention of the nation-state, the latter corroborates the colonial invention of civilizational boundaries. But both national cultures and civilizational boundaries are categorical inventions of the Enlightenment on behalf of capitalist modernity, the former to corroborate the national economy of capital, the latter to separate its operation from the colonial domain, both to alienate the abuse of labor by capital via the generation of a false and falsifying consciousness.

II *The Return of the Repressed*

4 *What's in a Name?*

You cannot lynch me and keep me in ghettos without becoming something
monstrous yourselves. And furthermore, you give me a terrifying advantage.
You never had to look at me. I had to look at you. I know more about you
than you know about me.

JAMES BALDWIN, *I Am Not Your Negro/Remember*
This House (2016)

In a landmark interview in 1965 Malcolm X was asked by his interlocutor why he preached "hate to meet hate." Malcolm X denied
having ever advocated hate. The white man questioning him persisted that he had. "No," Malcolm interjects, "that is the guilt complex of the American White Man that is so profound that when you
begin to analyze the real condition of the Black Man in America,
instead of the American White Man eliminating the causes that create that condition, he tries to cover it up by accusing his accusers
of teaching hate."[1] In that singular moment of rhetorical rebuttal,
Malcolm X stages a condition of dialectical reversal, where a Muslim critical thinker reasserts agency and reclaims history, not just by
confronting the White Man's monological premise but by epistemically overcoming the limitations of his moral imagination.

In that vein, what I am going to propose in this chapter is akin to what in his seminal book, *The Souls of Black Folk* (1903), W. E. B. Du Bois called the "dual consciousness" of the Black person, which he feared would burst any human being apart: the self-perception of the Black person and the internalized other's perception, the white gaze cast upon the Black person. Muslims of the "Islam and the West" gestation had fallen into a similar trap, their own historical self-perceptions pulling them from one end and the white gaze of "the West" they had internalized pulling them from the other. This chapter examines the delivery from that dehumanizing dual consciousness occasioned by the "Western" gaze when Islamism began to undo itself. To do so, I must first mark the violent disposition of "the West" itself, the commodified power of its fetish, and the political duress under which Muslims devoured their own faith. That will prepare the groundwork to see how Malcolm X's dialectical reversal of the epistemic foregrounding of white supremacy works.

In the third volume of his magisterial five-volume opus, *The Bourgeois Experience: Victoria to Freud* (1984–1998), Peter Gay's *Cultivation of Hatred* (1993) is a master class in exposing the violent underpinning of European bourgeois behaviors during the Victorian era.[2] The range of racist, colonialist, eugenicist, and xenophobic ideas and practices of the Victorian age boggles the mind and makes one wonder how the very assumption of "bourgeois morality" traced itself back to this age. From the other and earlier crucial text of this period, Steven Marcus's *The Other Victorians: A Study of Sexuality and Pornography in Mid-Nineteenth-Century England* (1966), we know of the more blatant sexual aggressions defining the same period.[3] Peter Gay's work, however, traces the political forces at work in the more global context of the rise of the Victorian age. Gay traverses the whole gamut of high European culture, from George Sand to Nietzsche, to map out a truly barbaric age, all embedded in the high and low cultures of the European and North American brutish power cast around the globe.

The geographical expanse of Gay's book ranges from the United States to England, France, Austria, and Germany in the period from 1815 to 1914, where three major "alibis," as he puts it, systematically cultivated hatred of others through (1) an ideology of competition, (2) the construction of inferior others, and (3) a violent cult of "manliness." It is in the section he calls "The Convenient Other" that Gay maps out the ease with which the Victorian age manufactured its cultural inferiors, the better to manage, hate, and dominate them.[4] Here we learn about a certain American divine named Josiah Strong who had written a bestselling book called *Our Country* (1885) in which he "praised the Anglo-Saxon race for its genius at colonizing and argued that its sterling qualities fitted it to impose its blessings on lesser, more shiftless races."[5] Strong's nefarious ideas represented a typical fusion of social Darwinism and racism. According to Gay, "the final competition that Strong and others foresaw would most likely be fought out in empires that the British and French, Belgians and Germans, Portuguese and Americans were amassing or consolidating in Africa, Asia, and the West Indies." Strong had observed that "the most ferocious bloodletting would be between colonizers and the natives they were struggling to subdue." Gay further adds: "Missionaries and explorers often mixed sexual excitement with their sheer aggressiveness. Homoerotic travelers admired the bodies of the local men, and lascivious heterosexuals admired those of the local women, reporting home about naked breasts, legs, and buttocks worthy of the artists pencils."[6]

The aggressive manufacturing of "Islam and the West," or "the West and the Rest," was the product of this violent period, integral to a bourgeois fixation on conquest and domination, predicated on humiliation and hatred. We are, however, all beyond those periods

of blind hatred—in part because of the revelatory scholarship of critical thinkers like Peter Gay. We can now see why and how such cultivation of hatred was meant to humiliate and rule over other people.
The false binary of "the West and the Rest" is exposed for what it
is, and "the West" is the main culprit in its construction. The future
of which Freud wrote is finally here, and the ideology of conquest
and domination at the service of the European capitalist modernity
is exposed as an illusion, a false and falsifying consciousness, as
both Marx and Freud considered "religion" to be. Marx and Freud
were talking about "the West" or "Western Christianity"—the combatant, concealed, camouflaged Christianity—when they wrote of
"religion." The end of the illusion is the end of "the West," the end
of history, as later scholars like Francis Fukuyama would call it, as a
condition of Christian eschatology where the resurrection of civilizational thinking is in fact the penultimate stage of Western (imperial) Christianity.

Now we need to ask ourselves the key question of how this false
binary became so predominant, and why we are ready to leave it. The
dangerously false binary that emerged as "Islam and the West" over
the last two centuries plus was a talismanic reference to two irreconcilably hostile nemeses. Although this binary is a recent concoction predicated on a false and ideologically distorted historiography,
it has been exceptionally productive in imagining enduring civilizational conflicts. In the course of various Muslim conquests around
the world, most of it to the east and north of the Arabian Peninsula,
a number of scattered encounters with "Europe" (when it was not yet
"Europe" as we now understand the term) are usually cherry-picked
and strung together as indications of military encounters that demonstrate an irreconcilable difference between "Islam" and "the West."
The Muslim conquest of Jerusalem in 638, taking it from the Byzantines; or the 673–678 Arab siege of Constantinople, at the time
the capital of the Byzantine Empire; the Islamic conquest of the

Iberian Peninsula in 711–718, followed by the Battle of Tours in 732, the Muslim conquest of Sicily in 827, and ultimately the commencement of the Crusades in 1095 following Pope Urban II's instigations— are all detached from their respective contexts to point to such presumed endemic hostilities. This has always been an ahistorical reading of those events, assimilating them forward into the later manufacturing of "Islam and the West" as two opposing metaphors. To counter this false narrative, we must remember how "Orientalism," as a discursive project, has been instrumental in fabricating, perpetuating, and authenticating this prolonged history of hostility and thus binary opposition. When Edward Said, in his *Orientalism*, exposed this mode of knowledge production as a colonial project, the categorical distinction between "Islam and the West" was in fact paradoxically ossified and categorically consolidated.

The condition of coloniality under which "the West" ossified and authenticated itself simultaneously forged and forced all its Others, "Islam" in particular, into a moral and imaginative metamorphosis in which the more they criticized "the West" the more they corroborated its metaphysics of authenticity. To reverse the thrust of that historical trajectory we must dwell on moments of the return of the repressed, when and where the fetishization of the false binary of "Islam and the West" begins to unravel. We need to show how the "Islam" of "Islam and the West" began to undo itself. As a world religion, Islam (like all other world religions) is real, but in their haste to oppose "the West" (as the epitome of capitalist modernity) Muslim ideologues from Jamal al-Din al-Afghani to Ali Shari'ati turned Islam into an illusion of itself. They began to turn their own historical consciousness into the mirror image of what they opposed, the very delusion of "the West"—until the "Islam" of "Islam and the West" epistemically exhausted itself—an event that was coterminous with aggressively globalized capitalism and the metamorphosis of imperialism into an amorphous empire. To see how the binary is dismantled, we need to look at it from the other side of the false divide, from the "Islamic" side, and from the starting point of perhaps its most spectacular manifestation in modern history.

The End of Islamism

The end of Islamism as a mode of ideological mobilization caused and conditioned by the "Western" colonial imaginary was evident precisely at the moment of its global recognition in a massive revolutionary uprising three-quarters into the twentieth century. By far the most spectacular—that last and longest flame of a dying candle—manifestation of Islamism was in the course of the 1977–1979 Islamic Revolution in Iran. After more than half a century of persistent ideological articulation and political action, Islamism finally succeeded where both nationalism and socialism had failed— the national liberation of a people from a corrupt monarchy and its US support. The culmination of Iranian nationalism was in the figure and phenomenon of Prime Minister Muhammad Mosaddeq (1881–1967), and when his democratically elected government was toppled by a CIA-sponsored coup d'état in August 1953, the moral and political prowess of the ideology behind it fell too. The Iranian experiment with socialism ultimately came to its most successful institutional achievement in the Tudeh Party, and so did its demise when in the course of the same coup it was at once ideologically discredited and politically dismantled. A decade into the successful return of the Shah back to power with the full support of the United States, neither the post-Mosaddeq Iranian nationalism nor the post-Tudeh socialism was able to stage a successful comeback. While the Muslim activists, inspired by the leadership of Ayatollah Khomeini, managed to startle the Pahlavi regime in a major uprising in June 1963, the ruling monarch managed to brutally suppress the uprising. But again, about a decade later, as the Shah was celebrating the

2,500th anniversary of the Persian Empire, Khomeini came back with a vengeance and, in a crescendo of revolutionary zeal, toppled the Shah. This was the beginning of the end of militant Islamism in political power.

The success of the Islamic Revolution was its failure. Khomeini used the smokescreen of the hostage crisis of 1979–1980 to have a theocratic Islamist constitution drafted and ratified and to establish an Islamic Republic against all sorts of ideological and political resistance to it. When Saddam Hussein invaded Iran in September 1980, Khomeini took advantage of the catastrophic war that followed, 1980–1988, to consolidate his power. In the process, he demolished the economic infrastructure of the country and destroyed its revolutionary disposition. Once again, toward the end of his life, when the crisis of succession to his charismatic terror was in jeopardy, Khomeini manufactured yet another diversionary incident in the Salman Rushdie affair and orchestrated a revision of the Islamist constitution to sustain the rule of the Shi'i clergy. By the time he died in 1989, Khomeini had at once achieved and discredited the highest aspirations of an Islamist revolution. The post-Khomeini decade of the 1990s further consolidated the historical evidence of how "Islamic ideology" came to a crescendo with the rise of the Islamic Revolution in Iran, and then came to an end with the fall of the Islamic Republic from the grace of legitimacy. Today, the office and institution of Velayat-e faqih—supreme and absolutist authority of the Shi'i Jurist—continues to reign supreme with no regard for any democratic principles, and the fragile steps of democratic institutionalization of the collective will of the nation, expressed in the successive presidential elections of Mohammad Khatami and other parliamentary and city council elections, are thwarted by a relentless succession of domestic and global quandaries. Militant Islamism, as the doppelgänger of "the West," came to its zenith and fell flat on its face with the Islamic Revolution of 1977–1979.

The failure of the Islamic Revolution in Iran brought the political aspirations of the Islamic Ideology to a calamitous end in terms domestic to the very doctrinal foundation of the faith. At the heart of Islam, Shi'ism is a religion of protest. It cannot succeed without failing itself. As the prototype of the noblest sentiments definitive to its doctrinal texture and history, there is a Shi'ism at the heart of Islam that is above and beyond sectarian divisions. At the center of this heart dwells a historical paradox that makes Islam at large triumphant at the moment of insurrection against it, defeated at the moment of its success.[7] Because it has historically spoken truth to power, it cannot be in power. Acquiring power, it robs itself of speaking the truth to power. The defining moment of Shi'ism—and with it Islam—is the doctrinal sanctity of *Mazlumiyyat*, of having been wronged, subjected to tyranny. From the controversy over the succession to the Prophet in 632, to the caliphate of Ali in 656–661, and ultimately to the battle of Karbala in 685, constitutional to the historical memory we call Shi'ism is the condition of its subalternity, its perpetual terms of disenchantment, its having been wronged. It ought to, and will always, remain that way. The instant it succeeds to power it negates itself. Shi'ism is either a religion of perpetual insurrection or it is the very negation of itself. It fails the moment it succeeds. It succeeds only in its defiant disposition. With the failure of the Islamic Republic as a legitimate state, Islamism—Islam articulated in potent political terms against colonialism and at a massive cost to its moral and intellectual imagination—came to a catastrophic end. And with that failure Shi'ism, as the charismatic core of Islamic insurrectionary disposition, was triumphantly released to roam freely the streets and alleys of the Muslim revolutionary imagination—from the slums of Casablanca to back alleys of Cairo, from Southern Lebanon to occupied Palestine, from the Persian Gulf to the Arabian Sea to the Indian Ocean, from Chechnya to Bosnia, from China to Somalia. The political failure of Islamism as the mirror image of "the West" was the fertile ground of the resurrection of Islam as a religion of protest.

Islam and Globalization

The collapse of Islamism as the mirror image of "the West" has a global context too. At the dawn of globalization, Islam has lost its interlocutor—the illusion of "the West" has exhausted its instrumental use value and is on its way to the museum of unnatural history. With the spiral crescendo of migratory labor defying the smokescreen of Orientalism and revealing its instrumental mutation into globalized capital, that binary opposition that once categorically separated the colonial from the capital is no longer valid or operative—nor is any illusory culture of civilizational divide that Orientalism manufactured to accompany it. With the collapse of the Soviet Union and the rise of the United States as a dysfunctional superpower, the world is at the cusp of a whole new global configuration of polity and power in which European nationalism, Soviet socialism, and by extension revolutionary Islamism have no place of power or systematic program of ideas. Colonialism now appears for what it has always been: the abuse of labor by capital—raceless, faithless, gender-neutral, and color-blind. It does not now, nor did it ever, make any difference whether capital abused the labor in its immediate neighborhood or colonized it in distant territories. Nike and Banana Republic go to Guatemala for cheap labor, cheap labor comes to Nike and Banana Republic in the sweatshops of Manhattan. Cheap labor moves from Turkey to Germany, German factories dodge and go after cheap labor in Turkey. Persistent and intensified patterns of labor migration—South Asians in Great Britain, North Africans in France and Spain, Turks in Germany and Holland, all of them joining Asians and Latinx in the United States—now correspond to the active de-sedimentation of all binary oppositions between "the West" and "the Rest" and, a fortiori, between "Islam" and "the West." The result is a variegated global texture to labor and capital and their character and culture, a texture that can no longer sustain any binary opposition between "Islam" and "the West"— and thus "Islam" and "the West" have lost each other and, with each other, themselves.

Signs of disarray and de-sedimentation are written all over Islam today. The reactionary appearance of jihadi cells in Central Asia before and after the collapse of the Soviet Union, the mercenary formation of the Taliban by Pakistani intelligence at the behest of the United States to fight against the Soviets (chickens that later came home to roost on 9/11), the catastrophic failures of the Islamic Revolution in Iran to deliver a minimum of its ideological promises, the fanatical rise of Islamism in Turkey and Egypt and other North African regions, the alarming rise of suicidal violence in Palestinian occupied territories, the clueless uprising of the Chechen separatists against Russia without any revolutionary agenda beyond sporadic skirmishes with the Russian army, and then the rise of the murderous ISIS in the aftermath of the US invasion of Iraq are among any number of cross-national indices that militant Islamism today is more an iconic dislocation of its once potent politics than a revolutionary political project. If militant Islamism emerged at the height of European colonialism code-named "the West," it is dying at the nadir of US dysfunctional imperialism, when "the West" has lost its iconic relevance.

With the material disappearance of "the West" as the principal interlocutor of Islam, so is vanishing any sense of continuity or purpose in the critical imagination of Muslim intellectuals. Today, there is not a single Muslim intellectual who commands the global attention of his fellow Muslims the way generation after generation of them did throughout the nineteenth and much of the twentieth centuries. Today, at the end of anticolonial Islamism, the Sudanese

Hasan Turabi has scarcely any knowledge of or anything to say about Iran or Pakistan. Hardly anyone has heard of the Iranian Abdolkarim Soroush in North Africa. Ali Abbasi al-Madani is known only in Algeria and Hasan Hanafi only in Egypt, where neither the Algerians nor the Egyptians have any clue as to what Abdurahman Wahid is talking about in Indonesia or Mohammad Kamal Hasan is up to in Malaysia. As the anticolonial position of the Islamists was taking effective shape in the early to mid-nineteenth century, the rising figure and torpedo character of Seyyed Jamal al-Din al-Afghani wove almost the entirety of the Muslim world together. He traveled widely from South Asia to Central Asia, to Asia Minor, North Africa, and Europe, crafting not only a wide web of solidarity among Muslim intellectuals and masses but also a global disposition to the texture of their language and project. Al-Afghani was of Afghan and Persian origin, but his principal follower was the great Egyptian reformist Shaykh Muhammad Abduh, who gave wide political currency to his mentor's ideas in much of the Arab and Muslim world. The Syrian Rashid Rida in turn became the great proponent of Muhammad Abduh's legacy. Shaykh Ahmad Khatib and Shaykh Muhammad Tahir extended al-Afghani and Abduh's ideas into a new generation of Sumatran and Malayan scholar activists. The pioneering Pakistani reformist Muhammad Iqbal (1875–1938) was deeply aware of these movements, and his groundbreaking writings on Islamic reform became extremely consequential for the leading Muslim ideologues in Iran like Ali Shari'ati (1933–1977), who was equally well-versed in ideas of such leading Egyptian revolutionaries as Hasan al-Banna (1906–1949), Shaykh Mahmoud Shaltut (1892–1963), and Sayyid Qutb (1906–1966). All that sense of revolutionary solidarity, political unity, and ideological purpose is now lost. Not a single Muslim intellectual today is known by anyone outside his immediate vicinity, nor do people outside that limit have any reason to get to know the self-referential meanderings of their astonishingly provincial concerns. Islam in the context of globalization has decoupled the false binary of "Islam and the West," and thus rendered entirely vacant the figure of a public Muslim intellectual with any claim to universal relevance.

The Rise and Demise of Islamic Ideology

To witness the end of Islamic Ideology as one of the most powerful modes of liberation theologies conditioned by the epistemic interface between "Islam and the West" in modern history, we may note two apparently contradictory but effectively complementary examples—the odd couple of Abdolkarim Soroush, perhaps the single most prolific Muslim intellectual from Iran, and Osama bin Laden, whose paramount mode of communication was not verbal but public affiliation with spectacularly iconic violence. Whether or not bin Laden was actually responsible for those acts of symbolic violence does not matter. What matters is that he had publicly celebrated their occurrence and taken credit for them. Soroush's verbal articulation of a systematic post-ideological hermeneutics and bin Laden's visual affiliation with symbolic sites of spectacular violence apparently contradict but effectively complement each other and mutually constitute a critical passage to misplaced hermeneutics and iconographic violence at the end of the progressive transmutation of Islam into combatant conversation with colonialism within the epistemic foregrounding of "Islam and the West."

Ever since the violent Islamist takeover of the Iranian revolution of 1977–1979, Abdolkarim Soroush has been relentlessly at work trying to safeguard what he considers to be the eternal tenets of Islam, "Islam Itself," as he calls it, from the political predicaments and ideological collapse that have been historically contingent on that metaphysical assumption—an Islam outside history. After an incomplete higher education in England as a pharmacologist, Soroush returned to his homeland in the wake of the 1979 Islamic Revolution in Iran, first to preside over its militant Islamist purges of higher education and then repenting his misguided membership in the upper echelons of the Islamic Republic by launching one of the most vociferous hermeneutic projects intended to separate the predicament of political Islam from its presumed metaphysical veracity. The result has been a singularly ahistorical conception of the faith and the social construction of its worldly realities.[8] In his famous thesis "The Contraction and Expansion of Religious Law," Soroush has argued that the essence of Islam remains constant, while its worldly attributes keep changing. This proposal is meant to perform two simultaneous tasks: (1) to save "Islam" from all its political ideologues, particularly those Muslim clerics who to this day rule over Soroush's homeland, and (2) allow for future, perhaps more progressive readings of the faith to succeed the failed experiments of militant Islamism.

Repeatedly in the course of articulating his thesis, Soroush argues that his principal concern is a hermeneutic and not a political or ideological project, and that he means to outline the main contours of a mode of interpretation that keeps the quintessential "essence" of the faith intact while allowing for the multiplicity of fallible readings of it. In this spirit, he believes that people as knowing agents are constitutionally disposed to "Progress" in their discovering of new things, and as such they are also in possession of an absolute and abstract "Reason." He accuses of Hegelianism those who believe in the historicity of this "Reason." Their judge, he believes, is History, not Reason. He exonerates himself from any attachment to Hegelianism or historical determinism. He believes Reason and the Progress contingent upon it are realities sui generis and immune to any subjugation to History. He denounces the Hegelians for the principality of History in their understanding of Reason. He maintains that his argument for contemporizing religious knowledge is not tantamount to collapsing his hermeneutics into what he considers to be Hegelian historical determinism. At one point in his main text, *Qabz-o Bast-e Teoric-e Shari'at* (Theoretical contraction and expansion of religious knowledge) he observes:

> The theoretical development of the religious knowledge (Shari'at) thus assumes an acceptable meaning. The proposition is not to add an item to what is doctrinally enjoined, or subtract an item from what is doctrinally forbidden, nor is it to abrogate a Qur'anic verse, or to distort a Prophetic or Imami Tradition. That which is being changed is the human understanding of the religious knowledge, and that which remains constant is the Religion Itself.[9]

Soroush then proceeds to suggest that the philosophical, juridical, or even the literary orientations in Islamic intellectual history are precisely the examples of multiple readings of one *Singular Sacred Reality*. History is silent, but historians make it sing different songs. Nature is silent, but physicists and biologists make it tell different stories. One needs to have a theoretically consistent awareness of these multiple readings. It is useless to compare a stagnant jurisprudence with a progressive jurisprudence when we still lack the principles of a hermeneutics that inform us as to what exactly is stagnant and what is progressive and why. Soroush considers himself as having provided that hermeneutics.

Soroush's project is contingent on resorting back to a medieval Islamic philosophical distinction between essence (*dhat*) and attributes (*sifat*) in an attempt to safeguard the metaphysical veracity of his faith from the vicissitudes of its historical predicaments—the most significant of which has of course been the colonial consequences of Enlightenment modernity. Equally absent from Soroush's deliberately, even militantly, ahistorical hermeneutics is the premodern Islamic intellectual history itself, with its multifaceted and multicultural character. In Soroush's hermeneutic project there is no room for premodern Islamic intellectual history or space for the colonial consequences of European modernity; nor is there a distinction between the effervescent premodern intellectual history of Islam and its colonial corrosion into a one-sided site of resistance to power. The result is a massive hermeneutic project with charming speculative attractions but very little historical correspondence to the globalized reality of Muslims today. This amounts to a monumental mausoleum of dead learning, archival and archeological in its long and languid homage to a once robust Islamic response to colonial modernity. In response to the ravages of colonial modernity and the rise of Islamic ideology (which he wholeheartedly served as an ideologue of the Islamic republic), Soroush in effect seeks to overcome a historical encounter that he had much anticipated and celebrated with a platitudinous and ahistorical hermeneutics. He protests too much: to cover up or make up for his detailed services to the Islamist tyranny he enthusiastically served, he now rushes to vacuous hermeneutics to muddy the water!

Not the Martin Luther (1483–1546) of the Islamic world, as he has been dubbed by some of his supporters, but more like a belated and outdated Meister Eckhart (1260–1327), Soroush strips his received faith of its historical resonance in search of some, for him, Eternal Word. In the mythic lexicon of that vocabulary, the political potency of an Islamism that over two centuries had given a colonially ravaged people a measure of moral resistance and insurrectionary defiance is finally historically vacated and politically spaded by an almost mystical hermeneutics.

Soroush's mystical retreat to an ahistorical Islamic hermeneutics is the metaphysical counterpart of Osama bin Laden's mutation of Islam into formulaic incantations addressed to fictitious audiences, drawing their attention to the symbolic sites of spectacular violence. Osama bin Laden's video messages represent the incantatory chanting of an iconic figure with no claim to any revolutionary project, ideological conviction, political program, or historical representation of a reading of Islam. The classical case of a berserk, inarticulate frenzy and amorphous rage are the defining moments of the fact and phenomenon of Osama bin Laden. His is the iconic demise of generations of Muslim ideologues who from the early nineteenth to the late twentieth century were instrumental in articulating a position of ideological conviction, political potency, and moral agency for Muslims' resistance to colonialism. Whatever major or minor acts of public violence he may or may not have been responsible for, bin Laden represented the catastrophic end, the last iconic flicker of a once vociferous political uprising, constitutional in the making of a systematic project of agential autonomy for a people. It is not accidental that Soroush and bin Laden happened almost at the same time at the two ends of "the Islamic ideology," one in hermeneutic the other in iconic terms, both of them post-historical, both of them placing two bookends around the historical rise and demise of militant Islamism.

Before his targeted assassination by the Obama administration on 2 May 2011, Osama bin Laden's public persona, in the age of dis/information, was squarely identified with a succession of spectacular acts of violence. He was known for having joined the anti-Soviet Afghan war of 1979–1989, trained by the Pakistanis at the behest of the United States in the interest of expelling the Soviets. After the Afghan war he is believed to have returned to Saudi Arabia, and soon after the Iraqi invasion of Kuwait he was incensed by the massive mobilization of US forces in Saudi Arabia. Because of his anti-Saudi and anti-US sentiments and activities in the course of the first Persian Gulf War (1990–1991), bin Laden was expelled from Saudi Arabia and sought refuge first in Afghanistan and then in Sudan, where he lived until 1996. The first spectacular act of visual violence attributed to bin Laden was when the World Trade Center in New York was the target of an unsuccessful attack in 1993. In

the same year, the brutal and public killing of eighteen US service-
men in Mogadishu, Somalia, had also been linked to Osama bin
Laden, as was the 1995 explosion of a truckload of ammunition in
Saudi Arabia in which five US citizens were killed. The 1996 explosion at Khobar Military Complex in Saudi Arabia, the 1998 bombing of the US embassies in Dar es Salaam, Tanzania, and Nairobi,
Kenya—with massive casualties—had also been attributed to Osama
bin Laden, and so were the 2000 attack on the USS *Cole* in Yemen
and the aborted attack against the Los Angeles International Air-
port. The simultaneous attacks on the World Trade Center and the
Pentagon (and potentially on other symbolic sites of US power) on 11
September 2001, were the last and by far the most visually spectacular events attributed to Osama bin Laden.[10] All of these deliberately
spectacular events came together to turn Osama bin Laden into public enemy number one for the United States and its European allies.

The United States and its allies have categorically failed to produce a shred of convincing evidence that persuasively and directly
links Osama bin Laden, let alone a ghostly apparition called al-
Qaeda, to any one of these incidents. But in a succession of carefully choreographed video installations—telecast, webcast, and
exhibited to a massive global audience with such alacrity that any
museum or biannual curator might be envious—Osama bin Laden
intimated solidarity with those who perpetrated these acts. What all
of these acts share is a site-specific mode of visual violence—at once
spectacularly imaginative and yet decidedly inarticulate. The terror
that is contingent on these acts of spectacular visual violence is precisely embedded in their disconcerting combination of ocular-centric
fluency and verbal infelicity. This is a generically emblematic phase
and the final sign of the end of a militant Islamism that, as the doppelgänger of "the West," once boasted a multiplicity of voices and
a variety of revolutionary visions across the Islamic world, articulated eloquently with clear ideological outlines, sustained political

programs, and elaborate economic plans. The current sporadic acts of visual violence—kidnapping of high-ranking officials, hijacking of commercial airliners, public assassinations, car bomb attacks, suicidal explosions in crowded commercial districts—are signs and symbolics in the arsenal of the concluding phase of more than two centuries of a robust and full-bodied history of Islamic resistance to colonial and imperial power. The Twin Towers of the World Trade Center and the Pentagon were selected neither as military targets— which they partially were—nor as civilian targets—which they partially were—but as *symbolic* targets: the tribal totem poles and the military emblem of an empire. This emblematic phase of militant Islamism marks the end of its legitimate claims on a sustained project of anticolonial and anti-imperial programs. What we are witnessing today is a talismanic escalation of visual violence on a purely symbolic plane, iconic in the range of its implications, figurative in the power of its destructive suggestions, with the vast repertoire of inarticulate sensation contingent on its political psychopathology, staging an *aesthetic* of violence to match Soroush's mystical hermeneutics.

A constant leitmotif in Osama bin Laden's video installations was his steady references to the Muslim sacred sites in Mecca, Medina, and Jerusalem, which he considers violated by the US and Israeli military presence. To the violated sanctity of these sites now should be added the sacred shrines in Najaf and Karbala, particularly potent in their memorial inviolability for the Shi'i Muslims: bin Laden hated Shi'is more than anyone. One more site ought to be placed next to these for a more complete picture: the two giant statues of Buddha in Bamiyan, Afghanistan, that were blown up by the brutish fanatical Taliban in March 2001, while Osama bin Laden was still there, just about a season short of the attack on their totem pole counterparts, the Twin Towers of the World Trade Center in New York. At the end of its demise, Islamism has become thoroughly emblematic, symbolically visceral, imaginal in its cosmic self-awareness and thus figuratively site specific. The sites that bin Laden kept referring to are the sanctified insignia of Islam, the seal and signs of its sacrosanct memories, the memento of its historical imagination, the hallmarks of its sacred geography. Mecca is where Ka'bah is, the House of God, while Medina is where the Prophet's house is located; and Jerusalem is where Muslims believe their Prophet ascended to the Seventh Heaven to meet the Almighty. The mere suggestion of the names of Karbala, Najaf, and Kufah run a naked electrical wire through the spinal core of a Shi'i. These sites are at once violated by forces alien to their sacred ceremony and violently defended against such intrusion. It is imperative to understand the visual intimation between the US and Israeli violation of the sacred Muslim sites in Mecca, Medina, and Jerusalem, and the violence that is targeted against the emblematic icons of the empire, the World Trade Center in New York and the Pentagon in Washington, DC. At such symbolic sites we have completely exited the realm of reality and reason and are squarely within the cyberspace of signs and signifiers, all emptied of their factual components, super-charged with their fictive significance. This is a battle of signs, one cultural constellation of symbolics against another, both vacated of their humanity and history, inundated with their talismanic allegories. As "the West" was the semiotic fetish of a civilizational totem, so did it alter any other civilizational category it had manufactured to belittle.

There is a catalytic effect that moves from these talismanic sites of contestation to emblematic effigies that rise to represent them. Figures like Osama bin Laden, Mullah Omar, Saddam Hussein, or Abu Bakr al-Baghdadi have appeared at the closing end of militant Islamism, when it has long since exhausted its normative ability to resist the moral colonization of Muslims by having categorically failed to provide them with any enduring institution of civil society, regional polity, viable economy, or cultural effervescence. The militant characters speaking on behalf of Islam—Sheikh Abd al-Rahman of Egypt, Mullah Omar of Afghanistan, Osama bin Laden of Saudi Arabia, Shaykh Fadlullah of Lebanon, Saddam Hussein of Iraq, Abu Bakr al-Baghdadi of ISIS—are all figurative in their rhetorical appeal to symbolic sites of public violence. As such, they lack the slightest ideological lineage with the generations of Muslim ideologues who, since early in the nineteenth century, were instrumental in providing a sustained program of thought and action in opposing European colonialism and the US and Soviet imperialisms. One searches in vain in their public pronouncements, video installations, and sporadic statements for any sign of a sustained program of action, ideological articulation of positions, or any theoretical awareness of where the Islamic world stands today, where it is headed, what its principal and peripheral ailments are, and what needs to be done. Instead, there is today a generic conflagration of ideas and sentiments—code-named "Islamic fundamentalism" by its detractors and "Islam" by its proponents—in which is consumed each and every trait of Islamic revolutionary thought and insurrectionary course of action over the last two hundred years. The inarticulate, vague, generic, and entirely iconic utterances of brutal tyrants, medieval potentates, highway bandits, and reckless adventurers like Mullah Omar, Osama bin Laden, and Abu Bakr al-Baghdadi have scarcely anything to do with the once-defiant rise of Muslim anticolonial struggles and everything to do with the pathetic demise of Islamic resistance to colonialism achieved at the great and irretrievable cost of Islamic moral and intellectual disposition. Scarecrows mounted on a dead and barren field, these pathetic shapes cut grotesque figures but attract no worthy attention, chase away no intelligent bird. The rise and demise of Islamism as the mirror image of "the West" remains the solid most compelling fact of Muslim predicament in the early decades of the twenty-first century.

It is crucial to see this epistemic exhaustion of militant Islamism as a dialogical failure—it was not only a mockery of revolutionary violence but in fact a testament to reactionary violence. Consider Georgio Agamben's reflections on violence:

> Fifty years after the publication of Walter Benjamin's "Critique of Violence," and more than sixty years after Georges Sorel's *Reflections on Violence*, a reconsideration of the limits and the meaning of violence stands little risk of appearing untimely. Today, humanity lives under the constant threat of its own instantaneous destruction by a form of violence that neither Benjamin nor Sorel could have imagined, a violence that has ceased to exist on a human scale. However, the exigency of rethinking violence is not a question of scale; it is a question of violence's increasingly ambiguous relation to politics. . . . We aim to determine the limits—if such limits exist—that separate violence from the sphere of human culture in its broadest sense. These limits will allow us to address the question of the only violence that might still exist on a human scale: revolutionary violence.[11]

It is the bizarre fusion of mock revolutionary and manifest reactionary violence that has sealed the fate of militant Islamism, which was formed as the mirror image of imperial violence that was coming to it from "the West," which predetermined an "Islam" very much akin to it.

"Islam and the West": From Militant to Iconic

The mutation of Islamic Ideology into iconic Islamism coincides with a similar transmutation of "the West" into identically iconic postures—virtually vacated and analytically abandoned. The publication of Samuel P. Huntington's 1993 thesis "The Clash of Civilizations?" might be considered a crucial marker in this categorical metamorphosis of "the West" from an invented illusion into a totemic icon. Huntington's thesis, noted for its psychopathology, was read far

more seriously than it deserved to be. In his self-sacramental ico-
nography, Huntington kept the United States as the besieged bas-
tion of Enlightenment intelligence while casting the rest of the
world into demonic indigenization and the diabolic revival of fanaticism.[12] "The West," he thought, was being challenged by Asia and by
Islam—but while the challenge of Asia was strategic and economic,
that of Islam was categorically civilizational. Predicated on a nonexistent knowledge of Islam or European colonial history, Huntington's 1993 thesis, later developed into a punishingly tiresome book,
was rooted in much earlier anxieties. The first resounding alarm was
sounded by Allan Bloom in his *Closing of the American Mind: How
Higher Education Has Failed Democracy and Impoverished the Souls of
Today's Students* (1987). The book became a sensational bestseller in
the United States; people obviously enjoyed reading Bloom telling
them how illiterate they had become, and how the masterpieces of
Western Civilization are no longer read with appropriate reverence
and required ritual.[13] Soon after the publication of Bloom's diatribe,
Robert L. Stone edited a collection of essays, *Essays on the Closing of
the American Mind* (1989), collectively celebrating Bloom's diagnosis. What becomes evident in this collection of essays was a systemic
orchestration of conservative will to reassert "the West" while thinking it in danger of corrosion. The iconic totem was indeed in danger.
Its delusional roots had been exposed.

Soon a Salem-style witch hunt began. Allan Bloom's bestseller
unleashed an avalanche of similar attacks on the US academy as
chiefly responsible for endangering Western civilization. Charles J.
Sykes wrote *Profscam: Professors and the Demise of Higher Education*
in 1988; Peter Shaw produced *The War against the Intellect: Episodes
in the Decline of Discourse* in 1989. Soon followed Roger Kimball's
*Tenured Radicals: How Politics Has Corrupted Our Higher Educa-
tion* (1990) and Page Smith's *Killing the Spirit: Higher Education in
America* (1990). Charles J. Sykes did not feel satisfied by one stab,

so he came back with another, *The Hollow Man: Politics and Corruption in Higher Education* in 1990. Dinesh D'Souza followed suit with his *Illiberal Education: The Politics of Race and Sex on Campus* in 1991. William Bennett made a splash with his *De-Valuing of America: The Fight for Our Culture and Our Children* in 1992. Martin Anderson went for the jugular in his *Imposters in the Temple: American Intellectuals Are Destroying Our Universities and Cheating Our Students of Their Future* in 1992. Richard Bernstein caught up with the bandwagon in 1994 with his *Dictatorship of Virtue: Multiculturalism and the Battle for America's Future*. The nervous meltdown was electrifying in the 1980s, and the temperature continued to rise in the 1990s. The US academy was targeted as the principal culprit in the evident decline and imminent fall of Western Civilization. "The West" was in danger and its valiant Crusaders had an air of missionary zeal and Divine benediction about their heroic march toward the Holy Land to rid it of the Mahometan heathens—with Alan Bloom, Francis Fukuyama, and Samuel Huntington at the helm, charging to smash the pagan idols of multiculturalism, postmodernism, poststructuralism, deconstructionism, postcolonialism, and a few other totem poles to pieces. "The West," the twin tower of the "Islam" it had manufactured on the colonial Ground Zero of "Islam and the West," was now equally in total iconic freefall.

These were no ordinary times in the heart of the sole surviving, however dysfunctional, empire. A strange cloud of menacing locusts had attacked, and in closer immunological examination its ghostly apparition was broken down to a bizarre combination of radical post-metaphysical thoughts from strange Europeans and recently naturalized darkly postcolonial intellectuals, commingling with Native and African Americans, instigating a dangerous condition in which an inadvertently acquired deficiency of certain culturally immune leukocytes had resulted in a variety of moral infections and even some forms of cancerous conditions, all leading up to the degeneration of the nervous system of Western civilization. All of these were thought to have been caused by an inconspicuous intellectual virus that infects the healthy cells of moral and upright Judeo-Christian characters, diabolically transmitted to their God-given health via illicit intercourse between monkey-looking recent immigrants and healthy-looking white Americans. AIDS was indeed soon discovered, while Ridley Scott and Sigourney Weaver made one frightful film after another about invading aliens. This was long before the outbreak of the COVID-19 pandemic around the globe, but the epidemiological fear of the foreigner had long been prepared for it.

The sum total of all these prognostications was the argument that higher education had been destroyed by a corrupt professor-ate (infiltrated by some infectious dark postcolonials) an illiterate student body (muddied by massive recent immigrants), and a complacent administration (staffed by gullible liberals.) But while Alan Bloom's book opened the complaints and suggestion box of the crusaders rising to defend Western civilization one contemptuous volume after another, the picture became clearer with the opening of another front. It was only two years after the publication of *Closing of the American Mind*, and in the middle of the collapse of the Soviet Union and the Eastern bloc, that Francis Fukuyama's essay "The End of History?" (1989) appeared in *The National Interest*.[14] We later discovered that in fact it was none other than Allan Bloom himself who, in the same year that his *Closing of the American Mind* appeared, extended an invitation to Fukuyama to come to his John M. Olin Center for Inquiry into the Theory and Practice of Democracy at the University of Chicago to deliver the essay that would later be known as "The End of History." While the agenda of Bloom's book was ostensibly domestic, the target of Fukuyama's argument became blatantly foreign. This somersault scissor attack by Alan Bloom and Francis Fukuyama defined the momentous rise of the iconic phase of Americanism (modulating itself on Islamism) completely taking over the cause and care of Western civilization—defending it against its domestic and foreign enemies. The morphed banality of "Islam and the West" had now found a decidedly American form.

Precisely at the time when Islamism was being persistently transmuted into an iconic mode of visual violence, its arch nemesis and historical doppelgänger, "the West," was on an equally emblematic course, aggressively metamorphosed by its custodians into a fragile relic in dire need of exceptional care and urgent protection against a gang of coarse and callous intruders and impostors. Harold Bloom's *The Western Canon* (1994) was a Miltonian reassertion of power at this point as to who and what counts in the august halls of the Western pantheon. Harold Bloom was dauntless against the onslaught of an army of nemeses he identified as multiculturalists, feminists, Marxists, or Afro-centrists. He championed himself as the defender of taste and of aesthetics independent of ideology—entirely blinded to his own ideology. The language of Bloom's account of the Western canon is inundated with exclusionary jabs like "our culture" and "our Western literary tradition."[15] He lamented with Yeats that "the center has not held" and that "mere anarchy" is upon the world. In September 1999, Bloom upped the ante and came out with *Shakespeare: The Invention of the Human*, no less. Humanity did not exist, could not exist, before the sixteenth Christian century, anywhere on the lonely planet. The Chinese, the Japanese, the Indians, the Arabs, the Persians, the Africans, the Latinos, the Eskimos, those native to the land Harold Bloom now calls "the West," and all other wretched subhumans of the world had to wait for the British Bard to invent them out of their bestiality. To invent the human was the retroactive task of the civilized and civilizing language and lore of "the West"— and Harold Bloom was there, one frightfully hefty volume after another, to make sure the world knew and humanity recognized who had invented it.

By the end of the millennium, a spirit of phantasmagoric doom and millenarian termination pervaded the soul of Western civilization— and there is no better place to see that sense of nostalgia and smell that air of antiquarian decay than in Jacques Barzun's *From Dawn to Decadence: 1500 to the Present; 500 Years of Western Cultural Life* (2000). As one of the most distinguished cultural historians of his time, Barzun wrote *From Dawn to Decadence* with a jeremiad sense of prophetic doom. Mustering a magisterial language at once oratorical and despondent, Barzun sets upon himself the obituary task of grieving the demise of Western civilization. "It takes only a look at the numbers," Barzun declares early in his massive volume, "to see that the 20th century is coming to an end. A wider and deeper scrutiny is needed to see that in the West the culture of the last 500 years is ending at the same time. Believing this to be true, I have thought it the right moment to review in sequence the great achievements and the sorry failures of our half millennium."[16] From there the tone and timber of Barzun's prose gets more mournful and meandering, somber in its elegant diction, woeful and grieving, as the sagacious historian canvases the desolate landscape of a once-glorious civilization. "Islam" and the "West" had forever lost each other as colonial counterparts and civilizational mirrors—each the specular apparition of the other. They had both ended. Barzun felt summoned to recite an appropriate and august obituary.

The Logic and Lunacy of Capital

Capitalism has a logic and lunacy of its own. The operations of labor and capital that had generated and sustained national economies, national polities, and their colonial divides in civilizational terms soon began to script a different story that commenced the fall of civilizational thinking. As the operation of capital began to transgress its artificially mandated national boundaries, economies, and polities, and as massive labor migrations from the global South to North and East to West began to confuse the forcibly nationalized sub-national cultures, a two-pronged critique of capitalist modernity emerged and proceeded to dismantle the very terms of civilizational thinking— one domestic to its European operation and the other launched from its colonial consequences. The transmutation of fabricated civilizational divides from militant to iconic had remained entirely oblivious to this fact.

It was first two eminent German Jewish intellectuals, Theodor Adorno and Max Horkheimer, who in the aftermath of the nightmare of Jewish genocide in the heart of the most "civilized" European nation, right at the very heart of "the West," began to question the promises of Enlightenment modernity. In their exilic home in California, Adorno and Horkheimer began a systematic dismantling of the Enlightenment project in what was later published as *Dialectic of the Enlightenment* (1944–1947), arguing how the aggressive mutation of instrumental reason under the violent logic of capital had come to turn humans into mere instruments. This observation of the mid-1940s in the wake of the European Jewish genocide was bracketed between Max Weber's ingenious diagnosis of capitalism and Protestant Christianity in 1905 and Martin Heidegger's similar conclusions in his 1957 essay, "Question Concerning Technology." It was finally brought to an orchestral crescendo in the 1960s and afterward with the rise of poststructuralism, postmodernity, and deconstruction, championed by the Franco-Algerian Jewish philosopher Jacques Derrida—a project that once and for all pulled the metaphysical rug from under the feet of the European Enlightenment and its philosophical antecedents, all the way back to the European re-manufacturing of Platonic dialogue. All the while, however, the colonial consequences of this project had never occurred to these European philosophers. It had to wait to be addressed by the generation of Edward Said and Gayatri Spivak in the rise of postcolonialism.

The poststructuralist critique of the logocentrism at the heart of both the Enlightenment and its engineered philosophical antecedents, as well as the postmodern critic of instrumental reason, coincided with a simultaneous critique launched against the criminal record of capitalism in its colonial operations. Postcolonial studies soon dovetailed and joined forces with poststructuralist and postmodern critiques and effectively paralyzed the positivist historiography at the heart of Enlightenment modernity. Valiant but ultimately feeble resistances to the poststructuralist critique of logocentrism and postmodern critic of instrumental reason were offered by such major European philosophers as Jürgen Habermas, who argued that the project of Modernity was still unfinished, and who offered a theory of what he called "communicative reason" as means of global recognition of it. But this theory was too vacated of the relations of power inherent in all acts of communicative reasoning for the poststructuralists and too Eurocentric for a postcolonial critique of modernity for it to be taken seriously.

The relation between knowledge and power that Michel Foucault had theorized in the 1960s and Edward Said brought home to factual fruition in the 1970s bloomed in the 1980s into a global flowering of similar studies, exposing the skeletons hidden in the closet of capitalist modernity. The impact of Edward Said's *Orientalism* (1978) followed by his *Culture and Imperialism* (1993) was global, despite the systematic demonization of him inside the United States (where he lived and taught) because of his defense of the Palestinian national liberation movement. It is impossible to exaggerate the liberatory significance of Said's *Orientalism* on generations of academics in a range of emerging sites in Latin American, Asian American, African American, and even Euro-American studies. Said's historic liberation of the silenced and cowed voices inside the United States then combined with massive waves of labor migrations into the country, and the result was that the self-appointed custodians of "Western civili-zation," or "the West," in the United States, now at the ripe age of their moral and intellectual retirement, began to be frightened out of their wits. It is in this context that Samuel Huntington's bureau-cratic directive known as "The Clash of Civilizations" thesis ought to be understood.

The target of Huntington's thesis, and an array of similar works published between the early 1980s and the late 1990s, was not *global* geopolitics at all. Huntington's essay and subsequent book are integral to a major reactionary backlash against some major demographic changes and discursive revolutions within the United States. After the change in US immigration laws in the mid-1960s, throughout the 1970s, for every eight Asian and Latino immigrants to the United States there was only one Western European; and throughout the 1980s it was a similar ratio of six to one. In the state of California alone, a principal site of Asian and Latino labor migra-tion, it was projected that by the year 2040 some 70 percent of its population would consist of Asians, Pacific Islanders, non-Hispanic Blacks, and Hispanics. These massive labor migrations and the demographic changes that they caused and projected alarmed the self-appointed custodians of "Western civilization," and an enor-mous propaganda war began against what was now code-named "multiculturalism."[17]

Consider in this respect the brilliant study by Catherine A. Lutz and Jane L. Collins, *Reading "National Geographic"* (1993), which exposed the racist horror at the core of the most popular US geog-raphy magazine, or Ronald A. T. Judy's *DisForming the American Canon: African-Arabic Slave Narratives and the Vernacular* (1993), in which he exposed the mind-boggling Negrophobia of the found-ing father of the European Enlightenment, Immanuel Kant. In her *Constituting Americans: Cultural Anxiety and Narrative Form* (1995),

Priscilla Wald carefully read through some of the masterpieces of US literary tradition and dismantled the normative category "American" and all the history of racism and sexism that had to be repressed for the category to become politically operative. What Donald E. Pease achieved in his edited volume *National Identities and Post-Americanism Narratives* (1994) was even more radical in its spherically finding a succession of alterities that the American identity has had to repress to make itself believable. The logic and lunacy of capitalism were changing places, and the emerging critical body of work was overcoming all sorts of received illusions.

Against this systematic dismantling of the fiction of "the West" and all its fabricated adversaries, the self-appointed custodians of "Western civilization" went berserk. Their conflicting and yet complimentary agenda of proclaiming "Western civilization" at once endangered and yet victorious suddenly turned an echo of their perturbed imagination, a delusional artifact of globalizing capital, as both precious and fragile, threatened by its poor and colored enemies who had now infiltrated the US academies. Their simultaneous pronouncement that "the West" was victorious but threatened by Islam had as its immediate domestic agenda the combating of what they now termed multiculturalism—namely, the rise of disenfranchised communities. Among them were women, who began a brilliant critique of the masculinist culture; the LGBTQ community, which launched an equally heroic attack on a constitutionally homophobic culture; African Americans, who started to restore dignity to their brutalized history; Native Americans, who began to tell their side of the genocide they had suffered; and Asians, Latinx, Muslims, and new African immigrants, who protested the indignity of their daily sufferings, as did Jews, who dropped their white-identified names and identity, as well as the ludicrous appendage of "Judeo-Christian" heritage, and proudly carried their Hebrew names and insisted on calling their sacred book the Hebrew Bible.

The Hobby Horse of Civilizations

The reemergence of Western-civilizational thinking evident in this set of militant defenses and mournful obituaries for "the West" during the last two decades of the twentieth century and at the heart of a global empire was a knee-jerk reaction, a defense mechanism, a futile attempt to save the defunct project of capitalist modernity, when Orientalism had invented the false binary of "the West and the Rest" to hide the integral relations between the accumulated labor called capital and the accumulating capital called labor. The categorical constitution of "civilization" has been a two-hundred-year-old Enlightenment invention for very specific reasons and objectives. But it had long since outlived its instrumental usefulness to the globalizing operation of capital by the time its defenders sought to revive it for the service of a new empire. The project was doomed to failure, not just because its practitioners were astonishingly illiterate when it came to reading the signs of the times, but also because the capital they thought they were serving—its amorphous texture vaporized into cyberspace—had no time or patience to waste on antiquarian ideologies that at earlier stages had served it well. Capital's notoriously charming body thrives on acquiring new and fashionable garments. It has a particular disdain for old-fashioned ideas and apparel. It discards them faster than the secondhand civilizational theorists and dying cultural historians can collect them. But the futility of their outdated agenda has yet to be fully recognized, as it is now aided and abetted by two diametrically opposed but effectively complementary forces: first, the prolonged pathology of jaundiced Orientalism, and second, a sudden and disturbing rise in New Age mysticism.

At the dawn of European colonialism, its military might was accompanied by a cadre of Orientalists. We may and we must oppose the epistemic foregrounding of their scholarship, but they were competent Orientalists. Today the rise of the dysfunctional US empire coincides with a spectacularly degenerate transmutation of Orientalism into outright propaganda pamphleteering, with no pretense to scholarship. The iconic rise of a talismanic "West" corresponds with the complete intellectual meltdown of classical Orientalism. As the intelligence arm of classical colonialism, Orientalism had a long and rather illustrious history, staffed by exceptionally competent philologists and historians. Today, that robust history of mercenary Orientalists has come to a sad and disgraceful end. Today the figure of Bernard Lewis (1916–2018), after his long and illustrious services to both British colonialism and American imperialism, looms large as the single most notable name in the sad saga of Orientalism. Whereas earlier in his scholarly career Lewis had a half-serious claim to being a historian of the Ottoman Empire, over the last few decades of his life his mental capacities degenerated, with one psychopathological symptom of his malady after another published for the whole world to see. The very titles of his books bespeak the severity of his ailment: *Islam and the West* (1993), *Cultures in Conflict: Christians, Muslims, and Jews in the Age of Discovery* (1994), *The Muslim Discovery of Europe* (2001), *What Went Wrong: Western Impact and Middle Eastern Response* (2001), *The Crisis of Islam: Holy War and Unholy Terror* (2003). The man was determined to stage Islam as a disease and Muslims as barbaric evidence of that disease.

Divisive, malicious, mean-spirited, and diabolic, the systemic mendacity on the pages of these books caters to the hateful banalities that a hysterical public wants to hear and harbor. With an astonishing ignorance of developments in an array of social sciences and humanities over the last half century, a frightful incompetence in any of the regional languages of the Islamic world and the culture they embody, and a narrative prose that reeks with hatred for the people who populate the world he examines, Bernard Lewis spent a lifetime producing one pestiferous text after another, with Muslims bearing the curse of his venom, and with a broken record spinning at the center of it all: Muslims have lost the game. In these books, Bernard Lewis completely lost any legitimate claim to sane deliberation; they can no longer be read even as pieces of pathological propaganda. Throughout his sad pages, Orientalism, once a rather respectable profession with a half-decent claim to serious scholarship, enters the realm of thaumaturgic voodoo, containing not even a pretense to rational argumentation, primary source references, linguistic knowledge of the sources, cultural familiarity with the region, firm groundings in any scholarly discipline, or familiarity with the state of scholarship in multiple fields. Distinguished scholars of Islamic history like Juan Cole have tried in vain to take these works seriously and write with clarity and precision against the insanity of their content.[18] But all such attempts are futile because these scholars are reading Lewis as if he were a serious historian who has made few factual errors or has not kept up with the most recent scholarship or is simply not aware of methodological and theoretical debates in various disciplines or harbors a particularly distasteful politics or has no moral qualms selling his outdated knowledge to military "intelligence" even more ignorant than he. This is not the case. With Bernard Lewis, Orientalism has officially exited the realm of colonial reason and entered the twilight zone of its unreality—it is now positively delusional, just like "the West" it defends and its habitual hobby horse of "civilization," which it takes out of the closet for yet another fantasy ride. In this hallucinatory project, Bernard Lewis is aided by an even sorrier gang of minions like Daniel Pipes on one side and self-loathing native informants like Fouad Ajami on the other. The collective wisdom of this platoon of abused souls is the continuous reiteration of "Islam and the West" as two eternal opposites and categorical imperatives with irreconcilable civilizational differences. Adding fuel to the fire of hatred and blindness, they create a thick, dark smoke of confusion and mistrust rising high above the fact and ferocity of a world that has no legitimate borders, a planet with no pole except the spiral gyration of abused global labor transmuted into obscenely cruel and amorphous capital.

As with all other historical phases when Islam experienced a moral shock, this latest phase of its evolving history has as its companion the soothing lullaby of mysticism. And this time around it comes in the compromised form of Seyyed Hossein Nasr—an expatriate Iranian Muslim, a former mystic philosopher at the Pahlavi court now devotedly committed to a monolithic and categorically ahistorical conception of his faith. A latter-day Muslim "mystic" in the New Age rendition of it, Nasr has published voluminously on the eternal truth of his Islam and how "the West" has gone wrong in betraying its Judeo-Christian truths in the course of what he calls "modernity." He believes in One Absolute and Absolutist Truth that has historically manifested Itself in one human form or another. Human fallacy has failed to recognize the Truth and Beauty of this Everlasting Revelation. Since 9/11, he has been taking pictures of himself smelling beautiful and aromatic flowers and publishing books with titles such as *The Heart of Islam: Enduring Values for Humanity* (2002). These books have a very lucrative market in a world terrified out of its wits by "Islamic Terrorism." Good-hearted liberals love to read a pious Muslim give a rosy picture of his faith. It soothes their fears, lulls their anxieties, and quenches their thirst for peace and prosperity in the universe. Not all Muslims are terrorists, they assure themselves when they read Seyyed Hossein Nasr. The Muslim mystic comes on the heels of a renewed interest in a generic kind of mysticism, with Coleman Barks's version of Rumi as national bestseller and competing with Deepak Chopra's *Golf for Enlightenment: The Seven Lessons for the Game of Life* (2003). The hobbyhorse of civilization has in these works found a lovely delusional garden of their Orient. It sells well.

Oracular Orientalism in tow and narcotic mysticism in mind, Bernard Lewis's regular visits to the Pentagon were a clear sign that the US generals were desperate to navigate the dead alleys of old-fashioned exotica for ways of measuring and monitoring their dysfunctional empire. One can only hope that they are more farsighted than to put all their intelligence eggs in this one threadbare basket. Once at the service of the British intelligence, Lewis still saw the world from the same set of outdated lenses. His mind was too nineteenth-century colonialist to be of service to a twenty-first-century empire. Sooner or later, the US generals would find out he was of no use to them. Empires change. If empires lasted, the whole world would be speaking Persian today. Empires change color with the changing condition of the material basis that has given rise to them. But there is always a lapsed period between the material and military rise of an empire and the emerging parameter of its hegemony. What we are witnessing today is a rare historical moment when a globalizing empire is falling, and the terms of its hegemony are yet to be assayed.

Today, at the twilight of its credulity, the binary supposition of "Islam and the West" is going out with a mystical halo of antiquity about its countenance. The ghostly apparition of an invented mystery called al-Qaeda is now the phantasmagoric insignia of an omniscient, omnipresent, omnipotent, and panoptic terror, capable of striking at the heart of normalcy, civility, and ordinariness at any moment and at any place. This frightful goblin is precisely the blueprint the US Pentagon is using to model its "open-ended war on terrorism," itself the very picture of terror, of "shock and awe," that it wants to defeat—and thus projects. The Pentagon has chosen its enemy very carefully, and it is becoming like it. The Pentagon is al-Qaeda. As the illusion of a binary opposition presumed between "Islam" and "the West" now enters its hallucinatory stage, with deadly violence on symbolic sites of power from one side and a megalomaniacal and predatory imperial imagination on the other, apocalyptic Christian fundamentalism is taking hold of the ideological disposition of the empire. All parameters of social reason and political prudence are washed aside, and both "Islam" and the "West" are reduced to their iconic meaninglessness, emblematic insignia of one mystic hallucination against another—at once apocalyptic and postmodern, surreal and metafictive, revelatory and delusional.

The Twain Collide and Collapse

"Islam" and the "West" have now been dismantled and become iconic, the symbols of each other's negation. But the end of "Islamism" that "the West" had occasioned and triggered is not the end of Islam. Islam is a religion of protest, the common faith of masses of human beings around the globe, always aware and confident of its hermeneutic wherewithal. It emerged as a revelatory language of speaking truth to power from the depths of the disposed and the heart of the forsaken. As a religion of protest, Islam rests on an irreconcilable paradox. It can never succeed in power without simultaneously corrupting and negating itself. Islam can never be in power—should never be in power. Islam is a moral authority, not a political power. For over fourteen hundred years, there has never been an Islamic empire that was not ipso facto opposed by massive revolutionary uprisings against it. Never in its history—from the Umayyad and the Abbasids early in its history to the Mughal, the Safavids, and the Ottomans at the dawn of modernity and throughout its encounter with European and American colonialism and imperialism—has Islam been devoid of its symbolic repertoire of a revelatory poverty, of a revolutionary asceticism, always speaking truth to power, never succeeding in power without simultaneously giving rise to its own negation. Islam, as a religion of protest, is never delivered, always protesting.

As for the dysfunctional US empire succeeding "the West," E. M. Cioran's prophetic vision almost half a century ago in *The*

Temptation to Exist (1956) still holds true, as it has come frightfully to pass:

America stands before the world as an impetuous void, a fatality without substance. Nothing prepared her for hegemony; yet she tends toward it, not without a certain hesitation. Unlike the other nations which have had to pass through a whole series of humiliations and defeats, she has known till now only the sterility of an uninterrupted good fortune. If, in the future, everything should continue to go as well, her appearance on the scene will have been an accident without influence. Those who preside over her destiny, those who take her interest to heart, should prepare her for bad times; in order to escape being a superficial monster, she requires an ordeal of major scope. Perhaps she is not far from one now. Having lived, hitherto, outside hell, she is preparing to descend into it. If she seeks a destiny for herself, she will find it only on the ruins of all that was her raison d'*être*.[19]

As I write these words late in April 2020 in self-quarantine in New York, I wonder if the coronavirus pandemic of 2020 is the first sign of that descent.

5 *The Monologue of Civilizations*

The European who goes from Persia to India, observes, therefore, a prodigious contrast. Whereas in the former country he finds himself still somewhat at home, and meets with European dispositions, human virtues and human passions—as soon as he crosses the Indus (i.e., in the latter region), he encounters the most repellent characteristics, pervading every single feature of society. With the Persian Empire we first enter on continuous History. The Persians are the first Historical People; Persia was the first Empire that passed away. While China and India remain stationary, and perpetuate a natural vegetative existence even to the present time, this land has been subject to those developments and revolutions, which alone manifest a historical condition.

G. W. F. HEGEL, *Lectures on the Philosophy of History* (1837)

In December 2003 I was invited to a conference in Rabat, Morocco, where the topic of our gathering was "Cultural Dialogues: Is It Possible?" The late Edward Said was also invited to attend this conference at its preparatory stages the year before, but he unfortunately passed away in September, just a few months before our meeting in Rabat. Colleagues were there from around the globe, mostly from the Arab world, but the event included, to my utter dismay, Bernard Lewis and his young protégé Noah Feldman, fresh from having evidently drafted what would be the constitution for the occupied

Iraq—as if Iraqis had no legal scholars of their own who cared about their democratic future more than a comprador lawyer at the services of an occupying force.[1]

Feldman and I were in the same plane flying from Newark to Casablanca, though I had no clue who he was. While waiting at the gate for our flight, I noted this loud obnoxious businessman-like character talking at the top of his voice on his cell phone as if he were in his own private office. Upon our arrival in Casablanca, we were picked up by our hosts and boarded a bus to be taken to our hotel in Rabat. Noah Feldman and another guest, the late María Rosa Menocal from Yale, were sitting behind me in the bus, and I overheard him talk about his nervousness when he first had to say a few words in Arabic in Iraq. Now I realized he was the infamous Noah Feldman who was invited to help write a new constitution for occupied Iraq! When we arrived at our hotel and disembarked from the bus, I turned to him and said, "So you are Noah Feldman who collaborated with Paul Bremer on the occupation of Iraq." He was taken aback and said he did not think working with one's own government was called "collaboration." I said I meant "collaboration" in the sense that no decent human being would participate in the occupation of another people's homeland. That was our one and only exchange on that trip: a non-dialogue.

The following day, when we boarded a bus to be taken to the location of the conference, I discovered that Bernard Lewis was also there, and this Feldman character spent the rest of that conference coat-tailing Lewis like a polite poodle. The displeasure of seeing these too characters, however, was more than compensated for by the pleasure of being in the company of a number of leading Arab intellectuals and scholars, including the eminent Iraqi literary critic Ferial Ghazoul, Algerian philosopher Mohammed Arkoun, and most importantly for me the towering Egyptian hermeneutician Nasr Hamed Abu Zayd, with whom I spent the rest of the conference talking about topics of mutual interest. Our dialogues were with our peers. We had nothing to say to or hear from our adversaries, Bernard Lewis and his sidekick Noah Feldman. They were talking to themselves, we to ourselves. There was no dialogue. How could the man who had spent his entire life manufacturing an insurmountable divide and hatred between "Islam" and the "West" and his young protégé possibly be part of any "dialogue" among civilizations? They were invested in this divide. During his talk, Lewis went out of his way to refer to Edward Said and his *Orientalism* as a dog sniffing in a garbage can, knowing only too well some of Said's closest and dearest friends were in his audience. We all had to sit there and pretend to be polite and civilized in reaction to that singular act of barbarity. So I asked myself, what was the point, what could possibly be the result of such conferences? I spent hours with Nasr Abu Zayd, learning from his grace and his wisdom, his unsurpassed knowledge of the Qur'an and his fierce critical intellect about its presence in the world. But in the midst of an abyss that the likes of Bernard Lewis and Noah Feldman had benefitted from manufacturing, not a word, not a sentence, could possibly be exchanged with them. So the question still lingered: who comes up with these ideas of "dialogues among civilizations" and for what purpose?

Foregrounding the impossibility of that dialogue is the globalized metaphor of "the West" itself and how the two sides of the binary have collapsed and unfolded upon each other simultaneously, like two parallel mirrors that never had anything between them to reflect except their own delusional fears. The material foregrounding of this dissolution of "the West" and all its Others has been evident in the formation of a globalized capitalism and the rise of an amorphous empire, as Thomas Hardt and Antonio Negri have detailed it in their seminal work *Empire* (2000). "The West" as a colonizing metaphor was the commodified product of a specific period in the formation of Eurocentric capitalism, which was a fiction from the very beginning. Capitalism never had a factual center or, therefore, a colonial periphery. There was always a capital in the colonial and a colonial in the capital. The beneficiaries of globalized capital were all over the world, East and West, North and South, as were those violently disenfranchised by it. "The West" became the fiction of an ideological center for that globalized capital, and "Islam" was among its manufactured peripheral Others, both material and imaginative, moral and normative. In the condition of postcolonial and postmodern capitalism, neoliberalism writ large, that fictive center was no longer operative or even necessary. The dissolution of "the West" was therefore the return of its repressed, the final dismantling of its originary fantasy when Europe had posited itself as the fictional epicenter of an already amorphous operation of capital. The world bought into that fiction under hegemonic duress—Muslims included, or perhaps in particular.

"Dialogue of Civilizations"?

In the aftermath of the events of 9/11, throughout the decade before 2010 and even later, similar conferences as the one in Morocco were held around the world, to some of which I was invited, for example in Lisbon, in Venice, in Istanbul, and in New York. My essay "For the Last Time: Civilizations" (2001), which is a critique of the whole phenomenon of civilizational thinking that I had written and published before the events of 9/11, was evidently the reason behind all these invitations.[2] In 2009 I was invited by Jorge Sampaio, the president of Portugal, who had just been appointed by the UN as its high representative for "the Alliance of Civilizations," a position he held till September 2012, to go to Lisbon, where we had similar conversations in the company of mostly European colleagues. Although this among many other events was far more pleasant and lacked the nefarious shadow of Bernard Lewis, still the thrust of the gathering was predicated on the presumption of the binary of "Islam and the West." Much of the attraction to my essay and my subsequent thoughts on the matter were precisely because it had gone upstream from this binary and had not fallen into the trap of civilizational thinking; it in fact effectively dismantled such thinking.

Despite the fact that they have much earlier gestations in previous times, international gatherings addressing questions such as "Is dialogue among cultures possible?" were mostly on the rise in the wake of the horrific events of 9/11 in the United States and the subsequent War (without end) on Terrorism, of which we have already witnessed two particularly catastrophic phases in Afghanistan and then in Iraq. The assumption was that "Islam" was there, "the West" was here, and misunderstandings between the two had to be resolved in a delicate, liberal, and civilized manner. This phase of "dialogue among civilizations" was of course entirely misplaced, for it operated via the notorious Huntington thesis of "the clash of civilizations" while, at the same time, the nonexistent dialogue had effectively ended civilizational thinking. I was and I remain convinced that the "dialogue of civilizations" was a liberal gesture against a militant "Westernism" that coincided with and matched militant "Islamism" in the final stage of "Islam and the West." But that presumed dialogue in and of itself was not dialogical—it was a monologue within the outdated parameters of civilizational thinking. It confronted "Western" fanaticism with Western liberalism, and most of the invitees were there in good liberal conscience to speak to the better angels of the others.

Soon after the translation of Huntington's essay "The Clash of Civilizations?" into Persian, President Mohammad Khatami of the Islamic Republic of Iran proposed the idea of a "dialogue among civilizations," and soon after that, Moroccan officials were wondering if "dialogue among cultures" was possible. The idea was then picked up by other well-meaning officials in Portugal, Italy, Turkey, and elsewhere. The very contrast between the belligerent idea of the "*clash*" of civilizations" as opposed to *dialogue* among them pointed to the bellicose rhetoric at the heart of a predatory empire and the conciliatory proposals that it solicited from a position of weakness at its peripheries. While the bizarre hubris of American strategists like Samuel Huntington speaks of *clash*, which is a military, militant, and arrogant term, Muslims and Europeans propose the possibility of *dialogue*, a gentler and more moderate term—and yet throughout the US media, it is the Muslims who are profiled as violent human beings, with books written about them as to "what went wrong with them." But in either case, clash or dialogue, what was constant was the unit of civilization and civilizational thinking at a moment in history when we witness the most barbaric acts of conquest and resistance in geopolitics of the globe.

It is not accidental that combative terms such as *clash* come from the United States at the height of its militaristic belligerence. The amorphous "response" to the event of 9/11 almost immediately led to the US invasion and occupation of Afghanistan and, soon after, Iraq. The excuse of ousting a ruthless dictator in Iraq flew in the face of, not only the fact that the US government had itself kept Saddam Hussein in power after he brutally massacred both the Kurds and the Shi'i Iraqis, but also the fact that the principal target of this terrorizing campaign of "shock and awe," in the language of Secretary of Defense Donald Rumsfeld at the time, was the Iraqi people and their national heritage. The use of flawed intelligence, mixed with cluster munitions and sub-munitions in heavily populated areas in so-called "decapitation attempts," failed to kill Saddam Hussein and the rest of Iraqi leadership; instead, the result was massive civilian casualties. That term *clash* in Samuel Huntington's conception of "civilization" is coterminous with the same imperial hubris.

As measured by that very conference I attended in Morocco or later in Lisbon on the possibility of a *dialogue* among cultures and civilizations, it was clear that those living in the shadow, at the mercy, and under the terror of the US empire took the original articulation of the idea, the "*clash* of civilizations," by a theorist in the United States as being aimed at them. My principal argument throughout these events was (and remains) that Arabs and Muslims have been entirely wrong in assuming that the primary target of Huntington's essay was them. The main objective of the argument is in fact quint-essentially domestic to the United States, and it belies a raging battle that has been waged inside this country, of which people outside it are entirely innocent. It was in fact the fear of sizable changes in the US demographic configuration due to massive labor migrations and the fear of so-called multiculturalism inside the United States that led people like Samuel Huntington and his cohorts to proclaim "the West"—the figment of their imagination—to be at once victorious and in dire need of protection—in both ideological and militaristic capacities. People like Samuel Huntington or Bernard Lewis (who later claimed that the idea of the "clash of civilizations" was actu-ally his), were not interested in any dialogue; they were interested in absolutist domination, in a triumphant declaration of the victory of "the West" over "the Rest." They were engaged in a soliloquy of power, of vindictive triumphalism, of the utter and total annihila-tion of their other in defeat and despair. But the arenas where they thought Muslims were sitting and listening to them in obedience had long been vacated. They had no clue where Muslims were.

The Making of an Amorphous Empire

Predicated on my essay "For the Last Time: Civilizations" (2001), my main contributions to these international gatherings on the "dialogue" of civilizations was in fact to question the very premise of their wish for dialogue, putting forward the argument that we were in fact living through the future (which is the present) of these twin metaphors of "Islam and the West"—in which they have concluded their outdated encounters and have collapsed onto each other. At the dawn of a phenomenon code-named "globalization," I argued, Islam has lost its principal interlocutor in the course of its colonial encounter with ("European") capitalist modernity. The metaphor of "the West" has now exhausted its instrumental use-value and is nothing but an archival, knee-jerk, and belligerent interest for white supremacists. With the spiral crescendo of migratory labor mutating into globalized capital, the binary opposition that once ideologically separated the colonial from the capital is no longer valid or operative. A shapeless schema of military domination and cultural control is now assuming the militant posture of a vacuous globalized empire without any claim to hegemony. The amorphous capital that it seeks to serve is too vicarious to function at the whim of any given hegemony. Neither the specifics of any hegemony nor the signs of the emerging modes of resistance to it are clear to this empire. The articulation of the ideological architecture of this amorphous empire and the defiant terms of resisting it are the elements of a whole different story, which I should tell at some other time. Here I was just pointing out the material circumstances in which the binary opposition between "Islam and the West" had in effect lost all historical relevance and run itself conceptually aground. The amorphous empire, incapable of "dialogue," was recruiting its main ideologues, like Bernard Lewis and Samuel Huntington, to annunciate its triumphalist soliloquy.

The sort of "dialogue" we were presumed to be conducting between civilizations actually cross-essentializes civilizational thinking—gives it a false sense of relevance when it in fact lacks it. Rejection of civilizational thinking is long overdue. Impossible "dialogue" in fact affirms and confirms "the West" and "the Rest" in their assumptions of differences. The far more expansive and enabling interplay among neighboring cultures that once existed eventually transformed during the European Enlightenment and finally came to a crescendo during the rise of capitalist modernity, where the manufactured clash became a head-on collision. During the rise of the European Enlightenment, aspects of non-European cultures and civilizations (from China, India, Egypt, and Persia in particular) were assimilated thoroughly into the making of the world historic period. But beginning with the project of globalized capitalist modernity, "the West" took on the self-universalizing measure of truth against all its colonized counterparts. The binary opposition between "Islam" and the "West" finds its strongest economic and political roots and cultural effervescence in this period. The transmutation of empires and imperialism into an amorphous empire effectively put an end to any possibility of "dialogue among civilizations."[3]

Something is changing in the very soul of a world when the Persian mystic poet Rumi (1207–1273) in its current English renditions appeals to an ever-expanding audience—a clear indication that across ages and continents, a single poet can demonstrate the traumas of our human condition mapped out in a spectrum of alternative modalities of being in the world. We are sensing an essential fragility in fabricated binaries like "Islam and the West" and finding that they simply do not represent but in fact conceal the truth. Early in 2020, when the world at large was in the grips of a coronavirus pandemic, all assumptions of civilizational divides collapsed in the face of a virus that was indiscriminate in its destructive power. The world revealed itself for the shrinking and endangered village that it is. The only dialogue that now mattered was between humanity at large and an invisible thing that demanded and exacted attention.

With the rise of the Arab Spring in the 2010s and the cataclysmic events that followed, Tahrir Square became the epicenter of an entirely different conception of our imaginative geography—for which reason in my book on those events I called them an occasion for a "liberation geography." The Egyptian revolutionaries took the heritage of the French Revolution to a different political domain, toppled an entrenched tyranny, and redefined the terms of any claim to total revolution according to the new horizons of an open-ended revolution. Soon squares from Europe to the United States were renamed "Tahrir Square," and groundbreaking events then began to turn Europe and the United States upside down. The binary illusion of "Islam and the West" was collapsing under the circumstances of a whole new topography of convictions and demands. The global environmental catastrophe, massive labor and refugee migrations, and the rise of nativist xenophobia that came in response together formed the fertile grounds of a whole new rendezvous with history. The only "dialogue" at this moment was between our humanity at large and our ravaged earth, between our ancestral follies and our hopes for our children's future.

With the disappearance of "the West" as a commanding allegory, evaporated under the amorphous nature of capital and all its hegemonic claims to a sovereign culture, the "Islam" that it had helped manufacture has also imploded, having lost its historical interlocuter. The proclamations of bewildered Sunni sheikhs and their Shi'i counterparts, the so-called "religious intellectuals," and violent terrorists like ISIS and al-Qaeda, as well as the fury of Islamophobia they have occasioned in Europe and North America, are all the ashes of what was once an enabling dialectical fire between "Islam" and "the West." Both "Islam" and "the West" have thus begun their systematic dissolution into far more violent material forces and a rather chaotic cultural disfiguration of authority, authenticity, and cultural essentialism. The future of those illusions is our present predicament, as the two metaphoric monsters are at each other's throats, evidently unaware of their final demise, their transmutation into potent fertilizers of a new growth in world historical consciousness. These are dying creatures, just like in the movie *Godzilla* (2014) where the two disfigured monsters fight a battle that spells doom for both of them. We are now beyond the binary, waking up after the nightmare and beyond the illusion. New, perhaps even more potent illusions may ultimately arise. But upon the horizon are the transnational public sphere, the postcolonial subject, alternative worlds that await their recognition and encounter.

The dissolution of "the West" and with it the "Islam" it had conjured up is rooted in the exposure of the fetishized commodity its dominant ideology represents. Here is how Marx exposed that fetishism:

A commodity is therefore a mysterious thing, simply because in it the social character of men's labor appears to them as an objective character stamped upon the product of that labor; because the relation of the producers to the sum total of their own labor is presented to them as a social relation, existing not between themselves, but between the products of their labor.... In order, therefore, to find an analogy, we must have recourse to the mist-enveloped regions of the religious world. In that world the productions of the human brain appear as independent beings endowed with life, and entering into relation both with one another and the human race. So it is in the world of commodities with the products of men's hands. This I call the Fetishism which attaches itself to the products of labor, so soon as they are produced as commodities, and which is therefore inseparable from the production of commodities. This Fetishism of commodities has its origin in the peculiar social character of the labor that produces them.[4]

What Marx describes here to define the nature of fetishized commodity is replicated in the realm of the fetishized ideologies that sustain the abusive relation of power between capital and labor extended to the colonial site. Marx borrows a metaphor from what he calls "the mist-enveloped regions of the religious world" to describe the nature of the fetishized commodity, entirely unaware that in effect he was describing the myth of "the West" as the very quintessence of those "mist-enveloped regions of the religious world."

Where Is the World in World History?

What kind of a *world* would that world be that brings us back to the factual domain of our humanity at large? In a recent book, *The Shahnameh: The Persian Epic as World Literature* (2019), I have taken issue with the manner in which a Euro-universal prejudice in the idea of "World Literature" as theorized by US and European literary critics has radically compromised the possibilities of other literary worlds that have existed but have been made alien even to themselves to inform a much more liberated and cosmopolitan understanding of both epic poetry and of world literatures.[5] Using the example of Ferdowsi's *Shahnameh*, I have put forward the idea that not just one but in fact a constellation of three worlds come together to form the worldliness of the Persian epic: the world in which it was created, the world it created, and the changing world in which it has been read. The existing debates within the Euro-universalism of "World Literature" could not accommodate such worldly reading of the Persian or any other non-European epic. During the spring term of 2020, I co-taught my regular course at Columbia, "Epics and Empires," with my distinguished colleague Sudipta Kaviraj in which we compared the two examples of *Mahabharata* and the *Shahnameh*, in the course of which we reflected on similar ideas in two non-European epics, not just one.

We can think of a similar frame of reference about the idea of "World History" that was of immense significance to German philosopher Johann Gottfried von Herder (1744–1803).[6] "Any history of the world," we read in a major recent essay on the issue, "at least of its last several centuries, must deal with the dominance of the West;

and the need to explain its ascendancy has been a major impetus to world history."[7] "The West," however, as an unexamined metaphor of the whole proposition has a very short history, only stretching across these very last couple of centuries. It is an ahistorical projection backward to think of "the West" anywhere before the French Revolution and the rise of a self-conscious bourgeoisie in opposition and contestation with the European aristocratic dynasties and the ecclesiastical order, for which *Christendom* and not "the West" was the overriding allegory. Plato did not think of himself as a "Western philosopher," nor did Aristotle or any other major literary figure until much later in what by then had declared itself as "Western history." If I were to walk up to Plato and tell him I was a "Persian," he might not like me and might even consider me his enemy, but he would know who I was. But if Herder walked up to him and said he was a "German," Plato would have no clue who he was. The issue as a result is this fictitious "world," ideologically predicated on a false consciousness, at the root of "World History," which has systematically covered up, denied, and denigrated other worlds that existed before, during, and after its imperial creation.

The author of this major recent essay, Raymond Grew, writes of explaining "some fundamental Western superiority. That assumption of superiority has increasingly come to be criticized, at first primarily on moral and cultural grounds and more recently as the result of historical research."[8] What "superiority"—"fundamental Western superiority" no less? "There is no document of civilization," Walter Benjamin writes in thesis VII of "On the Concept of History" (1940), "which is not at the same time a document of barbarism."[9] At what point in history has the history of this "West" not produced a document of any "civilization" that has not been at the same time a document of barbarism? That sense of "superiority" is an entirely manufactured ideological presumption with no basis in facts. The idea of "World History" will have to begin first by dismantling this terrorizing concept of "the West" and all the alterities it has manu-factured to believe in itself.

Raymond Grew cites Ranajit Guha's *History at the Limit of World-History*, in which he says, "Something still more fundamen-tal is at stake, and it applies to all of modern Western historiography. Whereas Hegel is traditionally honored as a founder of modern his-torical thinking, Guha finds in him the original sin polluting Western conceptions of the world."[10] More specifically, he adds: "Hegel's ideas of providential design, the centrality of the state, and the progressive development of ever-higher forms leads to a particular conception of universal history in which history moves according to the spirit of reason and creates increased self-consciousness."[11] We at Columbia know this book very well, for Guha delivered its initial lectures at our Casa Italiana in 2002 and subsequently published them with Colum-bia University Press.[12] But Guha's seminal critique of Hegelian histo-riography is one among many others coming at it from colonial and postcolonial, premodern, modern, and postmodern sites. It is neither the first nor the last nor indeed the most compelling of such critiques. Hegel was a philosopher of History for "the West," not *the* philoso-pher of History. It is indeed a symptom of that very Eurocentricity to consider Hegel as *the* philosopher of History and then pick just one critique of his historiography as evidence of an alterity, which is not even sufficient according to Grew. We need to expand the hori-zons of such pre- and post- and non-Hegelian thinking and think of a whole spectrum of critical reflections on the philosophy of history—ranging from Alberuni's writing on India, to al-Beyhaqi's theoretical reflections on Iranian and Islamic history, to Ibn Khaldun's mag-num opus *al-Muqaddimah*, all the way down to Fernand Braudel's rethinking of the Mediterranean basin as a unit of historical reflec-tions, to Américo Castro's revolutionary thinking on Spanish history, to José Martí's "Our America," to V. Y. Mudimbe's radical rethinking of Africa, to Enrique Dussel's liberation philosophy—to have a fuller view of alternative non-Eurocentric philosophical encounters with history. The assumption that there was Hegel there as *the* philosopher of history and then Guha here as a rebuttal is just categorically flawed and misleading.

The issue is very simple: the overcoming of the delusional bifurcation between "Islam" and "the West" requires a different conception of *the world* in world history. The world is no longer Eurocentric, nor indeed is it Europhobic, for Europhobia is the worst kind of Eurocentrism. That world is real, predicated on the factual evidence of our lived experiences. And it is to that real and evident world beyond the delusional impressions of "Islam and the West" that I will turn in the fourth and final part of this book. But before I do so I must turn the question of the "dialogue of civilizations" on its head, not to show that it is in fact just a monologue, but to transform it by exploring a dialogical thinking that will epistemically overcome this nasty entanglement of two conflating illusions.

From an Impossible Dialogue to Dialogical Thinking

When we were in Morocco in the midst of a non-dialogue, I thought a real dialogue meant a caring, critical, and creative conversation among Arabs themselves and then between Arabs and the Amazigh, between secular Moroccans and the demonized Islamists. That dialogue, in short, will have to be dialogical, contrapuntal. It is obscene for a Moroccan to dismiss his or her own fellow Muslim with the derogatory term "fundamentalist" simply because racist Islamophobes in European and US capitals do. The so-called "fundamentalists" are not from another planet. They are by and large from the poorest and most disenfranchised layers of Moroccan society—a number of which locations I visited while in Morocco. If there is an urgent need for any dialogue, it is for a mode of dialogical thinking within Morocco, within the Islamic world, between the opposing forces, to bring them to the fold of a communal conversation about a common destiny now threatened and terrorized by a predatory empire on one side and the violent adventurism of highway bandits it has occasioned on the other. Instead of such dialogical thinking when identity and alterity correlate, these conferences were an exercise in futility, for they were really not an occasion for any dialogue but the staging of a monologue within "the West," effectively neutralizing the alternative worlds that have always existed. From a futile and impossible dialogue, the shift must be toward a dialogical thinking within and without the Muslim world—in terms that are domestic to our global predicament, not uprooted from a sandcastle.

That dialogical thinking within and without the Muslim and non-Muslim world will include an intersectional encounter with race, gender, and ethnicity, a mode of critical thinking that will acknowledge and embrace varied and fluid conceptions of sexual orientations, that will include religious and ethnic minorities—with Jews, Berbers, Christians, atheists, and agnostics placed within a pluralistic conception of culture. This dialogical thinking places us beyond the colonially manufactured borders, deeper into Africa, across the continents into Asia, over the oceans into Latin America, including racialized minorities in Europe and the United States. This rampant and racist anti-Americanism widespread in both Europe and the Islamic world and elsewhere ignores the fact that there is a robust, powerful, multifaceted, and prolific coalition in the United States standing against the predatory designs of the US ruling elites. It is not just simplistic but irresponsible to disregard the millions of us in the United States who come from every walk of life—white, Black, Jews, Muslims, Catholics and Protestants, Hindus and Buddhists, atheists and agnostics, native or immigrant to this beautiful and bounteous land—who resist, who fight, who pour into the streets to protest, who demonstrate against injustice, who are beaten by the police and jailed. We categorically resent any self-righteous dismissal of us as docile collaborators in imperial designs. All these dialogues are necessary and critical—not in the vacuous emptiness of a jaundiced liberalism, but in our collective resistance to predatory empires and in the joyous celebration of life.

The dialogical reading of the world I envision here overcomes the illusion of "Islam and the West" by thinking of the world through its embedded injustices in class, race, and gender relations. Poverty, racism, and systematic gender discrimination are far more evident on the national, regional, and global scene than in fictive binaries such as "Islam and the West." The task at hand, a task to which I will now turn in the third and final part of this book, is to bring those crucial aspects of our lived experiences to the forefront, to replace the blinding delusions that have distorted the world and submitted it to the ruling regimes of power—East and West, North and South, from cyberspace to outer space, ruling over our common humanities, all at the mercy of an invisible virus that can turn the world upside down.

III *Where the Twain Have Met*

6 *Gendering the Difference*
From Metaphoric to Metamorphic

Well, children, where there is so much racket there must be something out of kilter. I think that 'twixt the negroes of the South and the women at the North, all talking about rights, the white men will be in a fix pretty soon. But what's all this here talking about?

SOJOURNER TRUTH, "Ain't I a Woman?" (1851)

Is Ibtihaj Muhammad an American woman, or is she a Muslim woman? Could she be both—or does she have to choose between one or the other? What happens when a Muslim American woman wins an Olympic medal and gets to represent her country on the global stage? Born and raised in Maplewood, New Jersey, to Muslim African American parents, Ibtihaj Muhammad eventually qualified to join Team USA and help win the bronze medal in the women's saber team competition at Rio 2016. She was the first American woman to wear a hijab while competing for the United States in the Olympics and the first Muslim American woman to win an Olympic medal.[1] How does that simple but compelling fact resonate in the echo chambers of "Islam and the West"? In the twisted taxidermic halls of "Islam and the West," her very gracious existence became a mixed metaphor, a contradiction in terms. American women were meant to be white, blonde, blue-eyed Barbie dolls. A Black woman, a Muslim, wearing hijab and swinging a sword, and then putting Team US on the pedestal? What was the world coming to?

My primary concern in this chapter is to show how a consideration of the question of gender in an intersectional perspective and across colonial boundaries and postcolonial borders effectively dismantles the civilizational divides presumed between "Islam" and "the West." The binary has falsely cast Muslim women as passive participants on a patriarchal grid from which they have no escape. This is a patently false assumption. The reality is far more complicated and the truth much more evident than such falsifications can allow. But the point here is not just to show examples of those who defy such clichés. The point, rather, is to bring together a constellation of critical thinkers, revolutionary leaders, and pathbreaking artists who have in one way or another effectively dismantled all forms of civilizational essentialism, particularly in this case that of "Islam and the West." In doing so, I would therefore argue, what these critical thinkers and artists show is a vision of "woman" not as emblematic metaphors of something else (chastity, piety, honoring of menfolk, etc.) but as metamorphic fluidity of the agential assertion of their own subjectivities.

For my critical thinking in exposing "Islam" and "the West" as two confounding and destructive illusions to be complete, I need to address first the defining issues of gender and race, and then the equally dominant factor of national narratives within which cultural and civilizational binaries are located. Turning first to gender, in this chapter I plan to put together the stories and the significance of a number of extraordinary women from both sides of this false binary of "Islam and the West" in order to show how their lives and achievements, rebellious characters and courageous deeds, revolutionary ideas and artistic practices, categorically dismantle the illusory wall that has been manufactured between them. I intend to bring together characters like the Mughal empress Queen Nur Jahan, Lady Mary Montague, and other iconoclastic figures such as Qorrat al-Ayn, Inji Aflatoun, Taj al Saltaneh, Rosa Luxemburg, Bibi Khanom Astarabadi, and Gertrude Bell to expose the bifurcation of "Islam" and "the West" as a simplistic cliché. There is something common among these uncommon women that defies civilizational divides and false cultural bifurcations. In their lived experiences these women crossed the imagined barrier between "the East" and "the West" and in their very lives proved it illusory and porous. The lives, characters, and achievements of these women are crucial not just because they were exceptional, but because in being exceptional they proved a rule: that their demarcation into two opposing camps was a deeply ideological and fraught proposition, effectively dividing them to rule them better, concealing the fact of a different kind of solidarity and sisterhood that has never been recognized for its defiant and subversive forces. In crossing these fictive frontiers, these women personify the fact of a gendered transnational public sphere and expose the masculinist bifurcation of any colonial divide as categorically flawed and even fraudulent. Even though they may never have even heard of each other, they form a world that was and remains real. It is the worldliness of that world that in and of itself dismantles all such false binaries as "Islam and the West." When women across all colonial divides stop being abused as metaphors of something other than themselves and begin to be metamorphic unto themselves, not just for self-representation but for self-generation, all such false binaries collapse upon themselves.

In this third and final part of my book, "Where the Twain Have Met," I turn to the evident deconstruction of the binary illusion of "Islam and the West" on the three intersectional sites of gender, race, and nationality—all of them predicated on the core issue of class consciousness and class warfare that crosses all national and civilizational boundaries. My underlying purpose in this part is to show how in the crucial issues of gender, race, class, and nationality the manufactured twain has already met and metamorphosed, and thus the two sides of the false binary have morphed into each other. In this chapter I wish to demonstrate how the question of gender injustice crosses borders and has given rise to the idea of transnational feminism overcoming the bourgeois feminism that is unaware of its white privileges, as perhaps best theorized by the eminent feminist theorist Chandra Mohanty. In a subsequent chapter I will show how the equally crucial issue of race dismantles the bourgeois notions of national and civilizational divides, and then in my final chapter I demonstrate how the very idea of "the nation" is always already "transnational" by virtue of the globalized patterns of labor migration and the formation of transnational public spheres where the very ideas of nations, cultures, and civilizations are formed. In the interpolated tapestry of class, gender, race, and nationality we discover the collapse of all false and falsifying national and civilizational boundaries.

"Feminism without Borders"

First, I need to borrow and expand for my purposes here from the seminal work of some feminists who have revolutionized our understanding of the politics of gender. Let me begin with the pivotal work of Chandra Talpade Mohanty collected in her groundbreaking volume *Under Western Eyes: Feminist Scholarship and Colonial Discourses*, originally published in her essay under that title.[2] With that essay and the follow-up volume, Mohanty revolutionized the field of feminism into a far more equitable and liberated domain. Her work has usually been characterized as "Third World" or "International feminism." But what her critical thinking and scholarship have exposed and enabled is far more important than these designations would warrant. She and a few other leading feminist scholars have been instrumental in liberating Eurocentric feminism and enabling the result to cover its historic blind spots. Before their work we did not have feminism. We had Eurocentric, white women, bourgeois feminism. She and her colleagues have effectively decolonized the feminist theory and successfully wedded it to a powerful anticapitalistic project. Both designating and overcoming "Western Feminism," these scholars have brought race, class, and national formations into critical focus, with a cogent critique of the corporatization of higher education as the foregrounding of the academic discourses that have occasioned and enabled them all. The significance of their work for my objective in this book is the manner in which they have radically reconceptualized feminism in a way that brings the two falsely bifurcated sides of "Islam and the West" critically together. Many of these theorists are neither Muslim nor "Westerners," and thus the power of their theoretical arguments overcomes both sides of the divide.

A key factor in Mohanty's critique of Eurocentric feminism is her systematic undoing of the concept of "women" as it is used indiscriminately and applied to "Third World Women." This is what she writes:

What is problematical, then, about this kind of use of "women" as a group, as a stable category of analysis, is that it assumes an ahistorical, universal unity between women based on a generalized notion of their subordination. Instead of analytically demonstrating the production of women as socio-economic political groups within particular local contexts, this move limits the definition of the female subject to gender identity, completely bypassing social class and ethnic identities. What characterizes women as a group is their gender (sociologically not necessarily biologically defined) over and above everything else, indicating a monolithic notion of sexual difference. Because women are thus constituted as a coherent

group, sexual difference becomes coterminous with female subordination, and power is automatically defined in binary terms: people
who have it (read: men), and people who do not (read: women). Men
exploit, women are exploited. As suggested above, such simplistic
formulations are both reductive and ineffectual in designing strate-
gies to combat oppressions. All they do is reinforce binary divisions
between men and women.[3]

It is precisely this denial of agency, this gendered politics of dis-
empowering, that underwrites the idea of "woman" as an unexamined category. What is lacking in the very idea of "woman" here
is not just "reductive and ineffectual"; it is also the premise of de-
subjection, when a human being by being designated as a woman
cannot exist as an autonomous agent of a destiny—in short, when
women have become metaphoric for something else. What Mohanty
says here about "women" is identically applicable to "Islam" in
"Islam and the West," and perforce particularly true about "Muslim women." This bizarre proclivity toward abstraction is endemic
to the epistemic production of metaphysical differences between
"the West" and "the Rest." Take away "the Rest" from "the West"
and "the West" collapses upon itself. Bringing history back to such
concepts as "Islam" or "Woman" or "the West" is precisely where
the postcolonial critique of our received epistemics has sought to
overcome the conceptual impediments of critical thinking. The production of "Muslim women" as docile and subservient is integral
to this project, entirely independent of class and gender dynamics, and merely reflects and cross-authenticates the presumed liberation of "Western women." That binary division between abstract
notions of "men and women" simply repeats and reiterates the binaries between "the West and the Rest," "White and Black," or "Islam
and the West." The Manichean dualism—the gendered, colored,
or classed codification of the relations of power—is at the mythical

foundation of the illusion of "the West." That Manichean dualism extends from the grand civilizational delusions of "Islam and the West" to "Western Women" and "non-Western Women." The epicenter of this hall of mirrors is the illusion of "the West."

Other key theorists in the field have extended Mohanty's crucial point even further. In her seminal essay on the idea of intersectionality, "Mapping the Margins: Intersectionality, Identity Politics, and Violence against Women of Color" (1994), Kimberlé Crenshaw has brought our attention to the simultaneous and cross-referential issues of race and gender, where in a key passage she writes:

> Among the most troubling political consequences of the failure of antiracist and feminist discourses to address the intersections of racism and patriarchy is the fact that, to the extent they forward the interest of people of color and "women," respectively, one analysis often implicitly denies the validity of the other. The failure of feminism to interrogate race means that the resistance strategies of feminism will often replicate and reinforce the subordination of people of color, and the failure of antiracism to interrogate patriarchy means that antiracism will frequently reproduce the subordination of women. These mutual elisions present a particularly difficult political dilemma for women of color. Adopting either analysis constitutes a denial of a fundamental dimension of our subordination and works to precludes the development of a political discourse that more fully empowers women of color.[4]

Here we have the same issue of the constitution of "women" independent of her race and class and nationality as the unexamined analytical unit of an epistemic of sanctioned ignorance. Unpacking that hermetic seal is precisely how the real world reenters history—as I have sought to do in this book with the dual delusion of "Islam and the West." We have had the mutually exclusive cases of feminism without race and critique of racism without gender. The result is the production of a kind of a generic bourgeois feminism that cannot go near race for the fear it exposes and dismantles its own racist privileges. Women of color here, as Crenshaw points out, stand between the two discourses of feminism and critique of racism as the subaltern of both, which is precisely the way actual Muslims have been lost in the colonially manufactured binary of "Islam and the West." What Crenshaw correctly identifies as "the failure of feminism to interrogate race" points to precisely similar kinds of blind spots that have made of nonwhite worlds a *terra incognita*. She brings to light the plight of real women of color exactly where they have been hidden in plain sight. That kind of revolutionary thinking is where dominant categories like "women," "the West," and its concomitant "Islam" are dissolved into concrete forces of history. Between Mohanty and Crenshaw, the case of transnational feminism beyond borders reintroduces race and class into our reading of a far more complicated understanding of gender discrimination and social injustice. That kind of dialogical thinking has enabled a far richer and more cogent reading of race, gender, and class—the combination of which enables a liberating thrust of the idea of "women" as metaphoric of something other than themselves toward the metamorphic regeneration of women as agents of history.

"Women without Men"

A quick thematic shift here in our perspective of how dialogical thinking might operate is to consider the body of work produced by the globally celebrated visual artist Shirin Neshat, who for over three decades has effectively transformed the metaphysics of Islamic logocentric doctrines and pieties into a tapestry of visual palimpsestic evidence. Her powerful move from the metaphysics of absolutist certainties to an aesthetics of visual allusions is where we see

the idea of women recapturing its own potent agencies. The transmutation occasioning dialogical thinking and seeing in Neshat's
work is from and through *verbal* to *visual*, reimagining instead of
rewriting doctrines and pieties on her canvas, where, from under
and over and through the visual, the verbal is still evident but subordinated, modified, humbled.[5] Neshat works the verbal into the
visual, reminds it of its own visualities as a trace of the metaphysics
of verbal certainty gives way to visual precarity. We are here in the
presence of the moment of visual revelation, where the verbal yields
its power and authority. Occasioning this revelatory ocularcentrism,
Neshat undermines the verbal masculinism of the Islamic metaphysical doctrines and pieties. The global spectatorship afforded Neshat
meanwhile has re-universalized the Islamic provenance of her art
beyond the cliché of "Islam and the West." She is from "Islam" and
she is from "the West," and she collapses the false binary upon and
into itself by altogether abandoning and overcoming all hostilities
of signs and signatures. As she shifts and moves to work through the
visual, all verbal binaries are left in ink.

Neshat's subsequent move from photography to film has staged
the ocularcentricism of her aesthetics and artworld even more effectively. In her signature film, *Women without Men* (2009), she carries
the visual registers of the Shahrnush Parsipur novella on which it is
based further, from metaphoric to metamorphic horizons.[6] In both
the exquisite novella and the film, the women of the story cease to
be metaphors of anything else and grow to become metaphoric of
their own existential realities. Central to both the story and the film
is the tale of five women who during the unfolding of the CIA-MI6
coup of 1953 in Iran opt to leave their ordinary lives in Tehran and
move to a garden in Karaj, where one of them plants herself in a garden and blooms. The novella reads on the borderline of magic and
realism and the film transforms that porous borderline into a visual
bonanza that overwhelms the little story that holds it together. The

masculinist politics of the coup of 1953 is the perfect backdrop of this decidedly feminist overriding of the male-centered historiography of the course of Iran's encounter with colonial modernity.

Shirin Neshat's dialogical disposition works through the interface of both recalling the original novella and yet straying from it. We see attempted traces of such a bold move also in the theoretical work of Gayatri Spivak, where she seeks to work through the noncommittal precarity of being and not-being a deconstructionist feminist. This is a critical passage:

> It is not just that deconstruction cannot found a politics, while other ways of thinking can. It is that deconstruction can make founded political programs more useful by making their in-built problems more visible. To act is therefore not to ignore deconstruction, but actively to transgress it without giving it up.... Feminism has a special situation here because, among the many names that Derrida gives to the problem/solution of founded programs, one is "woman." ... Feminism should keep to the critical ways of deconstruction but give up its attachment to that specific name for the problem/solution of founded programs.[7]

In this her most conciliatory reading of deconstruction, Spivak operates through her own particular form of dialogical thinking that neither fetishizes nor discredits, neither excuses nor accuses deconstruction, taking it not as a philosophical position but as a heuristic method. It is good that deconstruction cannot found a politics, for that is the only way that it can point fingers at those who do. But the point here is not political paralysis. Quite to the contrary. It is through imagining a dialogical disposition that she seeks to enable a more provocative politics—one that is both gendered and self-transcending. Thus feminism in her reading becomes at once critical and non-foundational, engaged and uncompromising. On other occasions, Spivak has called this theoretical strategy "strategic essentialism." The point is a kind of soft non-metaphysical reading of the world that is light and guerrilla style. Thus articulated, Spivak's provocative theoretical disposition becomes the summation of both Mohanty and Crenshaw, for she disallows the formation of any kind of "feminism" to script or legislate the feminine. Spivak oscillates between the politics of feminism and the power of deconstruction the way Shirin Neshat navigates between the certainty of the verbal and the precarity of the visual.

What all these theorists and Shirin Neshat's artwork effectively share is the constitution of a dialogical conception of "woman" as a human being who is real and worldly and, as such, impossible fully to represent, in and of itself disallowing any cultural, civilizational, or above all ideological essentialism. This is precisely the organic conception of the figure of the feminine that dismantles the ideological formations of "Islam and the West" or any other prefabricated dualism—which in the case of a Muslim woman involves choosing between being a "Muslim" or "Modern." It is also in this context that Judith Butler's primary concern in her groundbreaking book *Gender Trouble: Feminism and the Subversion of Identity* (1990) becomes useful to us. Here is a key passage:

> For the most part, feminist theory has assumed that there is some existing identity, understood through the category of women, who not only initiates feminist interests and goals within discourse, but constitutes the subject for whom political representation is pursued. But politics and representation are controversial terms. On the one hand, representation serves as the operative term within a political process that seeks to extend visibility and legitimacy to women as political subjects; on the other hand, representation is the normative function of a language which is said either to reveal or to distort what is assumed to be true about the category of women. For feminist

theory, the development of a language that fully or adequately represents women has seemed necessary to foster the political visibility of women. This has seemed obviously important considering the pervasive cultural condition in which women's lives were either misrepresented or not represented at all.[8]

That "full and adequate" representation is of course a red herring and a contradiction in terms, not just in the crucial matter toward which Mohanty's scholarship of a transnational feminism has immeasurably advanced us far beyond the limits of bourgeois queer studies and/or feminism and their contingent colonial divides, but perhaps even more crucially in what Foucault more generally called "the dividing practices" that foreground the constitution of (a fluid) gender and sexuality, in addition to race and ethnicity, all as the foregrounding of class struggles and class consciousness. Who is this subject, Judith Butler correctly interjects here, in need of representation? The category "women" both reveals and, in that revelation, conceals the complicated and un-representable truth it wants thus to represent. The point of this crisis of the subject here is not just the complexity, fluidity, and organicity of gendering people one way or another, or both or neither, by way of a mode of Foucauldian subjection that impersonates the gender and thereby incarcerates the person at one and the same time. Long before Butler, Michel Foucault articulated that the point of his entire project was to document "a history of the different modes by which, in our culture, human beings are made subjects." Foucault then identified "three modes of objectifications which transform human beings into subjects." First is in sciences such as philology and linguistics, economics, and biology. Second is the "dividing practices," as in the mad and the sane, the sick and the healthy, the criminal and the "good boys." And finally, the way a human being is turned into a subject, such as through sexuality.[9] Among those "dividing practices," what

Foucault did not consider is of course "the West and the Rest," the "European and the non-European," and in our case specifically "Islam and the West"—namely all kinds of civilizational divides to which the colonized world is condemned. "Muslim women" even more specifically are the most scandalous of all such "dividing practices"—leading to male fantasies of "white men saving brown women from brown men."[10] But there is no liberation of "Muslim women" by Muslim women themselves from the false consciousness of "Islam and the West" without opening the gates to a much larger frame of emancipation, where women cease to be the iconic representations of one thing or another and become actively metamorphic unto themselves.

"Ain't I a Woman?"

Let us recall the immortal words of Sojourner Truth in her revelatory speech "Ain't I a Woman?" (1851):

> That man over there says that women need to be helped into carriages, and lifted over ditches, and to have the best place everywhere. Nobody ever helps me into carriages, or over mud-puddles, or gives me any best place! And ain't I a woman? Look at me! Look at my arm! I have ploughed and planted, and gathered into barns, and no man could head me! And ain't I a woman? I could work as much and eat as much as a man—when I could get it—and bear the lash as well! And ain't I a woman? I have borne thirteen children, and seen most all sold off to slavery, and when I cried out with my mother's grief, none but Jesus heard me! And ain't I a woman?[11]

How could Sojourner Truth get a "full and adequate" representation in the body of feminist literature that came before or even after her? Hands that have ploughed and planted make a mockery of the sort of feminism that is satisfied by women being lifted over ditches. From Christine de Pizan's *The Book of the City of Ladies* (1405) to Abigail Adams's letter "Don't Forget the Ladies" (1776) to Mary Wollstonecraft's *A Vindication of the Rights of Woman* (1792) and countless similar texts, eloquent women have written persuasively to defend their rights. With one short stroke Sojourner Truth dismantled them all and exposed their class privileges, subverting their bourgeois etiquette, overcoming their structural limitations, introducing the crucial facts of race and class as the blind spot of the gender politics that had come before her. There is no "fully and adequately" representing Truth, and yet, Ain't she a woman? The question is unanswerable. With that simple question she has checkmated an entire history of bourgeois feminism—exposing its classed and racialized blind spots, and even more importantly enabling her vision of liberation to become self-generative.

The case of Sojourner Truth and the power of her towering presence in complicating the entire history of liberal feminism is replicated in the case of all other forms of non-White and non-European women's rights movements around the globe—the case for which was made persuasively by Mohanty. The towering voice of Truth is within the United States what her counterparts are all over the world—written off of the very texture of a liberal feminism that writes (for the) world. If we move from the iconic figure of Sojourner Truth to the much larger domain of mis/representation where a "Muslim woman" is imagined, we see how the binary "Islam and the West" has completely eradicated the fact of a living human being who happens to be a Muslim woman. Can a Muslim woman, thus designated, get a "full and adequate representation" anywhere on that gridlock of "Islam and the West"? The dividing practices evident in "Islam and the West" have made that very idea impossible. It is precisely in that impossibility that the crucial question of gender becomes the breaking point of the dual delusions of "Islam and the West," where Muslim women have overcome their abusive mis/representations, refused to be emblematic metaphors of anything else, and commenced to be metamorphic unto themselves.

In the course of colonial modernity, when Muslims like the rest of the colonized world were told to think for themselves at the gunpoint of European imperialism, the figure of "Muslim woman" became figurative, iconic, heteronormative, always something other than itself, standing for men's "honor," their religion's authenticity, their culture's truth. No woman could be a person in her personhood, for she was always already something else, a metaphor beyond her own control. What we have here is the simultaneous contraction and expansion of historical consciousness, when from Queen Esther in the Bible to the Queen of Sheba in the Qur'an to Queen Sudabeh in the *Shahnameh* all come together and contract with historical figures like Khadijah and Ayesha, the Prophet's wives, or Fatimah, his daughter, to fictional characters like Maral in Mahmoud Dolatabadi's *Kelidar* (1978–1984) or Zari in Simin Daneshvar's *Suvashun* (1969) to become the back- and foreground of actual historical people complicating the figure of the (Muslim) woman on metaphoric legacies. The image of Muslim woman therefore becomes productively paradoxical, on the borderlines of being both metaphoric and metamorphic, edging to dodge stereotypes. Not all women informing this figure of a Muslim woman are in fact Muslim. But they all have an active presence in the collective memory of a Muslim person. There could not possibly be any claim to a "full and adequate" representation of this "Muslim woman" always in the making, trapped inside her clichés, trying to run away from them all. She is always already liberated from all stereotypes, only to the extent that her creativity and agency warrant it. She is not a type, she is a character; she is not a subject without already being an agent in the definition of that subjectivity. Through this purgatorial birth to herself, the condition of the coloniality of this figure of woman made her self-generative.

Habitually we refer to quite a number of mighty women in positions of authority in Islamic history, figures such as queens and empresses who wielded extraordinary power in their own time and royal courts. Historical personas like Seljuk empress Terken Khatun (circa 1055–1094), wife of Malik Shah I and mother of Sultan Mahmud I, the next ruler of the Seljuk Empire, is usually cited as an example of such powerful women. The power and influence of Mughal empress Queen Nur Jahan (1577–1645), wife of Emperor Jahangir, perhaps even more influential than her husband, has become the stuff of fact and fiction for holding her own imperial court and having her own royal coin and seal. She very much enjoyed her political power and prestige. Born into a family of Persian nobility in Kandahar, she was a widow when the emperor fell in love and married her. She eventually emerged as a mighty ruler.[12] Historical figures like Terken Khatun and Queen Nur Jahan are neither exemplary nor exceptional, neither because nor despite the fact that they were royalty. They are part of a common repertoire of conduct that crosses class and privilege. They represent not what women should do but what they could do. Being royalty is here secondary to being capable and confident rulers. In the course of their historical recollections in later epochs, what mattered was the manner in which they were remembered in the constellation of figurative personae reconstituting the question of gender in the Muslim world.

What these powerful women among the ruling elite in the collective memories of Muslims represent is neither the rule nor the exception. They have been iconic and as such have become floating signifiers, having different meanings for different times and purposes. The legendary Persian vizier of the Seljuqids, Khwajah Nezam al-Mulk (1018–1092), devoted a whole chapter against women in his *Siyasatnameh* because of her rivalries with Terken Khatun. Their presence in Islamic history has made these women normatively iconic, parables of something yet to happen. What they represent is the inclusion of women among the ruling classes, thus pointing toward a similar position of power and authority among the revolutionary leaders on the opposite side of their politics, such as the case of the Babi revolutionary leader Tahereh Qorrat al-Ayn (circa 1814–1852), whom we might compare to the German revolutionary leader Rosa Luxemburg (1871–1919) of her own time. Together, these figures, Muslims and non-Muslims, present in the collective consciousness of both, vastly complicate the image of "the Muslim woman," crafting what effectively amounts to an authentic figure of liberation in culturally inauthentic terms. We must recognize the cosmopolitan worldliness in which a Muslim woman comes to variedly moral and imaginative self-consciousness, in which Islamic and non-Islamic factors and forces have a dialogical interface. This fact makes the dividing practices of "Islam and the West" entirely null and void, while giving birth to an authenticity of consciousness that is in fact culturally inauthentic, paradoxical, dialogical. There can never be a "full and adequate" representation of such an empowering paradox.

It is imperative to keep in mind that the rise of women's rights movements in the Muslim world, and therefore the formation of the figure of a liberated Muslim woman, is contingent on the formation of a transnational public sphere and therefore not entirely limited to Muslim women, that non-Muslim women visiting the Muslim world have had a profound effect on the scene. The presence of such European aristocratic women as Lady Mary Montague (1689–1762) among Muslims complicates the ideal-typical icons of a Muslim woman. Lady Montague's letters and poems, particularly while traveling in the Ottoman territories, are a two-edged sword—influential in what she wrote for her European audiences and what she meant for her Muslim contemporaries. She traveled through the Balkans when it was aflame with war, alongside her diplomat husband, leaving for posterity a compelling account of her observations.[13] When we place her next to her Iranian counterpart Taj al-Saltaneh (1884–1936), a Qajar princess, one of the daughters of Naser-al-Din Shah and the author of unique and pathbreaking memoirs, an entirely different constellation of images emerges.[14] Written eloquently from the vantage point of a secluded princess, the memoir of Taj al-Saltaneh reveals how the changing environment of the Muslim world at large had transformed the lives and aspirations of the younger generations. Once we place Lady Mary Montague and Taj al-Saltaneh next to each other, the very proposition of "the Muslim woman" as codified in "Islam and the West" completely disappears into thin air.

Here again we should not remain limited to aristocratic circles when navigating the contours of ideal types that enter the active imagination of reconfiguring a "Muslim woman." There is a literary elite that is equally if not more important for the emerging public sentiments. Bibi Khanom Astarabadi (1858–1921) was a pioneering figure in women's rights movements. She was a major figure during the course of the Constitutional Revolution in Iran and a leading reformist in women's and girl's education. She was a well-known public intellectual whose critical articles were published in reformist periodicals and whose seminal book *Ma'ayeb al-Rejal* (Failings of men) (1895) was a response to a widely popular pamphlet *Ta'dib al-Nisvan* (Edification of women) by an anonymous author.[15] Here the dialogical reasoning of Astarabadi against this misogynist pamphlet is the key character of her prose. Astarabadi opposes polygamy, criticizes men's exclusive legal right to initiate divorce, advocates for education of women and girls, and argues for their equal rights before point-by-point responding to the misogynist calumnies of the anonymous author of the "Edification" pamphlet. She then launches into a scathing critique of men's behavior, her prose and politics making it quite clear she is a member of the literary elite, well-versed in Persian prose and widely conscious of women's rights movements around the world. Astarabadi's mother was also an educator and her father a servant, both at the Qajar royal court. What we read in her politics is therefore the emerging liberal consciousness of an educated elite, dialogical in its encounter with the embedded patriarchy of their time. The prose of both the pamphlet and the response, for and against women, occasionally borders on cliché and generic satire, engaging in upstaging and finger pointing. The result, however, is emblematic evidence of the rising awareness of women of their inalienable rights, and even more importantly the authorial power of self-generation.

Even colonial officers like Gertrude Bell (1868–1926) had a lasting impact on the manner in which Muslim women saw and assessed themselves. While serving the imperial interest of Great Britain, the English writer, traveler, colonial officer, and archaeologist became interested in Persian poetry and produced a widely popular translation of Hafez (1897). Whether part of the ruling and/or literary elite or among the reformists or the revolutionaries, women were aware of these powerful colonial officers. The constellation of powerful or weak women that entered this collective memory soon assumed a logic and rhetoric of its own. By the time we get to figures like Nazik al-Mala'ikah (1922–2007) or Forough Farrokhzad (1934–1967), one a towering Iraqi and the other an Iranian poet and filmmaker, we know that the image of a "Muslim woman" is a deeply complicated character—always running away from her stereotypes, always ahead of her own aspirations. On the surface, Gertrude Bell's interest in Hafez and al-Mala'ikah's and Farrokhzad's iconic rise as defining poets of their time may appear unrelated. But in the dialogical formation of a public sphere and a collective memory in which Muslim women then saw themselves, there was no cultural authenticity, only the dialectic of a historical consciousness. In the revolutionary figure of Inji Aflatoun (1924–1989), an Egyptian Marxist feminist artist, the pre- and postcolonial worlds come to complicate the character of Muslim women, who have become authentic rebels precisely by being culturally inauthentic. They represent the world they inhabited, nothing short of the complexity of that world, overcoming "Islam and the West," which as a falsification of truth could not even come close to representing them. There was no "full and adequate" representation here or elsewhere, as all the "dividing practices" had come to naught. "Ain't I a woman?" these Muslim women would ask with Sojourner Truth, and their very rhetorical question was all the answer they needed, for the day they asked that question in their own terms was the day they became a woman in their own terms.

"The Day I Became a Woman"

The extraordinary testimony of the film *The Day I Became a Woman* is where through the filmic depiction of three stages of life—childhood, youth, and old age—the figurative constitution of the Muslim woman finally overcomes itself, and from being merely metaphoric of something else it becomes metamorphic unto itself.[16] Marzieh Meshkini's *The Day I Became a Woman* (2000) is a three-episode film depicting three stages of life, where we first encounter Hava as a young girl who on her ninth birthday is told by her mother and grandmother that she has become a woman, with particular mandates and responsibilities, among them the sudden injunction that she may no longer go out and play with her friends of the opposite sex and that she must now cover herself with a mandatory veil. Until noon that day she can be as free as a bird, and after that she must assume her womanly duties and corresponding modesty and chastity. From her childhood scarf she makes a sailboat and sends her dream off to other shores.

Ahoo is the subject of the second episode. She is a married woman out cycling with her friends—all female, all veiled, all preoccupied with the task at hand, a bit of cycling on a vacant road by the sea. Out of the blue appears an angry man who is Ahoo's husband, riding half naked on a naked horse, demanding she stop cycling and go back home or else he will divorce her. Ahoo ignores him; he goes and brings yet another half-naked man riding a naked horse to declare their divorce. Ahoo could not care less. She continues to cycle with her friends. The elders of her family now come and close in on her to stop her cycling, as her friends quietly ride away.

In the third and final episode we meet Hoora, an elderly widow on a shopping spree somewhere in the Persian Gulf, where consumer products abound and commingle with cheap child labor. She amasses a ludicrous assortment of household items by the beach awaiting a vessel to take her and her possessions to another shore. She floats away under the watchful eyes of Hava and Ahoo's friends from previous episodes.

The film is simple and solid, sedate, and cogent. It moves deliberately with full visual meditation, as if an allegory unto itself. The three interpolated cycles in the lifetime of a figurative woman, here split into three temporal registers and thus the very idea of a woman, projects a collage of three inaugural moments of childhood, youth, and old age. The tableau that emerges closes in and grows within itself. Paramount in the way we see the film is the abstract space where these events happen, off the coast of some island in the Persian Gulf or any other patch of water. The dialogues are minimal, and the mise-en-scène entirely virtual, thus giving ample space for the metamorphic images of the abstracted women to cease to represent anything or be the metaphor of anything else, a total and final devolution of the figure of woman from all it has been forced to represent or symbolize, to represent nothing but the inner dynamics of its own moral imagination, aesthetic possibilities, meditative horizons, and existential autonomies. This is the day that the abstracted metaphor of woman becomes a woman in terms rooted in her own existential realities—haphazard, conflicting, and yet, precisely as such, enabling, empowering, iconoclastic.

7 *De-racing Civilizations*

What, to the American slave, is your 4th of July? I answer; a day that reveals to him, more than all other days in the year, the gross injustice and cruelty to which he is the constant victim. To him, your celebration is a sham; your boasted liberty, an unholy license; your national greatness, swelling vanity; your sounds of rejoicing are empty and heartless; your denunciation of tyrants, brass fronted impudence; your shouts of liberty and equality, hollow mockery; your prayers and hymns, your sermons and thanksgivings, with all your religious parade and solemnity, are, to Him, mere bombast, fraud, deception, impiety, and hypocrisy—a thin veil to cover up crimes which would disgrace a nation of savages. There is not a nation on the earth guilty of practices more shocking and bloody than are the people of the United States, at this very hour.

FREDERICK DOUGLASS, "The Meaning of July Fourth for the Negro" (5 July 1852)

"White nationalist, white supremacist, Western civilization—how did that language become offensive? Why did I sit in classes teaching me about the merits of our history and our civilization?" This pointed and provocative question was rhetorically asked in an interview by US Representative Steve King (R-Iowa) in January 2019. The garrulous question was posed not to solicit any answer but to provoke an emotional reaction—an affirmation, in fact, that the US politician had learned about "Western civilization" in his college years and was here to defend it. Many liberal and conservative commentators were eager to rush to reprimand and censure the congressman for using "Western civilization" as a euphemism for racism and white supremacy. He soon issued a statement explaining further that he was not defending white nationalism, just "Western civilization."[1] But are the two any different? When and how were they conflated?

Among the responses to Representative King was one by two young scholars and journalists, David Perry and Matthew Gabriele, in the *Washington Post*, where they proposed: "Given that King has frequently used 'Western civilization' as a shorthand for whiteness, his defense is hardly credible, but the attempt is revealing. The term has been used to justify racism since it was coined."[2] That truth, thus put bluntly, reveals a whole different root to this passing political storm. The rest of this short piece reads as evidence of this genera- tion of young academics and journalists as products of a certain strand of critical thinking that must be traced back to the repressed and denied, but enduring and crucial, experiences of the United States in the 1960s—now resurfacing to confront a nasty return of militant and criminal racism. As Perry and Gabriele put it:

In the 21st century, violent white supremacists, including Anders Breivik, Jeremy Christian and other neo-Vikings, and the racists who marched in Charlottesville, all deploy this nostalgia for a mythical "West" in their fight to dominate the future. They insist that Europe has always been white, Christian, patriarchal and pure. They want to see Europe and its colonial children "return" to that imaginary state and are willing to go to extreme lengths to ensure it happens. King's defense of "Western civilization" does the same work, especially when placed alongside his long history of racist statements. It just does that work more politely.[3]

Other critical thinkers soon joined the conversation and aptly suggested: "It's time for classical scholars to recognize that 'Western civilization' is a similar dog whistle. We may think it means everything good about the classical past but to many people—including some, if you're a teacher, that may be in your class—it means a justification for racist politics and the 'defense' of a white ethno-state."⁴ Such sentiments and critical thoughts, however, did not go unanswered by right-wing outlets, and the website American Renaissance soon published a piece defending the term *Western civilization*, in fact proudly declaring it the product of white people: "Western Civilization is white civilization. No one can credibly claim to 'defend Western Civilization' without defending the people that created it."⁵ What was astonishing about this whole incident was the fact that this was not just a battle over the past but in fact a battle over the future too. From a piece in the *Atlantic* we learned about "a crypt of civilization" created and buried in a basement in a university in Atlanta, "designed to preserve a picture of life in the 1930s for humans thousands of years in the future."⁶ It turns out that the man behind this project, a certain Thornwell Jacobs, was a rabidly racist person. From the *Atlantic* piece we find out:

> Jacobs's curation makes the crypt more than a historical oddity: It inverts the current controversies raging in the United States about whether to retain Confederate statues and rename buildings and streets dedicated to avowed white supremacists. Literally underground, it carries a message for the future that many people today wouldn't want delivered yet that could still be seen as a valuable reminder of the past.⁷

Cast backward and forward, from a fictive past to a delusional future, the link between the very word and concept of "civilization" and race and racist sentiments are here most evident and in fact both publicly and archivally staged. "Civilization" was something that white people had. "Barbarity" was the exclusive plight of other people destined to be ruled and thus civilized by white people. Civilization was Western; Barbarity Eastern, Southern, global—and thus the "civilizing mission" of white people was to lead the world to slavery under their power. To be civilized the world had to learn to be slaves to white people. The "White People," thus self-designating, had invented civilization and had the burden of civilizing the rest of the world, very much like Christian missionaries who were out to save the wretched pagans. More specifically, "Western civilization" was a thinly disguised, massively choreographed ideology in which white people thought of themselves as God's gift to humanity and therefore considered all other people, whether in their own midst in "the West" or in Asia, Africa, and Latin America, as their inferiors, destined to be ruled by them, "for their own good." This dominating idea thus created an inadvertent link between traumatized "minorities" in "the West" and the colonially brutalized majorities in the rest of the world. Representative King was simply extending the colonial logic of European domination of the globe into the racist justification of the selfsame white people ruling in the United States. It was their civilizing mission to be racist, to believe in the racial superiority of their own "Western civilization."

What was happening under the radar of these "White People" and their civilization was the fact that the racialized minorities they wished to rule were systematically at work dismantling that ruling ideology, simply by their very lived experiences, which in fact had endangered the white supremacists who now were protesting too much. The case of the crypt in Atlanta was a powerful case in point. White supremacists' claim on civilization was preempting any future dismantling of its beleaguered ideology by projecting its racialized prejudices onto an unknown future, precisely because it found itself exposed for the fraud that it was. Before the month of May 2020 was over, and as I was writing these lines, the coldblooded murder of a defenseless African American man, George Floyd, in Minneapolis, Minnesota, by a white police office had triggered one of the most widespread uprisings against endemic structural racism in US history. As a racialized category representing the white Christian person, "Western civilization" was crumbling fast upon itself. The Black Lives Matter movement had become a defining moment of US history.

Within this contemporary context, in this chapter I wish to consider the underlying factor of race the same way I did gender in the previous chapter. The horrid history of racism and white supremacy in the United States, with its echoes in Europe and its genocidal consequences around the colonized world, brings us closer to the site where the struggle for racial justice has created a formidable space for overcoming false binaries like "Islam and the West." Was Malcolm X a Muslim, or was he from "the West"? Or both? The Islam of Malcolm X is the antidote for the "Islam" of "Islam and the West." His defiant character rising from the very heart of American experiences places Malcolm X and his homeland at a crosscurrent where a far different renewal of the historical Islam dismantles the false binary of "Islam and the West." From the rise of Malcolm X as a revolutionary Black Muslim to the unfolding of his legacy in the Black Lives Matter movement, perhaps the most popular social protest in American history, Islam has emerged at the very core of American historical experience.[8] And with that fact comes the reality of Islam and the United States charting their ways far away from the delusion of "Islam and the West." To come to terms with this enduring fact, let me begin at the very heart of American racism.

The Undoing of "Western Civilization"

However rhetorical and disingenuous, one key phrase in Representative Steve King's sentence is a perfect implication of far more than his own personal racism. "Why did I sit in classes teaching me about the merits of our history and our civilization?" That fair, rhetorical question brings us to the heart of the educational politics of the United States over the last century—and by extension the Eurocentric origins of it. By the early twenty-first century, the racist nature of the very term *the West*, short for "Western civilization," was open for full critical consideration—the term was not just a self-raising/other-lowering generic gesture against all other civilizations, which generations of Orientalists had invented as inferior versions of "the West." The term also exposed the racist roots and disposition of the ruling elite that had relied on its ideological foregrounding. As a result, it exposed the white supremacist disposition of this "Western civilization" and the ideological force of *Mission civilisatrice* that had animated it. Though deeply rooted in the classical age of European colonialism, the term *Western civilization* was resurrected especially in the aftermath of the 1960s when contesting it assumed more militant terms. The combined forces of the anti-war and civil rights movements made this "culture war" more evident, but it was 9/11 that gave a decidedly global and anti-Islamic twist to the battle cries! After that the Obama presidency offered a putative "post-racist" society, which culminated instead in the belligerent Trump presidency and the renewal of the white supremacist claim on the phrase.

From Native American to Latinx American to African American, to generations of more recent immigrants from Asia, Africa, and Latin America, there have always been alternative factual claims on the forces of cultural formations in the United States. Monopolizing the public sphere, the public space, the educational system, the national allegories, and higher education, the ruling elite linked "Western civilization" to an exclusively European origin. Thus it sought to silence, denigrate, and dominate all the other cultural claims on being American. *The West* and *Western civilization* were therefore coded terms seeking to sustain the white supremacist ideology of

FIGURE 3. Udo Keppler, *From the Cape to Cairo*. The caption reads: "Though the Process Be Costly, the Road to Progress Must Be Cut." Published in *Puck* 52, no. 1345 (10 December 1902). Courtesy of the Library of Congress.

European settler colonialists against both First Nations and subsequent immigrants from around the globe, especially those brought in chains from Africa. The educational system has been the cornerstone of this ideological hegemony.

Representative King's question takes us back to US university campuses and classrooms. His liberal and conservative critics can denounce and dismiss or celebrate and embrace him as they wish. But his question about the classes he and his ilk have attended remains valid. The history of the Core Curriculum at my own university is one key example of the contested legacy of teaching "Western civilization" to generations of students. Because of my own prolonged involvements with Columbia's Core Curriculum in multiple capacities (from teaching to serving on various committees), I have a firsthand knowledge of its inner dynamics over close to thirty years. The story of Columbia's Core Curriculum might be traced back to 1917 when, according to the university website, "spurred by World War I, the U.S. Army commission[ed] Columbia faculty to create a course for the Student Army Training Corps." The military origin of this curriculum is of crucial significance. We also know that Dean Hawke believed: "Its significance rested on the fundamental principle that in the long run man's accomplishment can rise no higher than his ideals, and that an understanding of the worth of the cause for which one is fighting is a powerful weapon in the hands of an intelligent man."[9] For the moment, we must put the gendered patriarchy of the prose aside and concentrate on its more obvious ideological force. Young Americans had just risked their lives overseas fighting in foreign lands, and the Core Curriculum at this point was to teach them the moral and intellectual foregrounding of what it was they were fighting to preserve. The project was both practical and ideological, with a potent propaganda purpose. The United States was being incorporated into a global imagery of itself, and American educators wished for the younger generation to have a solid grasp of what this world was and of "their Western civilization." Today the project may appear gaudy and even gullible. But the learned men (and they were mostly men) of US higher education wanted Americans to feel themselves part of this "Western civilization." For this very reason, soon after the war "War Issues" was changed to "Peace Issues," and the course was renamed "Introduction to Contemporary Civilization in the West." Representative King was therefore perfectly accurate when he cited his own education as the basis of his racist bigotry. He was born in 1949 in Storm Lake, Iowa, attended Northwest Missouri State University in the late 1960s, and was the product of these belligerent trenches of "Western civilization"—the celebrations of which were not meant for the defeated Germans or anyone else in Europe but for the Native Americans and African Americans and other non-European immigrants within the United States itself who may have dreamed of their own civilizational claims on the land.

The next significant change in the Core Curriculum at Columbia took place in 1968 during the anti-war and civil rights movements when in the spring semester Columbia faculty introduced a focus on "Revolutions." This hasty half measure was the sign of the turbulent times, but it did not much alter the rhetorical disposition of the Core. Columbia was the site of much political turbulence generated by what on US campuses passed for "liberal and progressive" sentiments.[10] Although only a watered-down version of anticolonial and antiracist uprisings around the globe, in Asia, Africa, and Latin America in particular, these events on US campuses had their modest influence on the curricular thinking of the administration.[11] The next significant event in the history of the Core occurred in 1985, two years after women were admitted for the first time to Columbia College, and when Jane Austen became the first female author to be included into the Literature Humanities course. This again was tokenism, an artificial gesture trying to address a far more structural issue at the heart of the Core. There is a scene in Spike Lee's film *Malcolm X* (1992), based on a factual incident. When Malcolm is about to enter a lecture hall at Columbia, a white female student approaches him and asks what she can do to help his cause. He hurriedly dismisses her and says, "Nothing." The incident is emblematic of a period of bourgeois liberalism when revisions to the Columbia Core tried to assuage white guilt without any serious challenge to its racist foundations. Still "the West" stood for "Western civilization" and "the Rest" only corroborated its unique superiority.

By 1990 the "Western Core" was being challenged by a new student body—far more entrenched in their critical thinking, far less flamboyant in their public politics. By then I had been at Columbia for about three academic years (first as adjunct and then as a tenure-track assistant professor) and had started teaching various components of the Core. The Standing Committee on the Core had created what it called the "Extended Core" requirement to cover cultures otherwise disregarded in Contemporary Civilization (CC) and Literature Humanities (Lit Hum), as they were then dubbed. The Core at this point included CC in philosophy, Lit Hum in Literature, plus Art Hum and Music Hum—all of them, without a single exception, devoted to "the West." The demographic disposition of the student body, however, was changing, and the Core was besieged with factual and rhetorical criticism. Under the new rubric of "the Extended Core" Columbia offered a list of courses on "non-Western" cultures from which students could choose to fulfill this requirement. Later this series of courses was called "Major Cultures"—which covered Asian, African, Latin American, or Native American regions. A committee on Major Cultures was created to address this requirement. I served on this committee for many years and know the difficult task its members faced in preserving the Core under pressure from the alumnae and responding to the new student body composed of radically different political sentiments. Still, "the Core of the Core," as we sarcastically called it, remained "Western," and on its peripheries "other cultures" were othered and offered.

But things were still changing—ever so imperceptibly. The racialized foregrounding of the whole Core Curriculum still troubled many among the faculty and even more among the incoming student cohorts. The administration was concerned about the deep pockets of wealthy alumnae who were committed to the Core and its standardized composition celebrating "the West."[12] Following a student hunger strike in protest of the Core Curriculum in 1996, then president George Rupp appointed a Blue-Ribbon Committee that Professor Ira Katznelson chaired and on which I served along with about a dozen other senior faculty, including Eric Foner, Manning Marable, Robert O'Malley, Karen Barkey, Patricia Grieve, Haruo Shirane, and others. This committee convened, consulted, met with student representatives, and then appointed a subcommittee that Eric Foner chaired and on which I served. We were tasked with producing a report to the Blue-Ribbon committee in which we would offer various possibilities for a department, center, or institute of Race and Ethnic Studies, as students had demanded. The work of this committee ultimately resulted in the establishment of the Center for the Study of Ethnicity and Race (CSER) under the direction of its first director, Professor Gary Okihiro. The result of this episode in the late 1990s was the Core Curriculum becoming more acutely aware of the rapidly evolving environment and the necessity of changing in more serious ways to adapt to campus life in North America. By the late 2010s the Columbia Core Curriculum had remained basically the same, with its emphasis on "Western Civilization," though the inclusion of what was now called "the Global Core" (still heavily understaffed) had gone a long way to addressing other cultures that had been hitherto ignored or even effectively denigrated.

By the late 2010s the critical disposition at Columbia, however, was ready and receptive to a Core requirement course, which I designed and offered, that knowingly and decidedly sought to overcome this racist divide between "the West" and "the Rest." I named my course "Critical Theory: A Global Perspective" and began offering it in the 2018 spring semester. The course had to go through various committees on which I used to serve, and it went flying through them, receiving enthusiastic support; it did so both because of my own record of commitment to undergraduate education and the care with which I brought the two components of the core together. My course, in which I had collapsed "the West and the Rest," neither dismissed nor privileged "the West." It began by dwelling on the Eurocentric moment of the rise of Critical Theory as developed by Theodor Adorno and other German Jewish philosophers in the aftermath of the Jewish Holocaust and then, in my reading of it, I went around the globe to Asia, Africa, and Latin America, mapping out similar traumatic events caused by European colonialism and generating a body of knowledge centered around the fact and phenomenon of collective trauma. I had in effect retrieved the history of anti-Semitism in Europe and the manufacturing of "the Jew" as the internal other of Europe and brought the Jewish experience back into the global context where it belongs. In this course I neither privileged "Islam" nor ignored it. Instead, I brought Islam into the bosom of larger global events and traumatic moments conducive to the production of art and literature, philosophy, and other forms of critical thinking. To this day, this course is one of the most widely popular courses in Columbia undergraduate education. Our registrar's office has to scramble for classrooms large enough to accommodate the number of students drawn to this course. When I offered the course in spring 2020, halfway through the semester because of the COVID-19 pandemic, we had to cancel in-person classes and continue our classes on Zoom. Representative Steve King's head would spin if he were to walk into my classroom. The undoing of "Western civilization" was here achieved via a retrieval and appropriation of one of its own traumatic moments, namely the Jewish Holocaust, and linking it to the larger global traumas caused by European colonialism.

Our experience with Columbia's Core Curriculum reveals the dynamically changing demography as well as the raced, gendered, and classed factors and forces that come together to contest the ideological forces at work in "Western civilization." By calling it "Contemporary Civilization" (CC), "the West" in fact seeks to colonize *the time* as well as *the space* of our worldly existence. The only "contemporary" that exists is "the West"; "the Rest" is nonexistent in the present. The Core Curriculum at Columbia began with a clearly racialized and in fact military underpinning to educate the ruling elite of the American political establishment. But it eventually evolved in response to massive social movements and demographic changes within the United States. What is missing in all those liberal-versus-conservative arguments regarding the link between race and civilization is the circuity of labor and capital and the underlying historiographic Hegelianism that has gone into a singular teleological emergence of civilizations and civilizational thinking—all of it "Western." As the republican epicenter of a globalized empire, the United States is a living organism, and every new wave of immigration from its colonial peripheries coming into its republican epicenter changes the dynamic of that circularity of labor and capital and the cultures it inevitably generates to keep itself in power with some impression of legitimacy. The term *civilization* cannot be exempted from the changing effects of this fact. Walter Benjamin's revelatory truth that "there is no document of civilization which is not at the same time a document of barbarism"[13] was completely lost in these tiresome debates between American liberals and their conservative interlocutors. Once we bring race, gender, and class together, the intersectionality of these crucial factors categorically dismantles the very proposition of civilizational thinking as we have received it and at the same time posits an entirely different disposition on how human cultural formations become materially grounded. De-racing "Western civilization," by exposing the factual evidence of its racist origins, effectively decodes enduring forms of cultural domination and dismantles their hegemonic power. Thus it opens people's lived experiences to horizons of far different conceptions of the world they inhabit.

Hiding in Plain Sight

De-racing the term *civilization* is like deboning a fish, taking out the structural supports of its racism and exposing it to critical examination. But even more important is to draw attention to the contemporary sites of powerful cultural formations that the Core at Columbia and elsewhere were actively ignoring. The sites of such cultural formations are in fact first and foremost inside the United States, not outside it. What discredits the way the term *civilization* alludes to "Western civilization," and tries in vain to conceal its racialized politics, is evident in much more than just the curricular changes at universities. The phenomenon is far more widespread and takes us to the core of the contemporary study of history that has overcome civilizational thinking and collapsed the presumed centrality of "the West" unto itself. The term *the West*, short for "Western civilization," and cross-authenticated in such binaries as "Islam and the West," loses all currency and relevance when we see how in our own present history the factual evidence of cultural productions crisscrosses the presumed opposition between "Islam" and "the West" in beautifully evident and yet politically denied ways.

In a beautiful essay on John Coltrane, Hisham Aidi asks his readers a pointed question: "Did Coltrane say 'Allah Supreme?'"[14] What in the world could this question signify? What has Allah to do with perhaps the most iconic jazz musician of his generation? We read further to find out that Hisham Aidi's essay centers around Coltrane's legendary album *A Love Supreme* (1964), which is widely considered his masterpiece. "Many an aficionado came to jazz through that classic album—a 32-minute-long composition organised around a four-note bass routine. The manuscript for the album is one of the National Museum of American History's treasures; the saxophone that Coltrane used to record the piece was recently gifted to the Smithsonian Museum; and former US President Bill Clinton, a saxophonist and Coltrane fan, is said to have 'A Love Supreme' set as the ringtone for when Hillary calls."

Scarcely anything could be more celebrated in this most American artform than this album, or more definitive to contemporary American music and performing arts, or more iconic of the living African American culture. From Hisham Aidi's essay we learn a central issue about this album. It has to do with the sacred Muslim phrase "Allah-u Akbar" (God is Great), which could also be rendered as "Allah Supreme," which in the Muslim mystic tradition could very well also be read as "Love Supreme." But what could the legendary jazz musician have to do with this iconic Muslim phrase?

The saxophonist Yusef Lateef, who died at the age of 93 earlier this year, worked closely with Coltrane between 1963 and 1966. In his autobiography, "A Gentle Giant," Lateef says: "The prayer that John wrote in 'A Love Supreme' repeats the phrase 'All praise belongs to God no matter what' several times. This phrase has the semantics of the al-Fatiha, which is the first chapter or sura of the Holy Quran. The Arabic transliteration is 'al-Humdulilah. . . .' Since all faithful Muslims say the al-Fatiha five times a day or more, it is reasonable to assume that John heard this phrase from [his Muslim wife] Sister Naima many times.[15]

By now we are deeply into the intertwined history of jazz and Islam. Who could have suspected this? So where is "Islam and the West?" Is jazz part of "the West," or is "the West" only Bach, Mozart, and Beethoven? If jazz is also "the West," then what is Islam doing at the very heart of it? We further learn: "What Lateef and others have noted is that 'gracious and merciful' is a translation of 'rahman raheem,' the opening lines of the Fatiha. Moreover, say the elders, when Coltrane begins chanting the album's title for half a minute it sounds like a Sufi breathily repeating 'Allah supreme.'" That brings jazz, the most iconic and celebrated American musical art, into the spiritual heart of Islam, into Sufism.

The relationship between Islam and jazz is almost a century old. It was in the 1920s that the Ahmadiyya movement, a heterodox Islamic movement that emerged in 19th century India, began sending missionaries to US cities, building a substantial following among African Americans in the decades to come. In a trend that still intrigues historians and music critics, after World War II, scores of jazz musicians embraced Ahmadi Islam.[16]

We will soon learn that the mystical dimension of Islam had in fact come to the American shores much earlier than 1920s. But for now, what is important is to see how "Islam" enters "the West," as it were, through the side door of American jazz, where the Muslim faith of some American jazz musicians has given them a creative space where the delusional binary of "Islam and the West" fades out and disappears. Hisham Aidi's conclusion is quite crucial here: "As the US celebrates and tries to mainstream figures from the turbulent 1960s, voices from the communities that produced the likes of Coltrane, Malcolm X and Muhammad Ali, should be heard—especially as the domestic and foreign policies that pushed African Americans towards Islam a century ago are still with us."[17]

Let's now turn to another iconic text in contemporary American literary culture, Toni Morrison's *Song of Solomon* (1997), a groundbreaking novel that thrives on its multicultural references, with allusions and elements from Native American and African American cultures framing rather bashful allusions to Islamic citations in the title "Song of Solomon." Who would have guessed? What does Morrison, a towering American novelist and winner of the Nobel Prize in literature, have to do with Islam? Again I emphasize that my point here is to detect the imperceptible, not the most obvious—for it is in the most imperceptible, in the casual matter-of-fact evidence in the creative subconscious of artists in particular, where the collapse of ideological binaries is most crucial. Considered one of the masterpieces of English-language literature of the twentieth century, *Song of Solomon* follows the life of Macon "Milkman" Dead III, whose creative crisis of identity very much carries the novel. Scholars of Toni Morrison's fiction have drawn attention to the possibility that "the flying Africans" motif in the novel could be a reference to Muslims. In particular they point to the following verse:

> Solomon and Ryna, Belali, Shalut
> Yaruba, Medina, Muhammet, too.
> Nestor, Kalina, Saraka cake.
> Twenty-one children, the last one Jake![18]

In Morrison's capable hands and creative soul all such African Muslim traces of course metamorphose and are transplanted in the southern United States and put to effective literary uses. But thanks to the historical investigations of scholars like Nada Elia, we have a more detailed understanding of the gifted American writer's casual allusions. This is how Nada Elia frames the question of Islamic references in Toni Morison's *Song of Solomon*:

> Decades before Morrison published Song of Solomon, the descendants of Belali Mohomet were interviewed over a three-year period (between 1936 and 1939), by the Savannah, Georgia, unit of the Federal Writers' Project. Despite the self-censorship they undoubtedly engaged in, as former slaves being interviewed by Southern whites, they clearly recall their ancestors following Muslim religious traditions, even if those traditions are never named, never identified as such.[19]

There are layers of remembered and forgotten memories at work here, all through the traumatic experiences of Black Muslim slaves who had been kidnapped from their homelands and brought to the United States to be sold into slavery. The trauma of being kidnapped, chained, shipped in bondage, and sold into servitude in and of itself robbed these Africans of the memory of who and what they were. Nada Elia gives us a detailed account of this early African Muslim experience in the Americas, and the differing attitudes of European slave merchants toward the faith of the human beings they stole and sold into slavery, where we learn, "still reeling from eight centuries of Muslim hegemony in their own country, the Spaniards were reluctant to introduce Islam into the New World." But disguised as Sufi slaves, these Muslims managed to bring their ancestral faith with them to "the New World."

> Traces of Sufi Islam, the mystic tradition quite distinct from the mainstream, orthodox religion, and which can be practiced without the outward manifestations of conventional religion, are to be found to this day in former Spanish colonies, where they tend to remain unacknowledged or, when detected, are attributed to "African animism."[20]

Meanwhile, the French and English slave traders had no particular qualms with what religion their possessions practiced. Thus Orthodox Islam was brought into the Americas. Nada Elia informs us:

> This is the brand of Islam that generally withered away within one generation, for it could not thrive without a mosque, a mu'ezzin, an imam, and the requisite Friday communal prayer. Yet enslaved Afrodiasporans who knew that their ancestors were devout Muslims tended to grasp at any survival of that religion in the "New World," and gradually, if unknowingly, they too shifted towards Sufi practices, making of the latter the dominant form of Africana Islam in the Americas, as it had become in many parts of Africa. Sufi Islam then merged with other hybrid Diaspora practices, including voodoo, providing the believers with the spiritual empowerment that sustained them in their enslavement.[21]

Whether mystics or legalists, Sufis or Sunnis, Orthodox or Heterodox, this earliest generation of African Muslims was brought to a world where their traumatized moral and cultural memories were systematically censured and/or erased. The force of that erasure, however, was never total or complete. It is telling that outside such painstaking scholarly investigations as those of Elia and others, literary giants like Morrison are left to their impressionistic awareness of the Islamic aspects of the characters they create. But just like Coltrane, in the case of Morrison it is precisely because of this vague, faded-out, metamorphosed, palimpsestic, and uncertain allusion to a repressed and denigrated past that the power of Muslim memory in African American experiences becomes ever more palpable, for the layers of those remembered/forgotten memories interpolate and make the traces of their presence even more powerful.

A Black Muslim Liberation Theology in America

My point here is to begin, not with the most immediately recognizable presence of Islam in the United States through the earliest generations of African slaves, but with the most imperceptible in the visual, performing, and literary arts, for by the time we get to the monumental revolutionary figure of Malcolm X we are on the ground of a solid collective unconscious that has brought back all those repressed memories.[22] The conversion of Malcolm X to Islam was not merely a spontaneous political move. It was equally a courageous act of remembering an African Islam that had been consistently debased and erased. But Malcolm X was no archivist of forgotten identities. Quite to the contrary. In my *Islamic Liberation Theology* (2008) I have already offered Malcolm X's political trajectory by way of an example to see how the active political presence of a Muslim revolutionary can recraft the world and history in which he transcends sectarian identity politics to become a global figure of revolt against injustice on the same platform as Che Guevara on one side and Mahatma Gandhi on the other. We ordinarily do not think of Che Guevara as Christian or Gandhi as Hindu when we imagine their revolutionary charisma. It is the same with Malcolm X, whose being a Muslim becomes subsumed and metamorphosed under his more universal revolutionary appeal. This I have argued by proposing Malcolm X's revolutionary *authenticity* was predicated on a cultural *inauthenticity*, or a kind of cosmopolitan worldliness that subsumed his faith into a liberation theology of a distinctly African American nature. Through Malcolm X, the long history of Islam in America links back to Islam in Africa, and by the time it reaches a global figure like Mohammad Ali it has assumed a distinct character very different from Islam in Europe, or Islam in the Arab world. At the time of Malcolm X's rise to political prominence in the United States in the 1950s and 1960s, there was no Muslim revolutionary figure anywhere else in the world that could match his charismatic presence—and he was a distinctly American phenomenon.

To be sure, long before the rise of Malcolm X, Islam had a pronounced presence in North America. The origin of Islam in America in transatlantic slavery brings Muslims to the heart of the American experience in a profound and enduring way, as Islam was systematically repressed, denied, and concealed until the emergence of Black Muslims in the 1960s triggered that repressed historical memory. Here we must see Islam in the United States as a uniquely American experience. In *Islam: An American Religion* (2017), Nadia Marzouki has shown how Islam has become a uniquely American religion, meaning it has become integral to matters of public debates and the negotiations between the sacred and the secular.[23] But the issue is not limited to contemporary debates. In *Muslims and the Making of America* (2016), Amir Hussain has put forward a cogent argument of how Islam has always been integral to *American* history.[24] In *Servants of Allah: African Muslims Enslaved in the America* (2013), Sylviane A. Diouf offers a history of African Muslims by following them from West Africa to the Americas, where their Islam flourished on the new and fertile ground.[25] Most of these studies were triggered in the aftermath of the rise of Malcolm X to revolutionary prominence. His presence and later his memory have been catalysts of remembering an Islamic history in the United States that had been hitherto denied, denigrated, or altogether dismissed, because the carriers of that Islam were not in any position of wealth, power, and authority to build mosques for themselves while others were making magnificent churches, synagogues, and temples for themselves. To this day, most mosques in New York are in rundown buildings; they are in Harlem or Brooklyn, not on Madison Avenue or Fifth Avenue, where we see magnificent churches and synagogues.

The case of Black American Muslims therefore offers the crucible of reimagining Islam in a manner far closer to its humble revolutionary origins some fourteen hundred years ago among the poor and the downtrodden in the Arabian Peninsula than in any rich and corrupt Arab state in the world today. Above all, Malcolm X's Islam was not trapped inside the delusional "Islam and the West." It was "in the West" but it was not "of the West." It was free in the mind and soul of a selfless revolutionary who lived for the restoration of the dignity of the people, Black people, to whom he belonged—irrespective of their being Muslim or otherwise. Malcolm X's Islam here was liberated from all the delusional trappings of false binaries. What we are therefore witnessing here is the infusion of Islam and its varied insignia and symbolic registers deep into the African American lived and aesthetic experiences—ranging from Malcolm X's revolutionary aspirations to John Coltrane's music and Toni Morrison's fiction, so much so that Islamic themes were not in need of being cataloged or scripted. If towering icons of American culture like Malcolm X, John Coltrane, and Toni Morrison have, each in their own different ways, internalized Islamic sentiments into the heart of their presence in "the West," then this "West" has imploded upon its own contradictions—so much so that the defenders of "Western civilization" are left only with the patently racist triumphalist hallucinations of people like Donald Trump and his diehard supporters who have lost reason and sanity and are engaged in mass apocalyptic hysteria so evident in American film and fiction.

Turning to the critical question of civilization and race, I have gone back to my central thesis of disentangling the false opposition between "Islam" and "the West," reasserting the contemporary consequences of this dangerous binary and drawing attention to its colonial and racial roots and underpinnings. Mapping out the alternative trajectories of far more fluid historical cultures necessarily pivots toward urgent global issues of environmental catastrophes and perilous human migrations without being bogged down by nervous preoccupation with false binaries. The issue is no longer a mere dismantling of false binaries like "Islam and the West." It is rather the opening of horizons of thinking on the unfolding domain of a transnational public sphere that is fully conscious of race and gender and has radically destabilized any false binary built to facilitate the ideological domination of one illusion over others it generates. It is important to address the racial factor, not just in manufacturing such binaries as "Islam and the West," but in keeping their exhausted relevance for racially codified modes of domination. It is imperative that we expand the analysis into African American experiences as Muslims on the site of US history, where the figure of Malcolm X would necessarily loom, pointing toward a systemic collapse of "the West and the Rest." This would eventually pave the way toward a post-Islamist liberation theology that will re-world Islam and release Muslims from any false opposition with the falsifying allegory of "the West." Dismantling that false binary in and of itself would be only preparatory to placing Islam and with it the world that the allegory of "the West" conceals on a leveled and liberating plane.

The interpolated connotations of blatant racism embedded in the discourse of civilization we witness in high-profile US politicians is squarely rooted in the articulation of the so-called Western canon mapped out in the core curriculum and distribution requirements of a majority of US and European colleges and universities. The very rhetoric of such canonicity overrides, ignores, and denigrates the active formation of real cultures and lived experiences, as evident in monumental figures like Coltrane or Morrison and brought to the revolutionary stage by Malcolm X. Overcoming the concept of "Islam and the West" here amounts to overcoming the dead end of sectarian Islamism, with the iconic figure of Malcolm X as a revolutionary figure of post-Islamist Black liberation theology. Here the American scene becomes the crucible of the historical dissolution of "Islam and the West." "Islam and the West" came to these shores in two divergent and diametrically opposed traces—Islam as Muslim slaves and "the West" as Christian settler colonialism that ultimately led to the formation of an evangelical imperialism. "Islam and the West" thus met on the broken backs of Muslim slaves from Africa—and in their lived and transcendent experiences African Americans have endured the brunt of a racism that is definitive to the very term *the West* and the civilization to which it lays claim. And at the same time, in the triumphant presence of Malcolm X a post-Islamist liberation theology dwells that has already overcome the false binary of "Islam and the West" that had occasioned it in the first place.

8   *Nations beyond Borders*

Yet Saadi loved the race of men—
No churl immured in cave or den—
In bower and hall
He wants them all,
Nor can dispense
With Persia for his audience;
They must give ear,
Grow red with joy, and white with fear,
Yet he has no companion,
Come ten, or come a million,
Good Saadi dwells alone.

RALPH WALDO EMERSON, "Saadi" (1842)

As I began preparing to write this last chapter, in mid-June 2020 when New York, like the rest of the United States, was engulfed in the massive Black Lives Matter uprising, I went to two specific shelves in my home library and, in the spirit of Walter Benjamin's legendary essay "Unpacking My Library" (1931), began taking down books I had collected over so many years on the theme of "Islam and the West." The sadistic murder of George Floyd on 25 May 2020 in Minneapolis, Minnesota, had triggered a massive protest around the country—and in fact around the globe. This collective uprising against white supremacist racism was thus very much on my mind. Whereas Benjamin's books had been in boxes and he had to unpack not just his books but the recollections embedded in them, in my case the colonial context of the manufacturing of a binary of "the West and the Rest" (the white and the nonwhite) came down from the shelves with the accumulated memories of how and when and why I had started collecting them.

My writing of this book was coming to an end, and the books I had collected in my home library had been with me for many years and had fulfilled their individual purposes. But now it was in their collection, in their totality, that they presented a gestalt view of the field of scholarship that had preoccupied me for so many years. "Every passion," Walter Benjamin famously wrote in his beautiful essay, "borders on the chaotic, but the collector's passion borders on the chaos of memories."[1] This is true. But for me the chaos of memory of how and why I began chasing after these books, reading them, taking notes on them, and finally writing this book to conclude my reflections on their subject matter all yielded to the singularity of the purpose that the term *the West* has exercised on my mind as a single object of curiosity. I am not "from the West" but I am "in the West," with all its delusional presence wreaking havoc around the globe, and yet in my lifetime of scholarship I have read Benjamin, a German Jewish thinker of unsurpassed subtlety and power, as my own kindred soul. We are both not "from the West"—he for being Jewish and I for being Muslim.

Following a clue from Benjamin's essay, the chaos of memory hovering over these books for me spans the cities where I have purchased them. For Benjamin's library, he tells us, it was Riga, Naples, Munich, Danzig, Moscow, Florence, Basel, and Paris.[2] For me, it has been from Philadelphia, Boston, New York, London, Lausanne, Munich, Geneva, and then to cities where I have carried them with me as I was reading them—Beirut, Cairo, Damascus, Casablanca, Rabat, Marrakesh, Mexico City, Buenos Aires, Tokyo, Gwangju, St. Petersburg, Jerusalem, Ramallah, Istanbul. These geographies are where "Islam and the West," as a vintage sample of "the West and the Rest," began to collapse for me as I was collecting and reading these books. From my own lived experiences there was neither a West to collecting these books nor an East to reading them; nor was there a North to their wisdom or a South to their follies, and the whole ideological production of "Islam and the West" thus imploded under the factual memories of these books. But I needed to write a detailed account of emancipation from this dual delusion—and thus this book.

Spain, the Crucible

As I looked at my collection of these books, I noticed how at one particularly liberal moment in the history of Orientalist learning suddenly European and North American scholars began to pay closer attention to Islam in Spain, for that particular span between the eighth and fifteenth centuries seemed to comprise the long history of manufacturing "Islam" as the absolute other of their "West." The presence of Muslims in Spain or Sicily now seemed an apt object of curiosity to scholars, in fact to have been integral to European continental experiences. The effect of this body of scholarship, however, was exactly the opposite of what might have been expected. Attention to Spain or Sicily further fetishized both "the West" and "Islam" as realities unto themselves and entirely sui generis. As such, they were worlds apart and now and then had "interactions" or "influences" with and on one another. At the roots of all such civilizational anxieties was the centrality of nations and their preferred narrations, of regions and continents suddenly becoming culturally coded— Asia is this, Africa the other, and Europe was always on the other hand. It is to this colonial concoction of nations and their imagined locations that I wish to turn in this last chapter of the book—to argue that the formation of all nations is always already transnational.

A typical example of this genre of books about Islam in Spain is L. P. Harvey's *Islamic Spain, 1250-1500* (1992), which offers its readers a detailed account of Muslims in Spain from the fall of Seville to the Christian reconquest. Another classic example of the genre is Rheinhart Dozy's *Spanish Islam: A History of the Moslems in Spain* (1913), which is an even more comprehensive account of Muslim Spain until the reign of Ferdinand and Isabella in the late fifteenth century. There is a certain romanticism at work in these books, perhaps best evident in Elmer Bendiner's *The Rise and Fall of Paradise: When Arabs and Jews Built a Kingdom in Spain* (1990). But there were cooler heads at work too, such as in the classical work of W. Montgomery Watt and my late Columbia colleague Pierre Cachia's *A History of Islamic Spain* (1996), which offers a more balanced account of the period. All of these studies were still performed in the larger context of "Islam and the West," as best evident in Norman Daniel's *Islam and the West: The Making of an Image* (1993), or R. W. Southern's *Western Views of Islam in the Middle Ages* (1962), or Larry Poston's *Islamic Da'wah in the West: Muslim Missionary Activity and the Dynamics of Conversion to Islam* (1992). So the epistemological foregrounding had still remained "Islam and the West," but a nostalgic and romantic period was now carved out inside the binary within a few centuries of Spanish history.

There were, to be sure, some skeptical minds at work, such as Vassilis Lambropoulos in *The Rise of Eurocentricism* (1992), in which he distinguished between "the Hellenic and Hebraic" modes of thought—considering one analytic and the other hermeneutic. I was not quite sure if the dualism worked with such marked differences. But it was a cogent argument that went against the spirit of Eurocentricism I had found in such classical texts as Ali-Akbar Siyasi's

La Perse au Contact de L'Occident (1931). However critical in its spirit, Philip D. Curtin's *The World and the West: The European Challenge and the Overseas Response in the Age of Empire* (2002) was still categorical in the binary it proposed between "the West" on one side and "the Rest" on the other. Be that as it may, the fusion of the two works by Lambropoulos and Curtin marked a critical turning point in understanding the very term *the West* and all other terms that had come to consolidate and corroborate it.

In the same spirit, Richard Hodges and David Whitehouse's *Mohammed, Charlemagne and the Origins of Europe: Archaeology and the Pirenne Thesis* (1983) was a fine study that drew our attention to the Mediterranean basin as a unit of cultural and economic investigations. Whereas Albert Hourani's *Islam in European Thought* (1992), learned as it was, again posited "Islam" and "Europe" as an analytical binary. With studies such as Hourani's the two worlds of Islam and non-Islam and Europe and non-Europe were further consolidated. The same is true of María Rosa Menocal's *The Arabic Role in Medieval Literary History: A Forgotten Heritage* (1990), where we read all about the ways in which Arabic culture was instrumental in shaping Medieval Europe and yet how this influence was downplayed and ignored. Again, this was a laudatory intervention that also inadvertently further pulled the two sides apart. The same is true with Khalil I. Semaan's edited volume *Islam and the Medieval West: Aspects of Intercultural Relations* (1980), where eminent scholars like George Makdisi, Claude Cahen, J. Van Ess, Albert Dietrich, Vicente Cantarino, and Anwar Chejne documented the exchanges between "Islam" and "the West." These studies were all done in good faith to show the exchanges between the two constituents of the binary, and yet inadvertently their epistemological and historiographical foundations maintained that binary.

Crucial in this period, however, was a text like Larry Wolff's *Inventing Eastern Europe* (1994), where we read a cogent argument regarding the manner in which during the eighteenth century "Europe" as an idea was divided between "Eastern Europe" and "Western Europe." This conceptual overriding of North and South was a product of Enlightenment modernity, where Paris had become the epicenter of the world from which an inferior "Eastern Europe" was distanced and invented. The invention of "Eastern Europe" was therefore the extension of the invention of "the Orient" as the domain of unreason to define the Reason at the heart of Enlightenment modernity. It is crucial to keep in mind that this "Eastern Europe" was mostly the domain of the Ottoman Empire, with Vienna as the purgatorial domain that could have gone one way or another. First the domain of the Ottomans and then the realm of the Soviet influence over socialist Europe, the region's fusion of Islam and Communism thus defined "Western Europe" as Christian and Capitalist. Berlin was the divided city that until the fall of the Berlin Wall in November 1989 marked this bifurcation.

Classic Eurocentric texts like William McNeill's *The Rise of the West* (1964) were still very much dominant in European historiography. But Dimitri Gutas's *Greek Thought, Arabic Culture: The Graeco-Arabic Translation Movement in Baghdad and Early 'Abbasid Society* (1998) had also advanced far more grounded arguments in the Greco-Arab environment of the early Islamic history in the Mediterranean domain, while at the same time texts such as Aziz Ahmad's *A History of Islamic Sicily* (1975) were far more aware of the local and regional contexts of the same territories. In other words, the grand narratives of "Islam and the West" were still dominant, and yet they were also being implicitly challenged by alternative modes of thinking about the region, where the trope of *interaction* was yielding to more full-bodied accounts of common domains that overcame the binary construction and implicated alternative historiographies.

There were, to be sure, still knee-jerk reactions to received clichés. In Amin Maalouf's classic text *The Crusades through the Arab*

Eyes (1989) we have an over-interpretation of the Crusades from the Arab perspective. Just because the Crusades were an important episode in European history, it does not mean they were the same in Islamic history, at a time when the epicenter of Muslim empires had shifted to the East, to Khurasan of the Seljuqids and beyond, deep into Central Asia. But Europe was the measure of historiography, and "an Arab eye" was devised to consolidate Europe in its Eurocentricity. The same was true with Eugene A. Meyers's *Arabic Thought and the Western World* (1964), which examined the Islamic "influence on the West." "The West" was there to be reviled, to be revered, to be emulated, or else to be influenced. Such tired and old clichés had their heyday in the 1960s through the 1990s. That brings us back to Bernard Lewis's *The Arabs in History*, published first in 1950 and last in 2002, basically arguing the platitude that Islam was once something of a civilization in its olden and golden ages but had ultimately lost to "the West."

Against the ideological grain of much of this literature, in this final chapter I wish to show the circulatory dispositions of labor and capital around the globe, where "the West" goes east to conquer, plunder and trade, and the "East" goes west as cheap labor and raw material, and thus the world is made to go around an entirely different "logic" that the delusion of "the West and the Rest" cannot fathom. The circulatory logic of labor and capital in turn translates into capital and culture, which offer a much richer and more robust reading of the world than that of imagining a fictional center for all its presumed peripheries. The logic and rhetoric of a transnational, parapublic sphere is where the economic underpinning of that circulation translates into a syncretic culture accommodating the whimsical pleasures of capital. The ideologically formed "nations" are the by-products of this circulatory logic of capital, a mere bookkeeping mechanism overriding the dynastic histories they replace and in which every element of a national consciousness is already transnational.

In my *Persophilia: Persian Culture on the Global Scene* (2015) I offered the concept of parapublic sphere as a location on which in colonial contexts people have used the ideas generated on the transnational public sphere to revolt against domestic tyranny and foreign domination at the same time. Habermas's notion of "public sphere," I have proposed, is both Eurocentric and stagnant. I have put a global spin to it. My purpose here is to go beyond both Edward Said's *Orientalism* (1978) and Raymond Schwab's *La Renaissance Orientale* (1950) to look at "Orientalism" as not just a site of cultural domination or exploitation, but in fact definitive to the most consequential social and intellectual movements throughout the world. In other words, the European encounter with their "Orient" became definitive to groundbreaking and historic changes both in Europe and, because of its cultural hegemony, also around the globe. This is a far different perspective than giving Europeans the sole agential power and casting "the Orientals" as a passive recipient without any agency. It places both Europe and non-Europe on the more leveled bourgeois public sphere upon which major social and intellectual movements have been launched with far-reaching global and regional consequences. That dialectical reading of our condition of globality is a far more realistic assessment of the encounter between multiple cultures, where the site of the "nation" begins to expose its transnational origins. The delusion of "Islam and the West" evaporates on this transnational disposition of the nation.

From Orientalism to Persophilia

Let me now give some more specific examples. How do we remember Aeschylus (circa 525–455 BC) today or read one of his dramatic masterpieces, *Persians* (472 BC), if we indeed care to remember and read him at all? Many of the literary masterpieces of classical antiquity are now either subjects of recondite academic scholarship or else frequented by literary connoisseurs for the sheer pleasure they offer. They have significantly disappeared from the literary map of our political consciousness—what occasioned them, who read them, how were they staged, and why (or if) they still matter. But when these classical texts appeared they were indices of a much different world whose imaginative geography is now hidden under a thick layer of the fiction of "Islam and the West." Aeschylus's play is plotted around the Battle of Salamis (480 BC) with the Persian emperor Xerxes as its chief protagonist. The Greek dramatist was himself a veteran of the Battle of Marathon (490 BC), and thus he wrote from the depth of his own experiences. When those battles were waged and those literary masterpieces were written, there was no bifurcation between any fictional East and West, for the Persian Empire and the Greek city-states were integral to an antiquity entirely alien to these terms—and certainly there was no "Islam and the West." Remembering those distant times recasts the imaginative geography dominant today in an entirely different light. We need a wider and longer global imaginary, a deeper historical memory, a more embracing emotive universe to overcome the false bifurcations that are today ripping our world asunder. We need actively to remember that not all Muslims are Arabs, not all Arabs are Muslims, and that nations now under the two opposing camps of "Islam and the West" have in fact had variedly longer histories before reaching this particular juncture in our current predicament.

With those geographical maps now long since erased and forgotten, today there is an inaccurate and ahistorical conflation of Arabs and Muslims, and Muslims with the rest of the world, from Asia to Africa and Latin America, against which the imperial allegory of "the West" is ideologically posited as a measure of truth. Muslims are not the only people at the receiving end of the global colonial project launched by Western Europe and later North America in the aftermath of Industrial Revolution and the commencement of the European Age of modern empires. Asians, Africans, Latin Americans—they have all been subject to European imperialism and colonialism and their concomitant cultural accoutrements. This confusion has confounded the enduring hostility presumed between "Islam" and "the West." This binary, as a result, has placed the abstracted entity "the West" against everything and anything its ideologues wish to other and exoticize, dismiss and denigrate, over-rule and dominate. The underlying economic logic of globalized labor, raw material, markets, and capital is completely hidden under the ideological power of the term and the binary it keeps generating.

This conflation of Arabs and Muslims is a key conceptual confusion, informed by a politics of racialized domination. Today we need to complicate Islamic history and remember that the last major Muslim empires were decidedly non-Arab. The Ottomans were Turks, the Safavids and the Qajars were Persianate empires of Turkic descent, and the Mughals were of Central Asian descent and entirely sub-continental Indo-Persian in their cultural habitat. Arabic language was of course integral to the ritual and doctrinal dimension of the Islam these empires practiced, but not Arabic culture. Their Islam was of a syncretic and cosmopolitan disposition. The ascendency of a very short-lived major Arab empire was a very long time ago, from the middle of the seventh century (656), with the rise of the Umayyads, until about a century into the Abbasid Empire (751–1258). But with the rise of the Turkic Ghaznavids (977–1186) and the Seljuqids (1037–1194), both deeply Persianized in their courtly cultures, the Abbasids declined in power, never to rise again. Even at the height of the Abbasid Empire in ninth-century Baghdad, the dynasty was instrumental in the rise of a manifestly cosmopolitan culture that included non-Arab and even non-Muslim (Zoroastrian, Jewish, and Christian in particular) elements from across the Muslim-majority world. Though the Arabic language endured in significance through-out many though not all these empires, beyond its Qur'anic sanctity for all Muslims, this was entirely due to its function as one of the four major lingua francas of the Muslim lands, which included Persian, Turkish, and Hindi/Urdu. As we must de-Arabize the Muslim world to have a larger and more accurate conception of Islamic civilization, which certainly includes Arab nations but is not limited to them, so must we de-Islamize the juxtaposition of "the West and the Rest" so that no undue significance is given to the false binary of "Islam and the West." Closer attention to the economic forces of globalized capitalism/colonialism is a key factor in seeing how binary civilizational thinking has infused our reading of "nations."

If Greeks, Persians, and in fact Egyptians were so intimately intertwined within the larger Mediterranean culture, as they were, then when and how did the idea of "the West" emerge in opposition to "the Orient," and in turn how did that "Orient" become almost exclusively associated with Arabized "Islam"? The fact that there was a much larger, far more flexible Mediterranean exchange—in which the towering Jewish philosopher Maimonides wrote his magnum opus, *Guide for the Perplexed*, in order to place it in dialogue with Averroes and Al-Ghazali and through them with Aristotle—became an inconvenient fact in the making of this false binary, which emerged solely and entirely in the context of European imperialism. The conditions that facilitated the material foregrounding of capitalist modernity was so pervasive, so global in its abstraction of power of domination that it cast a long and distorting shadow over the entirety of human history, and nations and their histories were thus plotted within the falsifying binary of "Islam and the West."

Today, more than ever in living memory, "Islam" and "the West" appear as two principal forces set on a permanent collision course. Scholars and foreign affairs analysts ranging from Samuel Huntington, Francis Fukuyama, and Bernard Lewis to Gilles Keppel, Olivier Roy, and Niall Fergusson have written extensively on the historical and strategic encounters between "Islam" and "the West," or even "the West" and "the Rest." They have conflated Islam with Arabs, Arabs with all Muslims, categorically disregarding the instrumentality of the colonial encounter in which "the West" was manufactured as an ideological trope pitted against all its colonial sites (including but not only Muslims) to give it normative and moral authenticity and superiority. As all other mythical claims, these two colliding metaphors have repressed and/or forgotten their historical origins. Nations have been formed and presumed eternal, their usually illegitimate ruling states have been assumed representative, while the underlying material and ideological forces confining these countries within fixed boundaries has been ignored and the fact that the very formation of nations is transnational has been disregarded.[3]

In his now classic *Orientalism* (1978), Edward Said attributed the rise of this civilizational encounter to the ascendency of European colonialism and the concomitant cultural and academic knowledge production conducive to that relation of power. This colonial construct, he believed, normatively sustained the political superiority of "the West" over "the Orient" it had invented to rule. "The Orient," in other words, was a politically modulated discursive construct, the civilizational other of "the West," there to fantasize, conquer, exploit, and "civilize"—to beat into obedience. In his even earlier diagnosis, *Oriental Renaissance* (1950), Raymond Schwab, however, had an entirely different take; he considered the rise of European Orientalism as integral to the period in European intellectual history he termed "Oriental Renaissance," an eighteenth- and nineteenth-century movement that effectively augmented and expanded upon what in European historiography we call the "Renaissance" proper. In my recent study, *Persophilia* (2015), I offer a radically different perspective than both Said and Schwab, though obviously building on their respective insights. In this book, I have proposed the site of a European—and by extension non-European (India, China, Persia, more specifically)—bourgeois public sphere that was conducive to major social and intellectual movements with global consequences. From the European Enlightenment to Romanticism and even American Transcendentalism, I demonstrate, literary, poetic, and artistic elements from "Persia" were instrumental in the making of the most transformative events in European and, by extension, global history. I have offered the idea of a *parapublic sphere* as a location where colonized people have revolted against domestic tyranny and foreign domination at the same time. My purpose here has been to go beyond both Said and Schwab to look at "Orientalism" not as a site of cultural domination or exploitation, but in fact, quite paradoxically, definitive to the most consequential social and intellectual movements throughout the world. In other words, the European encounter with "the Orient" became definitive to groundbreaking and world historic changes both in Europe and by extension around the globe. This is a far different perspective than giving Europeans the sole agential power and "the Orientals" a passive receptivity without any agency. It places both Europe and non-Europe on the more consequential bourgeois public sphere on which major social and intellectual movements have been launched with far-reaching global consequences. These bourgeois public and subaltern parapublic spheres were not (and this is my main difference with both Said and Schwab) mere political accoutrements of power but, rather, the social consequences of the economic logic of the circulatory disposition of labor, raw material, market, and capital.

Persophilia was my first attempt at decoupling "the Orient and the Occident" as two adversarial sites prior to and subsequent to their colonial encounters by way of showing there is a tertiary space where "the West" and its manufactured alterities meet to create a whole new and very liberating set of critical occasions. In this book, I have offered a much deeper and wider historical viewpoint that transcends these radically contemporary perspectives. History has brought us to this cul-de-sac, and history will deliver us from it.

With hindsight we can see how Edward Said's insights were in fact very much animated by the Arab-Israeli conflict placed in a larger European colonial context, while Schwab's point of departure was to complicate our understanding of the European Renaissance by bringing a non-European, Indian in particular, element into our considerations. While Said's insights considerably advanced our understanding of European colonialism, they embedded his *Orientalism* in a largely Arab-centric and perforce a radical contemporaneity. While Schwab's insights deeply complicated our understanding of the social and intellectual history of the European Renaissance, they categorically disregarded the transnational public and para-public spheres on which such cultural developments had global consequences. Arabs and Muslims are relatively recent factors in the equation of "the West" and "the Rest." We have always been in need of a much longer historical context to assess this perception, a period in biblical historiography and classical antiquity when neither the Arabs nor in fact Islam even existed as the civilizational other of this "West," for "the West" itself did not yet exist as a potent metaphor. This wider angle will make it possible for us to see how very recent the fusion of "Islam and the West" has been.

Once we frame "Islam and the West" in a pre-Islamic and pre-Western context, as it were, we can mark the way to a post-Islamist and post-Western world that has already dawned upon us and is rapidly spreading its claim on our contemporary history. My purpose here is threefold: (1) to disentangle the false binary of "Islam and the West," (2) to re-historicize the relationship, and (3) to map out alternative trajectories of far more fluid historical cultures, an understanding of which is necessary in order to confront the urgent global issues of environmental catastrophes, perilous human migrations, and frightful pandemics without being bogged down by nervous preoccupations about supremacy and insurgence. Consider the fact that in his July 2017 visit to Poland, President Donald Trump, who had just withdrawn the United States from the Paris climate agreement and promised to ban Muslim immigration and build a wall on the US-Mexico border, once again flagged the battle between "Islam" and "the West" as the hallmark of his presidency.[4] It is precisely such catastrophic uses of the false binary that is deeply disconcerting and compels us to disengage it. Exposing the ideological roots and material conditions of economic exploitation and political domination of this binary are the preconditions of this dismantling that I have pursued in this book.

I have proposed that the false rivalry now presumed between "Islam" and "the West" is the end result of a flawed civilizational narrative present at the height of European colonial conquest and the rise of militant ideologies of resistance ranging from Islamist to Zionist to Hindu to Evangelical militancy. The "Islam and the West" narrative soon began to assimilate itself backward into history. One can easily pick and choose certain scattered memories of the Muslim conquest of Spain or the Crusades or even, anachronistically, the Greco-Roman encounters with Persian empires as evidence of such normative, moral, or even cosmic battles. Despite all his own warnings, Edward Said's *Orientalism* perhaps inadvertently exacerbated that false binary. The result has been a dangerous geography that pits the illusion of "Islam" against the illusion of "the West" in a faux Manichean battle with catastrophic consequences. Dismantling this situation requires precise historical recollections.

Persian Empire as a Prototype

Let me now be more specific: When Alexander the Great (356–323 BC) conquered and put an end to the Persian Empire, he entered the fertile soil of Persian literary imagination until such point where the master epic poet Ferdowsi (940–1020) gave him the last word as he brought the heroic age of classical antiquity to an end and commenced the historical epoch of his and our own time. What is the fictionalized character of the historical Alexander the Great doing in a Persian epic—especially under such loving and ennobling light? Ferdowsi did for the Macedonian world conqueror what Xenophon did for Cyrus the Great, Alexander's model! How did that happen? Was "the Orient" always the "Orient"? When did "the Orient" become "the Orient," and "the West" "the West" such that we were told "the twain shall never meet"? Why would Alexander the conqueror of Persia become Alexander the chief protagonist of Persian epics and romances? Why are moments of effervescent cultural fusions around the Mediterranean Sea, revealing alternative historical maps, now completely forgotten or camouflaged? Partially responsible for distorting and simplifying the complicated history of the world is a decidedly wrongheaded misreading of Edward Said's seminal work *Orientalism*, where a critical assessment of a mode of European colonial knowledge production is wrongly extended to exacerbate the presumed civilizational demarcations between "Islam" and "the West" even before Islam had entered the historical stage or "the West" had been coined as a civilizational cornerstone of world history. I contend that we can correct this abusive historiography by looking to the place of Persia, China, or India—integral as they have been to European self-understanding—doing so not to mark "influence" but to map alternative topographies of knowledge, sentiments, and culture.

Since the biblical age and then Greek antiquity, what today we call Iran but Europeans knew as "Persia" (as did Arabs, who called it "al-Furs") has been a site of consistent "European" fascination and fantasy—feared, envied, emulated, rejected, copied, and cursed, but never ignored. I place "European" in quotation marks because the term itself and what it means is a gradual historical product. Neither Arabia, nor India, nor even China has had as long an antiquity as Persia in the European imaginary. The extended shadow of the

Persian empires, particularly the Achaemenids (550–330 BC), on both Greek antiquity and before it the Hebrew Bible marks the longest physical and metaphoric presence of "Persia" in what would later be called "Europe" as we understand it today. Imagining Persia was not just something that Europeans did. Imagining Persia is what made Europe "Europe." The figure of the "Persian" has always been a familiar foreigner in the ever-expansive European imagination, near its geographical neighborhood but kept far from its changing sensibilities, known to its normative parameters, but made alien to its own evolving political purposes. At every major critical juncture in European (and subsequently North American) history, the figure of "the Persian" and the land of "Persia" have provided the self-centering metaphor of "Europe" with ample allegories to envision and reinvent itself.

The attraction of Europe to Persia was primarily because of its place in the Bible and then its imperial heritage—from the Achaemenids down to the Sassanids, contemporaneous with the Greeks and the Romans, respectively, in the European chronology of itself. These empires were known to Europe from the Bible and Greek and Roman sources. It was precisely the imperial pedigree of the Achaemenids, and their domination in a global and regional context that included Europe, that had made them significant both in the Bible and for the Greek and Roman antiquities. The Book of Esther, where King Ahasuerus/Xerxes has a key role, is usually dated to the third or fourth century BC, while Aeschylus's *The Persians* was composed and performed in 472 BC, and Xenophon's *Cyropaedia* was composed circa 370 BC. Imagine that historical expanse from Athens to Jerusalem and you'll have a sense of the place of Persia in the very origin of European self-perception. In the biblical and classical ages and texts—Hebrew, Greek, and Latin—Persia and Persians were familiar foreigners, neither Hebrew, nor Greek nor Roman, nor a fortiori Christian, and yet they were a dominant imperial order with their own Zoroastrian, Manichean, and Mazdakian antiquities. The Persians were never complete strangers, and thus they could not be categorically estranged and "othered." Persians were known to Europeans before Europeans knew themselves as "Europeans." Indeed they were known long before the rise of Islam and Christianity—and therefore not as Muslims or Arabs. This distinction is critical if we are to de-fetishize this ahistorical bifurcation between "Islam" and "the West." In his magisterial text *Orientalism*, Edward Said almost completely disregards this crucial factor and pays very little to no attention to the Chinese, Indian, or particularly Persian presence in the European imaginary. He is almost entirely Arab-centric in his legitimate critical stance vis-à-vis "the West." His enduring insights in his *Orientalism* are contingent on that blindness.

Of all the ancient cultures (China, India, and Egypt), Persia and the Persian Empire were of particular interest to Europeans in their age of empire building, especially through their own remembrance of Alexander the Great. With the publication of Montesquieu's *Persian Letters* (1721), however, the figure of the Persian as a familiar foreigner enters the European age of Enlightenment, of capitalist modernity proper. In this seminal work, the two traveling Persians, Usbek and Rica, are foreigners who are familiar with the changing Europe. The proverbial question asked in this book, "What does it mean to be Persian?," is really in reverse. It means to ask: "What does it mean to be European?"—which is the central question of Montesquieu's entire philosophical project as one of the key architects of Enlightenment modernity. It is crucial for us to keep this figure of the inquisitive Persian in mind at this inaugural moment of European modernity as we witness the eventual rise and expansion of the European bourgeois public sphere. Montesquieu's *Persian Letters* therefore is not just a piece of Orientalism. It is also the evidence of trying to define Europe as "Europe" at the crucial crucible of Enlightenment modernity. As thus Europe defines itself in non-Persian terms, Persians define themselves in non-European terms. The two have become the yin and yang of each other.

What is extraordinary here is how (on the model of the Persian embracing of Alexander) many times in the course of European Enlightenment modernity we witness the multiple transfusion of the Persian and the European into one speaking soul. The linguistic and philological theories of William Jones (1746–1794), the eminent Indo-Iranian philologist of his time, made those foreign Persians more familiar to the Enlightenment age. Jones took a Persian name—"Jones-e Oksfordi/Jones from Oxford"—and capitalized on a theory that categorized Persian as an Indo-European language. Persian-speaking people around the world woke up one day and discovered that, unbeknownst to themselves, they were really speaking a European language! The philological theory of Indo-European languages had of course nasty racial undertones that later went on to wreak havoc in Europe, but it still managed to create an elective affinity among Europeans, Indians, and the Persian-speaking world, including Iranians. These crucial moments in the history of European modernity punctured the assumption of a sustained hostility between "Islam" and "the West."

Given the predominance of Iran in the regional and global geopolitics where the country is incessantly over-Islamized in a particularly Shi'i context, it is hard to imagine—but necessary to do so—a time when Persian and German poets were integral to a whole different topography of sentiments and emotions. We now need to recall how soon successive pairs of European and Persian poets and literati came together to form a veritable duet—as did Goethe (1749–1832) and Hafez (1325–1389), for example, defining German Romanticism in terms domestic to a liberated geography far beyond the intellectual cul-de-sac of "Islam and the West." Goethe furthered the course of familiarizing the foreign Persians through his attraction to and rendition into German of the towering Persian poet Hafez and composing lyrical poetry in his fashion. Soon many other European Hafezes were created on the model of Goethe. Hegel (1770–1831) comes right after that and brings Persians into the fold of world history, where in Persian empires Europeans feel already at home. Through his philosophy of history Hegel makes Persians further at home in the historical habitat of Europeans. But Hegel still denies these Persians and the rest of "Orientals" any possibility of thinking. For him, Persians were not capable of philosophy. So Goethe and Hegel complement each other—sustaining the familiar foreigners, as both European and yet not completely so, and therefore inhabitants of a tertiary space that holds them together. The task of bringing Persia and Persians into the philosophical space will have to wait for a while. At this point Goethe's discovery of Hafez's poetry, centuries after the death of the Persian poet, has a profound and enduring impact on the character and disposition of German romanticism. Keep in mind that with Goethe and Hafez we are right in the heart of German Romanticism at the epicenter of European poetic revolt against rigid Enlightenment rationalism.

Ralph Waldo Emerson (1803–1882) and Sa'di (circa 1210–1292) would soon follow in Goethe's and Hafez's footsteps as yet another pair of poets across continents and centuries, categorically dismantling the fake bifurcation between "Islam and the West." Just as the preeminent Indo-Pakistani thinker Muhammad Iqbal (1877–1938) took Goethe's version of Hafez from Germany (where he was a doctoral student) to India and added Rumi and Dante to it and turned it into the cornerstone of his Pan-Islamism and renewed interest in Islamic philosophy, North American Transcendentalism took the same European Romanticism to America and led to Ralph Waldo Emerson (1803–1882) considering himself a reincarnation of Sa'di, another iconic Persian poet. Upon the expansive domain of the European bourgeois public sphere, Persia and Persians were now towering historical metaphors. Rumi (1207–1273) and his American translators Coleman Bark and Robert Bly would replicate the self-same reincarnations generations later. Again, the point is not to mark the *influence* of one poet on another between East and West— but to mark the compelling common space that such pairs create to craft a tertiary space, where the binary opposition between East and West has already disappeared.

This consistent Persophilia, meanwhile, remained integral to the rise of the most provocative ideas and philosophies in Europe. From the bosom of the Hegelian denial of Oriental philosophy emerged Nietzsche's reincarnation of the Persian prophet Zarathustra combined with his love and admiration for Hafez—so that his prophet, which is a combination of an imaginative Zoroaster and a Germanic rendition of Hafez, becomes the new European figure of philosophical revolt. The historic revolt of Nietzsche against the whole Platonic tradition of philosophy culminating in Hegel in his seminal book *Thus Spoke Zarathustra* (1883–1885) assumes the symbolic force of two Persian figures (a prophet and a poet): Zarathustra and Hafez, who in the German philosopher's mind mutate into a singular force of Dionysian revolt. Edward Said's *Orientalism* cannot begin to address this figure of a Persian prophetic/poetic allegory at the heart of the most revolutionary European philosopher of his time. What part of that is "Orientalism" in the sense of knowledge at the service of European colonial interest? In Nietzsche's subversive philosophy Persia and Persians further expand their inroads into European critical consciousness. In the philosophical subversion of the Platonic tradition, so consequential in the aftermath of Nietzsche all the way to the philosophical works of Heidegger and Derrida, two seminal Persian figures, Zoroaster and Hafez, become definitive, as similar figures in the formation of German Romanticism. Where exactly is "Islam and the West" here—as a pre-Islamic Persian prophet and a Muslim poet (Hafez's name means "the one who has memorized the Qur'an") become definitive to a key philosophic moment in Europe?

The transnational bourgeois public sphere is where these world-historic intellectual movements are taking place.

Examples abound and each offers a whole new spectrum of the Persian presence in the most progressive and provocative aspects of European arts, literature, poetry, and philosophy during the most revolutionary age in Europe, such as in Mozart's daring and pathbreaking opera *The Magic Flute* (1791), where again the figure of Sarastro/Zoroaster has a key and transformative role. Meanwhile, Edward FitzGerald (1809–1883) became the reincarnation of yet another Persian poet when he published his Rubaiyat of Omar Khayyam as a counter-Victorian poet for "the other Victorians," as literary historian Steven Marcus would say in his seminal work *The Other Victorians: A Study of Sexuality and Pornography in Mid-Nineteenth-Century England* (1964). This Khayyam offers a de-gendered homoeroticism to Europeans that suspends both ecclesiastical and worldly authorities and opts for an erotic asceticism that not only best fits FitzGerald's own mostly repressed homosexuality but also dovetails with a kind of Protestant ethics at the heart of both European capitalism and British imperialism. The global popularity of Omar Khayyam in effect follows the footsteps of British colonialism—they go together. In the poetic persona of Omar Khayyam, FitzGerald produces a new European prophet not quite unlike Goethe's Hafez and Nietzsche's Zarathustra—all varied models of Dionysian revolt against Christian bourgeois ethics and its underlying ressentiment. Take Persia and these European "Persians Prophets" away from Europe at these crucial stages and something serious in all such spectacular social and intellectual movements collapses. The two tropes of "Persia" and "Europe" here are not antagonistic. They are metamorphic. On that metamorphic space we witness the most compelling and transformative changes on the transnational bourgeois public sphere.

Soon Matthew Arnold (1822–1888) too would find his way into the Persian epic poet Ferdowsi's soul. In Arnold's turn to Persian poetry, manifested in his classic poem "Sohrab and Rostam" (1853), he went for the anti-Oedipal trace, putting into his own poetry the famous epic *Shahnameh* by the tenth-century Persian poet Ferdowsi, where the chief hero, Rostam, inadvertently kills his own son—and thus the earliest origin of Arnold's major essay "Culture and Anarchy" (1869), which would make little sense without paying attention to the cultural paradox at the heart of this seminal poem. In his famous phrase on culture, that it is "the best which has been thought and said in the world," there is a worldliness about Arnold that defies any false civilizational divide. In Arnold's cornerstone bifurcation between the "Indo-European race" and "any Oriental and polygamous nation like the Hebrews," Ferdowsi's *Shahnameh* was a breed apart. It is from here and other European *Shahnameh* scholarship that a renewed interest in the Persian epic eventually goes back to Iran to the Pahlavi state-building monarchy and the recruiting of Ferdowsi for a forced formation of "the fatherland," a violent twisting of the central trauma of the *Shahnameh* that has systematically abused the epic to this day.[5] But the more important point here is how upon a transnational public sphere Persian classics were being re-canonized, and how Arnold and Ferdowsi became kindred souls in a seminal moment in both European and Muslim cultural histories. There is scarcely a poetic text more seminal to the formation of modern Iran as a nation-state, and yet its contemporary canonization was a decidedly cosmopolitan proposition formed on a transnational public sphere.

My assessment of the end of "Islam and the West" with a specific reference to Persophilia as a particular twist to Orientalism is therefore markedly different from the mere detection of the illusion of "the West" as precisely that—an illusion. At least since Edward Said's *Orientalism* (1978) we have known that "the West" is a productive metaphoric illusion, despite the fact that his primary concern was not with "the West" itself but with its ideological consequences on "the Orient." But even before Said, the Jamaican critical thinker Donald Hinds in his bold and beautiful book *Journey to an Illusion: The West Indian in Britain* (1966) had detailed the contours of this illusion from an entirely different angle. After Said, writers like Kwame Anthony and Seyla Benhabib have mapped out ideas of cosmopolitanism that underlie the centrality of this reproductive illusion. But perhaps more pointedly than all of them, Walter Mignolo in his brilliant text *The Darker Side of Renaissance* (1992) reveals the hidden side of this epistemic catalyst of colonial knowledge production. What these and many others have missed, however, is how the pairing of "Islam" and "the West" has also been a devious decoy concealing the place of pre-Islamic "Persia" as the hidden desire of imperial Europe, its secret wish, its political blueprint—a fact evident at least since Xenophon's *Cyropaedia* (circa 370 BC) and even before that in Aeschylus's *The Persians* (472 BC). What this much later European camouflaging of "Persia," the historic nucleus of its own ressentiment, reveals is the structural consolidation of its own repressive regime of desires, while what it has actually unleashed in the Persian reception of that desire is a Dionysian outburst of energies otherwise hidden to the naked eyes of this delusional abstraction dominant in the European bourgeois consciousness.

The Adventures of James Morier of Smyrna

The experience of "Persia" as hidden imperial desire, though, is not entirely unprecedented. The notorious cable TV show *Shahs of Sunset* (2012–) had its antecedent in James Morier's nasty Orientalist picaresque *Adventures of Haji Baba of Isfahan* (1824). In the capable hands of its Persian translator Mirza Habib Isfahani, however, this colonial cliché buffoonery was turned around into a cornerstone text of the Constitutional Revolution (1906–1911).[6] Mirza Habib Isfahani's habitat for that feat of literary rendition was Istanbul, the remissive cosmopolitan space between the changing Europe and turbulent Iran, the space where European Persophilia yielded to the constitutional revolution of 1906–1911 and Morier's Orientalist prose inadvertently produced the Persian revolutionary discourse of Mirza Habib Isfahani. The Persian translator had happily infiltrated the nasty soul of the English colonial officer and transformed it inside out into a cause of revolutionary good in his own homeland. Examples abound, but the point is simple and consistent: the fictional binary "Islam and the West" does irreparable epistemic violence to the historical facts and sustained truth of ulterior spaces beyond and above such misconceptions where realities have mapped out a far different geography for our contemporary history. James Morier's *Adventures of Haji Baha of Isfahan* was a vicious piece of European Orientalism. Its Persian translation was a seminal text in the course of the Iranian Constitutional Revolution. That paradox is where the wisdom of overcoming both Orientalism and "Islam and the West" resides.

There is another lesson in the unanticipated consequences of a colonial fiction. The fictive character in James Morier's *Adventures of Haji Baha of Isfahan* becomes a real literary historian, as E. G. Browne (1862–1926), who goes back to Iran to offer Iranians an enduring gift. Browne was the European figure of Persophilia incarnate closely familiar with that figurative foreigner. His travelogue to Iran is the complete reversal of Morier's literary racism. As a literary historian, Browne's monumental four-volume *A Literary History of Persia* (1902–1924) emerged as a key text in the transnational canonization of Persian literary humanism and the process of postcolonial nation-building.[7] He was closely affiliated with such leading Iranian literati as Mohammad Qazvini, Seyyed Hassan Taghizadeh, and Mohammad Ali Jamalzadeh, and such leading periodicals as *Kaveh* and *Iranshahr* that were laying the foundations of the emerging literary public sphere upon which Iran as a postcolonial nation was founded. Upon that public sphere, Persophilia was a common trope of a familiar foreigner holding any assumption of "West versus East" tightly under erasure.

The cycle of European Persophilia comes to a contemporary crescendo with the French Islamicist Henry Corbin's (1903–1978) journey from his youthful fixation with Martin Heidegger to Iran to translate (with remarkable scholarly tenacity) his attraction to the German mystical philosophy into Shi'i Gnosticism. In Iran, Corbin had become the French reincarnation of his beloved Persian philosopher Shahab al-Din Yahya Suhrawardi (circa 1154–1191), with the same fascination evident in another French scholar, Louis Massignon, for Hussein ibn Mansour al-Hallaj, as evident in his monumental book *La passion de Hussayn Ibn Mansur an-Hallaj* (1975)—effectively translating his own Catholic fascination with Jesus Christ onto a Muslim mystic. Corbin's major project, fully funded by the Pahlavi royal court, was successfully resisted by the appeal of the Italian Marxist thinker Antonio Gramsci to the far more potent force of such leading public intellectuals as Jalal Al-e Ahmad, as it was by the streak of rebellious Dionysian joy of Nietzsche flowing in the robust veins of the defiant poetry of Forough Farrokhzad and Ahmad Shamlou and other similar poets. All of that Dionysian revolt fell on its face in the aftermath of the Islamist takeover of the Iranian revolution of 1979, when Iranians became foreigners to their own familiarity, awaiting a renewal and resurrection of an entirely different vintage. The point here is to see how major European scholars like Corbin or Massignon or Ignaz Goldziher had become integral to Islamic intellectual history far beyond a passing Orientalist curiosity. A committed and proud Jew, Goldziher in fact intellectually identified with his Muslim interlocutor's past and present.[8]

This entirely natural but now repressed pairing of a Persian and a European poet or thinker progressed apace—and thus made the very formation of the ideas of "Europe" and "Iran" integral to each "there." Staging playfully the familiar foreignness of the Persian becomes the uncanny sight of a soprano castrato (now done by a mezzosoprano or countertenor) singing the mighty Xerxes in Handel's *Serse* (1738). The Persophiliac opera anticipates Nietzsche's critique of Wagner, in *Nietzsche contra Wagner* (1895), and his denouncing of *Parsifal* as the triumph of asceticism over sensuality generations later. The fascination of Matisse and Gauguin with Persian paintings extended that early operatic Persophilia into the groundbreaking sights of European artistic revolutions of the nineteenth and twentieth centuries. The mirror image of all this soon appeared on the Iranian cultural scenes. Where exactly was this presumed animosity between "Islam and the West" in the midst of all these groundbreaking events in European and Iranian cultural history? Nowhere. The same arguments can be made about Europe and China, or Europe and India, or Europe and ancient Egypt. The crucial point here is not to suggest Europeans were totally enamored of Persians, Indians, Egyptians, or Chinese. The point is to identify the European bourgeois public sphere when it becomes transnational and upon which all of these "Oriental" resonances (Persian or otherwise) became integral to the structural transformation of a revolutionary class that by being the vanguard of global capitalism carried its cultural preoccupations around the world.

The cultural interplay among nations and their cherished heritage intensified during the Enlightenment period and reached contradictory ends during European colonial encounters with the world. Undoing the military narrative of a sustained hostility between "Islam and the West" is therefore necessary but not sufficient. The enduring cultural proximity of multiple nations in and around the Mediterranean regions speaks of alternative sites of reality, alterity, and identity. Once we specify the grand narrative of "Orientalism" to the European interest in sites such as Persia, India, or China, such cultural interplays come into full view and we see how in fact the very idea of "Europe" or "the West," as we understand and use these terms today, is entirely rooted in cultural interstices that are neither exclusively "Western" nor "Eastern." It is such sites "in-between" what today we have imagined as civilizational divides that completely dismantle the assumption of those divides. Here we come to realize how the very notions of "Europe" and "the West" are in fact so thoroughly contingent on historical developments outside the imaginative geography of what today we consider "Europe" or "the West." The Arab-centrism of Said's reading of Orientalism need not be matched or augmented by Chinese- or Indian- or Persian-centric corrections, but in fact by corrective lenses that override all such manufactured civilizational divides that play into the hands of cross-authenticating the myth of "the West" and all its alterities. What we witness on such geographical and cultural interstices is not the habitual claims of "influence," that Indian, Persian, or Chinese cultures have "influenced the West." Any such cliché claim will in fact corroborate and exacerbate the assumption of a civilizational divide between "Islam and the West." The point is rather to mark social and intellectual spaces upon which different visions of the world were articulated above and beyond any such false divides.

Among these visionary alterities are the occasions of Europeans coveting imperial blueprints, as evident in their multifaceted Persophilia. What in effect I am proposing here, which is entirely hidden to the camouflage of "Islam and the West" or "the West and the Rest," is the counterintuitive discovery that such anxiety-laden pairings have served as a deceptive smokescreen obscuring the place of "Persia" as the truly desired imperial other of Europe. This realization in turn procures a potent Nietzschean Dionysian revival of rebellious energies that have been repressed by the false abstractions and exploitative operations of the European bourgeois fantasies.

One Last Word

The task of overcoming both Islamism and Westernism as the twin by-products of colonial modernity must begin and dwell on those critical moments in race, gender, class, and national formations when all the received Muslim epistemics of knowledge production come face-to-face with the imperial reality of a colonial encounter with the master metaphor of "the West." The trope of "the West" had once enabled but now has depleted itself and all its alterities as its others, and now leads a parasitical life in the mind and fury of racist pockets of resistance to reason and sanity. If we have inherited the Islamic metaphysics, the sum total of its scholasticism and humanism, from the moment of a precolonial encounter in the wide spectrum of Muslim intellectual history, over the last two hundred years, then that metaphysics has positively degenerated into the fateful encounter and subsequent exhaustion of that triumphalist revolt of one final victory over "the West"—the figment of its own imagination—at all costs. The battle was delusional and self-defeating. Muslims today are liberated from the delusions of Islamism that "the West" cross-authenticated.

The question of why there is a God instead of no God is not meant to solicit any answer—but to suspend the inaugural moment when theology commences and seeks to answer itself in history. The question is no longer a theological question and thus as an ontic pause can hold the entire course of Islamic metaphysics—from its scholasticism to its humanism—at bay. In the same vein, when Heidegger questioned and dismantled what he called "Western metaphysics" by asking the bizarre question of why is there something instead of nothing, we might rethink the question of "nothing" in other (non-European, non-Greco-Roman, or Greco-Christian) contexts by wondering what happens to the nature of thinking when the metaphysical gridlock of Muslim thought comes to a standstill with European colonial modernity or with what calls itself "the West." Liberation from "Islam and the West" is the moment when the metaphysics of post-Islamism and post-Westernism both at one and the same time announce themselves.

The question of Arab, Iranian, Muslim, Asian, African, or Latin American modernity is categorically misplaced. Today, as we bid the colonial project of European modernity farewell, those Arab, Iranian, Muslim, African, etcetera modernities do not, nor could they, stand for any ethnic, linguistic, or metaphysical authenticity or underpinning of identity. Today, as the European project of modernity self-destructs and implodes—somewhere between the Holocaust and colonial savagery, the two towering calamities of this European project—those Iranians, Turks, Armenians, Kurds, etcetera can only stand for the generated and sustained shared memories of resistances to European and now US imperial power. It is their will to resist power—not the will to power—that makes the postcolonial world what it is and turns the site of "the Rest of the World" into a citation. Moreover, the question and crisis of modernity are historically and epistemically exclusively European phenomena, and the world at large has nothing to do with them except when it seeks to tabulate an inventory of its miseries. But the critique of colonial modesty is no longer a necessary or even legitimate project. The paramount project at hand is the critique of Muslim metaphysics, a moral and imaginative reassessment of where and wherefore we are in the world, free from the delusion of "the West" that had for a very long time colonized our minds.

Today I am convinced that fortunately there is no pure anything. "The West" was never just "the West" except for the lunatic fringe of the racist reading of world history, nor indeed was "Islam" ever just Islam pure and simple, except in the murderous minds of militant criminals like ISIS who keep European and other racists determined in their racism. For the overwhelming majority of the rest of us, the happy and healthy body of humanity at large, a part of our Selves has positively been an Other. In this active splitting of our entire selves into others, all the inherited binaries of colonial modernity have self-destructed—and we are all more liberated and enabled by it. It was the crucial task of my lifelong scholarship and critical thinking once and for all to put an end to the dual delusions of "Islam and the West."

Conclusion

"The Inverted Consciousness of the World"

Alice laughed: "There's no use trying," she said; "one can't believe impossible things." "I daresay you haven't had much practice," said the Queen. "When I was younger, I always did it for half an hour a day. Why, sometimes I've believed as many as six impossible things before breakfast."

LEWIS CARROLL, *Alice's Adventures in Wonderland* (1865)

Time to sum up—and learn from the Queen in *Alice's Adventures in Wonderland* how she believed "as many as six impossible things before breakfast." In this book I have put forward the proposition that the constitution of "Islam and the West" as a civilizational divide was a colonial concoction, an ideological chimera, a mode of false consciousness that centers "the West" (where capital is believed to have accumulated) and marginalizes "the Rest" (where cheap labor and raw material are thought to be located). Both capital and its abused labor and ravaged earth, however, are global and rapidly globalizing; neither has any center or periphery. Abused labor and raw material also exist in "the West," and accumulated capital and the rich and powerful classes it entails abound in "the Rest." Thus constituted,

the binary has then been falsely and ahistorically assimilated backward into time immemorial. Suddenly Plato has become a "Western
philosopher," and the *Bhagavad Gita* an "Oriental epic." This relatively recent ideological concoction, however, has been rooted in the
material forces of capital, labor, raw material, and markets. At work
has been the accumulated capital that required a normative center and correspondingly the dispersed labor and raw material that
were at the service of that accumulated capital. "Islam and the West"
was perhaps the most potent component of "the West and the Rest"
that facilitated and enabled the operation of that relation of power.
I have also put forward the argument that we are no longer trapped
at the moment of simply pointing out the abusive mode of knowledge production called "Orientalism" that this "West" had crafted
about "the East," about "the Orient," about "Islam." The far more
urgent and liberating task of moving forward and thinking, knowing,
and being beyond this trap has in fact been long at work. This is not
mere wishful thinking, or political positioning, or counterargument
against the lingering ideologues of "the West." This is based on the
fact of the dissolution of any center for the operation of accumulated
capital or any fixed continental location for abused labor and raw
material. Massive labor and refugee migrations, global pandemics
such as COVID-19, and the dismemberment of the planetary environment are among the indices of the disappearance of any meaningful
and authoritative "Western" Self to craft any stable Other to believe
in Itself. Donald Trump tried to do in the United States what Abdel
Fattah el-Sisi did in Egypt and before him Augusto Pinochet in Chile.
The streets of Seattle and Ferguson and New York in 2020 looked
like the streets of Buenos Aires and Alegria or Myanmar during their
military coups.

Two towering critical thinkers stand tall in our reading of the
colonial construction of all forms of selves and others. Edward Said
(1935–2003) in his *Orientalism* (1978) and before him Frantz Fanon

(1925–1961) in his *Wretched of the Earth* (1961) have radically challenged such colonial constructs and altered our reading of any allegorical relation of power assumed between the colonizer and the colonized. As critical thinkers, Said and Fanon were the products of colonial cultures that had dominated their births and upbringings, Said's in Palestine and Fanon's in Martinique. For one, the British colonial domination of the Arab world was the defining moment of colonialism, and for the other the French domination of the Caribbean had a similar importance. The *theoretical* insights of Said and Fanon were therefore paradoxically coterminous with their *historical* blind spots. They could both see so sharply what was so close to them for they had blurred out of their sight what to them appeared to be too far away. Any corrective lenses put upon their enduring insights will have to bring the history they had to repress more into focus. They were both too much in the trenches of critical encounter with European colonialism to see the deeper historical roots of such encounters or the emerging paths of epistemic liberation they were instrumental in opening beyond their own insights.

To disengage "Islam" and "the West" at the stage of their entanglement, I needed necessarily to pick up from where Edward Said ended in *Orientalism* and seek to reorient our historical consciousness. It is crucial now to remember that Edward Said was an intellectual product of the Arab-Israeli conflict and his *Orientalism* very much the result of the animus between the 1967 and 1973 wars. His theorization of Orientalism, pathbreaking as it was, was almost entirely oblivious to any serious sense of history prior to the rise of European colonialism in the eighteenth and nineteenth centuries, and perforce was limited specifically to the colonial encounter between crumbling Muslim empires and rising European imperialism. Said was no historian. He was a towering literary theorist with an ingenious ability to theorize and universalize the unjust dispossession of Palestinians, wedding it to larger colonial contexts. Even within such contexts, Said was fixated within the Arab nationalist animus against the continued carnage of European colonialism. His global references to other parts of Asia, Africa, and Latin America have been justly influential in the rise of postcolonial thinking. But they have at the same time categorically contorted our historical consciousness of the fateful encounter. While Said's fixation with a particular phase of European imperialism in the Arab world is perfectly logical and points to a serious site of colonial contestation, it also summons a much more multifaceted historical reality into a potent but limited nexus of identity politics and subject formation. The radical contemporaneity of the Arab-centrism of Said, in short, replicated the Eurocentricism of his ideological nemesis and radically de-historicized the longevity and globality of the encounter.

Between Fanon's critique of colonialism and Said's critique of Orientalism there is a third space, a neglected historical hiatus that is not fixated with either the place of "the Orient" in "the Western" imagination or with the place of "the West" in the captured colonized mind of the world at large; instead, it is a space in which "values," in Nietzsche's words, are "transvalued" and the full force of what he theorized as ressentiment has come to light. This ressentiment is a tango, a danse macabre in which the partners have in their recent history defined each other in each other's distorting mirror. We should not be concerned with those false mirror images but with the reality of that danse macabre itself, which needs to stop. My principal proposal here is that we are way past the point of pointing a finger at the "the West" from a location that is ipso facto its fabricated "Orient." The more we point a finger at "the West" from precisely the fictive space it has created ("the East," "the Orient," "Islam"), the more we corroborate it and thus fetishize beyond recognition our own alienated selves. Europhobia, in other words, is the worst kind of Eurocentricism. We must stop cross-authenticating that fictive location, which is paradoxically the most enduring legacy of Edward Said's critical thinking. No matter how you do the finger pointing, and how deconstructive you might think you are, you are, in effect, counter-essentializing the two components of the false binary, corroborating and thus authenticating them. The time is long overdue to step out of that bicameral cul-de-sac and dismantle the whole worldview that keeps spinning around to catch its own tail, pointing fingers that in effect mark its own dead end. "Islam" and "the West" are not two separate but one bifocal metaphor, created and sustained under conditions of coloniality. To dismantle that metaphor, we need to actively historicize it and show that it has now finally overcome itself. We must, in short, dismantle "Islam and the West" as a single allegorical trope, and stop pointing a finger at "the West" for having misrepresented "Islam." "The West" did not misrepresent "Islam." "The West" coinvented an "Islam" best suited to serve its colonial interests by sustaining the illusion of its own civilizational superiority. This dual false consciousness was not merely a product of a sense of racial superiority; it was also a requirement of the economics of robbing continents of their wealth and wherewithal.

To dismantle this false binary for good, as well as to achieve a more detailed reading of history, we also need a more liberatory theory, or a more theoretically critical conception of history, which requires a shift from the condition of coloniality not just toward postcolonialism but also, far more importantly, toward a moral and imaginative decoloniality, where we reverse the false historical consciousness of an imperial imagination that has overwhelmed the geographical divides we have been led to take for granted.[1] Any and all acts of decolonization are entirely contingent on dismantling all such civilizational divides as "Islam and the West," "the First and the Third World," "the West and the Rest," in all of which the ruling ideological powers of the world have robbed continents of their material and labor resources and the centrality of their place in the world and have rendered them second-rate inhabitants in their own worldliness—or, in my terms, the "Islam" of the "Islam and the West" was always already a figment of a colonial imagination. Without de-fetishizing "the West," which has fetishized all its others, none of those fetishized others, particularly Islam, will ever resume their moral and material historicalities.

Why Decolonized History Matters

To achieve this de-fetishization of a fictional "West," historicity must come to the fore to dismantle the myth of civilizational divides. To put an end to the disorienting power of the assumption of such civilizational divides, we must collapse the binary upon itself. Though long in the making, the intensity of the hostility presumed between "Islam" and "the West" reaches a newly alarming pitch every time there is a global crisis between the United States and its European allies on one hand and the population of a Muslim land on the other. This dominant and distorting discourse disregards all other colonial and postcolonial conditions, and the debilitating democratic deficiencies and consequent calamities they have created. Consider a Muslim revolutionary figure like Jamal al-Din al-Afghani (1838–1897) and ask yourself if his life and career as a widely popular transnational public intellectual matches the fixed opposition we assume between Muslims and non-Muslims. Afghani was an Iranian Shi'i who pretended to be a Sunni who hailed from Afghanistan. He systematically and consistently assumed varied identities in order to appeal to multiple audiences. He gathered some significant Muslim followers from India to Iran to Ottoman territories, before he traveled to Europe and engaged in philosophical debates with his European contemporaries, and in doing so he became definitive to his post-imperial Muslim world. Figures like Afghani, who are representative of many more, are the historical evidence of a world we have now systematically erased and overwritten under the false binary of "Islam and the West."

Disregarding such facts, perhaps no other ideologue has done more than the late Bernard Lewis (1916-2018), most emphatically in his *What Went Wrong? The Clash between Islam and Modernity in the Middle East* (2002), to posit "Islam" and "the West" as two irreconcilably opposite entities: cultural, civilizational, moral, and normative. Based on Lewis's ideas, Samuel Huntington later developed his notion of "the clash of civilizations" (1992), which was also predicated on a similar notion of the triumphant victory of "the West" that Huntington's student Francis Fukuyama had prematurely declared in his *End of History* thesis (1989) soon after another of his teachers, Alan Bloom, had mourned the decline of "the West" in *Closing of the American Mind* (1987). Compared to these senior scholars, Niall Fergusson is a relative newcomer, whose hefty volumes have exacerbated that tension and hostility between "Islam" and "the West" by upping the ante in books like *Civilization: The West and the Rest* (2012). The binary was and remains so powerful that even the master of deconstruction, the French philosopher Jacques Derrida, fell into its trap when sitting for a conversation that would later appear as *Islam and the West: A Conversation with Jacques Derrida* (2008). The active hostility is therefore not something presumed merely on the daily headlines. It extends deeply into the scholarly and intellectual debates of our time. Predicated on bad history, the metaphors assume allegorical and even philosophical power.

To be sure, in the more recent scholarship that categorical binary has been studied in far more critical terms and its underlying assumptions exposed and discredited. The publication of two significant books in 2015 marks a turning tide in the understanding of Islam as the doppelgänger of something beyond its own internal dynamics and history. Predicated on the groundbreaking work of Edward Said, Sophia Rose Arjana's *Muslims in the Western Imagination* (2015) and Joseph Massad's *Islam in Liberalism* (2015) bring out the place of Muslims and Islam in the making of "Western liberalism." These two polemical books and the body of scholarship they best represent are markedly positioned against the sort of scholarship represented by Bernard Lewis, Samuel Huntington, and Niall Fergusson. Arjana's and Massad's studies expose the central significance of "Islam" as a definitive trope that has enabled the fictive fetish of "the West." Their books are studies in kind. They reciprocate argument by argument and document how "Islam" has been essentialized into an antagonistic trope, but stop short of taking "Islam" out of the scare quotation marks and placing it in its own historical dynamics. Two ancillary tasks remained: (1) taking "Islam" and "the West" into two respective historical domains that demythologize and historicize what they refer to and designate, and (2) subjecting the very "Islam and the West" binary itself to deconstructive scrutiny to overcome its corrosive power.

It is imperative to note here that without the groundbreaking work of Edward Said and some of his most prominent followers and students—like Joseph Massad, Gauri Viswanathan, Amir Mufti, Sophia Rose Arjana, and others—we would not even be in a position to write a book like what I have written here. But the issues that Said and his followers have raised have persisted and morphed into new directions, which require fresher and even more critical angles. In addition to Said, by academic training I am drawn to Marx and Freud as two other seminal thinkers whose works are definitive to the way I think and write.

The kinds of deconstructive gestures that Edward Said and his followers have made, crucial as they have been in their time, have also paradoxically (not intentionally) strengthened the metaphoric power of "the West" and thus critically compromised the path ahead for an entirely different mode of emancipatory thinking that seeks to dismantle, not to merely criticize, "the West." The same is true of "Orientalism in reverse," a concept advanced by critical thinkers ranging from the Syrian intellectual Sadik Jalal al-Azm to Lebanese academic Gilbert Achcar, which has used that false cross-essentialization to discredit the whole colonial interjection between Eurocentric Marxism and Europhobic nativism evident in militant Islamism.[2] If for Said and his followers their reading of colonialism has overtaken and overshadowed the global operation of capitalism, for their critics their mechanical reading of capitalism has vitiated the centrality of colonialism—and thus their legitimate critique of nativist Islamism borders dangerously with Islamophobia. In between these two diametrically opposed and ossified positions stands the monumental intellectual legacy of Rosa Luxemburg, whose liberating Marxism overcame Marx's colonial blind spot—which Said had exposed—and foreshadowed the field of postcolonial theory by half a century.[3] For my way of thinking, the critical fusion of the best of Marx and the best of Said is found in Rosa Luxemburg.

To keep recentering the metaphor of "the West" will continue to conceal the liberating thinking that the pre-Islamist and pre-Western history of the Mediterranean world and its larger frame of references entails, as, I contend, the post-Islamist and post-Western world anticipates. I am therefore not concerned with the fact that manufacturing a fictive "Islam" or "Orient" was definitive to the discursive construction of "the West" in general or "Western liberalism" in particular. My concern is rather with the manner in which the binary itself disappears once placed against a longer historical context, both before and after the colonial construction of the "Islam and the West" liaison. In addition to that act of necessary historicity, I also propose that the very constitution of "the West" functioned as a Freudian *illusion*, perforce making catalytically *illusory* any other abstraction like "the East" or "Islam" that it touches to cross-authenticate itself. The culprit, in other words, is "the West" itself, the false consciousness of capitalist modernity that has been pulling this smokescreen around itself and all its alterities to camouflage the historical foregrounding of its moral and material forces of self-consciousness and resistance. Seeking to dismantle that false consciousness is precisely to restore that self-consciousness and its ancillary historical agency.

In this task, I have taken my point of departure from Frantz Fanon's famous phrase that "Europe is literally the creation of the Third World." That phrase places our critical dismantling of the "Islam and the West" binary at the forefront of contemporary postcolonial history and theory.[4] I therefore balance Fanon's insight with Edward Said's fixation with how the Orientals and Muslims were imagined in "the Western imaginary," of both the liberal and the conservative vintage. This twist will bring us closer to the crucial postcolonial critique of Eurocentric knowledge production, but it will also allow us enough distance to understand the structural transformation of the European bourgeois public sphere on which much of this Orientalism took place. I therefore propose moving beyond that dialectic and working toward the dynamics of a transnational public sphere that these European developments generated, upon which postcolonial subjects have been formed, and from which they are yet to be liberated. Bringing down the false binary of "Islam and the West" is the first crucial step in that emancipation.

Reorienting History, Reimagining Geography, Liberating the Postcolonial Subject

Reorienting history as I have sought to detail in this book also requires a different imaginative geography of our creative and critical thinking. Consider the career of the eminent French scholar of Islamic philosophy Henry Corbin (1903–1978) and ask yourself why he would, at the top of his academic career, pack and leave his homeland for Iran, where he revolutionized our understanding of Islamic intellectual history. Corbin became fascinated with the intellectual history of Shi'ism from the Safavid period forward. His monumental work, *En Islam iranien* (1971–1973), became a potently philosophical engagement with Islamic philosophy. As one reads Corbin today and places him next to generations of other similar thinkers before and after him, it is impossible to avoid the intellectual intimation that the French scholar had in fact become a "Muslim philosopher" himself. In this sense, Corbin was very much similar to the other towering European scholar of Islam Ignaz Goldziher (1850–1921), whom Edward Said in his *Orientalism* terribly misunderstood and misrepresented, and whom I have written extensively about, restoring the memory of that giant Hungarian scholar.[5] In rethinking the Muslim postcolonial subject, we will have to take such seismic events like Corbin or Goldziher seriously. Another crucial example, similar to Corbin and Goldziher, is Louis Massignon (1883–1962), whose enduring masterpiece *La passion de Hussayn Ibn Mansur an-Hallaj* (1975) is the closest approximation of a martyred Muslim mystic to the figure of Jesus Christ. As this seminal work helped a devout Christian to better understand the figure of Christ, so does it help Muslims understand Christianity more intimately. Where is "Islam and the West" in this towering example of French scholarship—and how has *Orientalism* in fact contributed to distorting such truth? My point here is not to find fault with Edward Said's masterpiece, which in many ways has enabled my generation of critical scholarship to see things better, but simply to build on what he has done and to think further ahead. To dismantle the terrible binary of "Islam and the West" we must overcome the intentional and unintentional consequences of the false interface.

The critical point must therefore be taken further away from Edward Said and moved far closer to the enduring insights of Frantz Fanon as a precondition to expanding on retrieving a historical consciousness that in fact entirely predates European colonialism. We have spent an entire generation of scholarship not just documenting but in fact fetishizing that "West." Edward Said's Orientalism is about "the West," not about "the Orient"—and as such, it helps fetishize "the West." We need to be liberated from that fetish. Via a systematic reorientation of our historical consciousness, in this book I am after a liberation of the postcolonial subject from the very notion of "Islam and the West," instead of further exacerbating the fortification of "the West" by relentlessly criticizing what I consider to be a dead interlocutor. We need to see how Fanon's concern was less about the place of the Orient in the European imagination, while Said was entirely fixated with that location. Fanon's focus was from the other end and about what "the Third World" counter-invents and calls "the West," and then how that invention becomes instrumental in the making of a colonized mind and thereafter (I wish to add) an entrapped postcolonial subject. Said and the Saidian project were and remain critical. Fanon's project was and remains emancipatory, liberating, and revolutionary—its full potentials yet to be realized. But these are two very different projects. More than Said himself, his followers have exacerbated that critical fixation, bordering it with a retrograde nativism. It is long overdue that we free ourselves from that debilitating nativism.

My preoccupation with this falsifying fusion of "Islam and the West" is ultimately rooted in a larger frame of thinking—namely, the texture and disposition of the public sphere upon which the postcolonial subject takes shape and assumes agency and authority. Two particular studies I have done in this domain are the immediate predicates of this book. One is *Persophilia: Persian Culture on the Global Scene* (2015) and the other *Reversing the Colonial Gaze: Persian Travelers Abroad* (2020). In the former I mapped out a globalized transnational public sphere that European Persophilia created, and in the latter I detailed Persian travelers' mobile and nomadic subjectivity found in their travel literature. This book on "Islam and the West" puts a radically different spin on this body of work. As I have argued in the book, "Islam and the West" has been the most destructive false consciousness subverting the formation of any meaningful Muslim subject through the course of colonial modernity. Without dismantling this false consciousness and exposing its delusional nexus with an illusory chimera that calls itself "the West," no Muslim person can ever find peace of presence in being in the world. The being of a Muslim has been rendered contingent on this falsifying and internalized gaze—very much on the model of what W. E. B. Du Bois called "double-consciousness" about the existence and the moral imagination of the Black person. The Muslim person too has found his and her very personhood contingent and shadow-shaped after the chimeric consciousness of "the West." People on the right who continue to sustain this double-consciousness and those on the left who keep corroborating by critiquing "the West" are equally at work to sustain its parasitical existence and binary persistence. The issue is no longer critiquing "the West"—for the more you critique it the more you corroborate it. The issue is to overcome all the binary oppositions this "West" has historically manufactured to center and believe in itself—most specifically "Islam and the West." Consider Du Bois's insight:

> It is a peculiar sensation, this double-consciousness, this sense of always looking at one's self through the eyes of others, of measuring one's soul by the tape of a world that looks on in amused contempt and pity. One ever feels his two-ness, an American, a Negro; two souls, two thoughts, two unreconciled strivings; two warring ideals in one dark body, whose dogged strength alone keeps it from being torn asunder. The history of the American Negro is the history of this strife—this longing to attain self-conscious manhood, to merge his double self into a better and truer self.[6]

In the case of the Muslim person, this double-consciousness has amounted to an impossibility of not being able to be a Muslim in the world when it is thus defined by the chimeric hegemony of "the West." The more Muslims have fought this chimera of "the West" the more they have empowered its psychopathological power over them. It is precisely this false consciousness that will have to be dismantled for the Muslim person to be liberated from a false, falsifying, and terrifyingly overwhelming consciousness.

My primary concern in overcoming the ideological, conceptual, and metaphysical force of the formula "Islam and the West" therefore points toward examining the historical circumstances that have been colonially constituted and then periodically reconditioned, and thereby refocusing our attention on the real history of people whose lives, experiences, shared memories, institutional affiliations, cultural traits, and intellectual trajectories are radically opposed to any generic meaning that "Islam and the West" could possibly generate and/or entail. I propose that the specter of "Islam and the West" is like a nightmare from which people are waking up, yet the memory of which is still haunting them. What I have done in this book is offer an interpretation of that dream, to continue with the Freudian take on the matter. The necessary and potent critique of Eurocentricity and mis/representation of "Islam" and "the Orient" over the last half a century has finally hit a plateau, if not faced a cul-de-sac. It is now completely useless and in fact counterproductive to continue to insist that "the West" has misrepresented "Islam." All empires generate a kind of knowledge that sustains them in power and legitimizes that power, and European or American imperialism is no exception. Far more urgent is the dismantling of that false binary that has actively misremembered history and sustained its hegemonic foregrounding of how the world understands itself. It is necessary to pave the way for a manner of thinking no longer trapped in the exhausted matrix of that epistemic dead end; thus liberated, we can rethink the world toward a more democratic truth and on a more even footing.

The proposition of "the West" as an illusion in fact links the insights of Freud to those of Marx and his idea of "false consciousness," and ultimately to Gramsci's idea of "hegemony." All these master theorists of Europe were in fact theorizing the condition of capitalist modernity in whose colonial shadows the rest of the world was cast. What Freud was unveiling in 1927 in his *Future of an Illusion* was not a reading of "religion" as such but in fact the diagnosis of any illusion, such as the myth of white supremacy, or the frenzy of fascism that was destroying his world as he wrote that book. It is "the West," as the code name of that imperial hubris of capitalist modernity, that is the paramount illusion that Freud was diagnosing, the combative Christianity in its imperial posture in action, the very hegemonic illusion that had turned Islam and any other civilizational other it touched into its illusory nemesis. Freud was actually diagnosing fanatical fascism as a modus operandi of that capitalism, but he gave the whole spectrum of unfounded conviction that this link needed the generic term of "illusion."

The same, we might say, was what Marx was doing in his critique of religion as false consciousness. For both Marx and Freud, combative Christianity was the simulacrum of the illusion that had called itself "the West." They were both doing a critique of "religion" within the domains of capitalist modernity, which had squarely centered itself in "the West." "The foundation of irreligious criticism," Marx proposed, is: "Man makes religion, religion does not make man." To which he then famously added:

Religion is, indeed, the self-consciousness and self-esteem of man who has either not yet won through to himself, or has already lost himself again. But man is no abstract being squatting outside the world. Man is the world of man—state, society. This state and this society produce religion, which is an inverted consciousness of the world, because they are an inverted world. Religion is the general theory of this world, its encyclopedic compendium, its logic in popular form, its spiritual point d'honneur, its enthusiasm, its moral sanction, its solemn complement, and its universal basis of consolation and justification. It is the fantastic realization of the human essence since the human essence has not acquired any true reality. The struggle against religion is, therefore, indirectly the struggle against that world whose spiritual aroma is religion.[7]

Here Marx is doing his signature critique of the false consciousness that distorts reality for the ruling class to rule better. It is also crucial to keep in mind that "the man" Marx uses here is "the Western man," "the European man," the prototype of humanity for him as for all other European thinkers. So "the state and society" he chooses as examples are equally European and thus "Western." That state and society have indeed produced a religion, "which is an inverted consciousness of the world," as he correctly says, and that "religion" is not Christianity, Judaism, or any other religion, except in their renditions in the course of capitalist modernity. It is what has happened to these religions in the crucible of "the West," in the metaphysical, almost magical, belief in "the West," that has damaged these religions' historical memories of themselves. This "West" therefore did indeed become "its encyclopedic compendium, its logic in popular form, its spiritual point d'honneur, its enthusiasm, its moral sanction, its solemn complement, and its universal basis of consolation and justification." That is the Hegelian Geist of the world that was coming to a finale and a closure in "the West." Following this argument, then, "the struggle against religion is, therefore, indirectly the struggle against that world whose spiritual aroma is religion." Marx was never too far from his earliest stages as a Young Hegelian, and what here he calls "religion" or false consciousness is in fact the Hegelian Geist (Spirit), Eurocentric to its epistemic bones, bringing the whole history of humanity to serve "the West." Whatever Marx and Freud wrote and theorized about "religion" is even more poignantly applicable to the religion that capitalist modernity invented and called "the West." They were both theorizing "the West," the very prototype of "religion" that was defining their age, entirely unbeknownst to themselves.

If we thus subject Marx to a Freudian and Freud to a Marxist reading of each other, we see them both deeply engaged in revealing "the West" as the single most potent illusion that had indeed clouded even their own theorization of "religion." They were pitch perfect in their theorization—not of "religion," but rather of "the West" as the single most convoluted myth of their own time, and in which they were themselves integral and implicated.

Rooted in this reading of Marx and Freud, Fanon and Said, one against and for the other, once we look at them through the bold insights of W. E. B. Du Bois, I wrote this book to map out the argument that the "Islam" of "Islam and the West" is a fetishized fiction the Muslim ideologues have wholeheartedly bought into, a chimeric delusion that has nothing to do with the lived experiences of millions of Muslims living a quiet and mostly dignified life around the globe. But even more to the point, I have written this book to argue that "the West" itself is a commodified fetish that capitalist modernity concocted, like the illusion of the color of white in white supremacy, to rule the world with a metaphor that corresponded to a predatory capitalism it sought to serve and sustain in power. The desire to render the condition of capitalist modernity as preternatural translated into the fetishization of its paramount commodified ideology of "the West and the Rest." The unfolding Islamophobia plaguing France as I write this conclusion, and the enduring Islamophobia that culminated in the nefarious hatred in Donald Trump's Muslim ban, are the most recent examples of the "Islam" that the fictive binary of "Islam and the West" has produced. Muslims trapped inside this Stockholm Syndrome who have internalized this "Western" gaze and continue to keep justify themselves accordingly are integral to this systematic distortion of their own faith too. In this book I have sought a deeper and more historical understanding of how and why this dangerous fiction of "Islam and the West" has come about, how it finally self-imploded, and how and upon what specific features of a transnational public sphere do we have the evidence of a far more liberating conception of our contemporary history, of Muslims and their history, and of the changing demography of people all over this earth.

Epilogue
2021: After Gaza and Afghanistan

I began this book by citing the most recent front-page news cover-
age of our current history featuring an eternal opposition presumed
between "Islam and the West" before I proceeded to dismantle that
protracted illusion by tracing the false binary back into the deepest
layers of our historical memories. In May 2021, as I was preparing
my typescript to submit to my editor, yet another deadly development captured our global attention. The terrorizing Israeli military
strike against Palestinians in Gaza resulted in yet more lethal consequences for a nation trapped inside its own homeland. How does yet
another frightful fact assaulting the moral conscience of the world
around us figure in my arguments in this book? Soon after that, in
August and September the spectacle of US forces leaving Afghanistan and the Taliban taking over the entirety of their country marked
the twentieth anniversary of the events of 9/11. Does the proposition put forward in my book have anything to say about such terror-
stricken parts of the world—from Palestine to Iraq to Afghanistan?
What do the two words *Israel* and *Hamas* or the terms *US* and the
Taliban mean and signify beyond their immediate contexts in the
"Arab-Israeli conflict" or the US "War on Terror"?

The "Arab-Israeli Conflict"

In this book I have set myself the urgent task of dismantling what I propose has been the most dangerous delusions of our time, the presumed hostility politically projected between two vastly fetishized abstractions: "Islam" and "the West." How does the horror inflicted upon Palestinian men, women, and children figure in the fictive opposition presumed between "Islam and the West"? In this configuration, Israel is projected as part and parcel of "the West" ("the only Democracy in the Middle East," or else "a villa in the jungle" as Israeli officials like to say), and Palestinians are subsumed under the talismanic mantra of "Hamas" and thus stand for "Islam." But has the historical presence of Jews in Palestine anything to do with the fiction of "the West"? And how do we account for the fact that Palestinians are both Muslims and Christians—and in fact, Jews are Palestinians too? My principal argument in this book has been geared toward dismantling the dangerous delusions manufactured about "Islam and the West" that have historically distorted the facts and mapped out a fictional divide in a vast stretch of human misery from Asia and Africa to Europe and the United States. Palestine today is perhaps the single most important spot on earth where the fictional battle between "Islam" and "the West" is waged. Palestine has always been home to Jews, and should always remain home to Palestinian Jews, in the company of their Christian and Muslim neighbors, in the framework of a free, equal, and democratic state. What has that simple fact to do with a colonial project of European settlers that has called itself "Zionism" and catapulted its colonial conquest of Palestine into the false binary of "Islam and the West"?

Let us consider some details. The flare-up of hostilities in early May 2021 was focused on the Sheikh Jarrah neighborhood of occupied East Jerusalem, where six Palestinian families were being forced by Israeli authorities to leave their homes to facilitate the further colonial conquest of the city. This is what the Palestinians call their "continued catastrophe," their dispossession begun in the nineteenth century and sealed in 1948, now writ large. The violence was then extended to the al-Aqsa Mosque compound in Haram al-Sharif, which Israeli forces stormed with full force, reaching deep into the West Bank, and from there to Gaza, as Palestinians inside Israel joined the protests. Never in recent memory was the fact of Palestinian unity more potently on display, exposing the utter failure of the Israeli strategy of divide and rule. Between 10 and 21 May, Israeli forces bombed Gaza, as the Palestinian militant groups Hamas and Islamic Jihad targeted Israel with their flimsy rockets. Some 250 Palestinians including 66 children were killed by Israeli forces, exponentially more than the few casualties in Israel. When Israelis finally stopped bombing on May 21, once again Gaza was left in ruins, and Palestinians were more determined and unified in their defiance of the military occupation of their homeland.

When the bombing and shelling finally stopped, both Israel and Hamas declared victory. But they in fact both lost in irreversible and definitive terms. The repeated moral defeat of Israel and the habitual military defeat of Hamas amount to the same factual premise: a future for all the inhabitants of Palestine—Jews, Christians, and Muslims—beyond the calamitous adventurism of Zionism and all the mirroring nemeses it has generated in response. While the slaughter of Palestinians and destruction of their homes and habitat was centered in Gaza, the reverberations of the massacre spread across Palestine and indeed worldwide. After this attack, Gaza was in fact liberated from the Hamas-Israeli nexus of misplaced binary and was reconnected with the rest of Palestine. The same is true in equally irreversible terms about the decoupling of Judaism and Zionism. No human being, let alone a people who have been the systematic target of abuse and harm throughout history, could in good faith identify with an ideology that can perpetrate and justify slaughter of children. The massive evidence of Jewish solidarity with the Palestinian cause means the moral authority of Judaism and the sacred memory of the Jewish Holocaust have joined the Palestinian aspirations that have always embraced the historic Jewish homeland as part and parcel of their dream of liberating their country. Palestine has always belonged to Palestinians: Jews, Christians, and Muslims alike. Zionism was always a colonial sideshow distracting from this simple fact.

In this context, singling out Hamas to define Palestinian resistance to occupation of their homelands is a deliberately false and falsifying synecdoche—making one militant group stand for the entirety of the Palestinian national liberation movement—a cause that has been overwhelmingly peaceful in decidedly cultural and apolitical terms. Palestinians have resisted the colonial domination of their homeland in their attachments to the Arabic language and culture, in their pride in their habits and forms of civility, in their songs and folkloric traditions, cuisine and customs, music and poetry, art and literature, theater and cinema—of which the dominant European and North American media have made sure the world knows very little, so that "Hamas" stands for the entirety of Palestine, just as they once made sure the PLO had an identical function. A systematic Islamophobia first informs what the world understands by the term "Hamas," and then this very "Hamas" stands like a firm but false synecdoche for the entirety of Palestine— so that all Palestinians are identified with this "Islam" that stands in diametrical opposition to "the West," which now Israel represents. Any people subjected to enduring military occupation by a foreign force is entitled to any form of resistance available to them—no matter how feeble and pathetic. But if we dismantle that false synecdoche between Hamas and Palestine and do not allow it to stand for the entirety of the nation, then something extraordinary happens. The cosmopolitan disposition of Palestine emerges as the single most potent metaphor of our world dreaming of its own liberation in nonsectarian, nondenominational, and entirely life-affirming and worldly terms.

To be sure, there is no moral equivalency between the colonizer and the colonized, between the oppressor and the oppressed, between the occupier and the occupied, between a massive, astronomical military industry that tests its newest weapons on Palestinian targets before selling them around the world and a few flimsy rockets Palestinians throw at it. Israel's moral failure as a settler colony is of a different rank and order than Hamas's miserable military failures. Hamas's military failures however are symbolic of its ideological exhaustion—of its irrelevance to the future of Palestine. Representing an entirely depleted ideological site of militant Islamism, Hamas can never represent the totality of the Palestinian struggles for self-determination, but nor can the PLO or PA or any other fake state blueprints feigning authority under occupation. An "Islamic Republic of Palestine" is a nightmare mirror image of "the Jewish State" it opposes. The "Islam" of the "Islamic Republic" and the Zionism that lays a false claim on Judaism at the heart of the "Jewish State" are both the products of the "West" they either oppose or seek to appease, respectively. But unless and until Palestinians are all free from colonial domination and able to choose their own future, there can never be a free and fair election to see what political formations earn that trust. The moral authority of the Palestinian cause does not translate into ideological legitimacy for Hamas or any other political posturing for ruling over an occupied people. When you trap millions of people in their own homeland under brutal military occupation, of course Hamas and Islamic Jihad and PLO and PA claim to be their representatives. They are not.

Instead of thinking of Hamas as synecdoche for Palestine, we should think of Gaza as a metaphor for the world at large—as a floating signifier for liberation from wanton cruelty and colonial conquest everywhere. This is precisely what the collection of essays brought together in *Gaza as Metaphor* (2016), edited by Helga Tawil-Souri and Dina Matar, does by expanding the factual evidence of the besieged open prison into far-reaching metaphoric dimensions. If we do that, Palestine is placed in the assembly of national liberations beyond its own immediate context. The false identification of Hamas with the entirety of the Palestinian cause is a by-product of the belated order of "Islam and the West." If Hamas here stands for "Islam" and Israel for "the West," then the mutual defeat of Hamas and Israel—one in military and the other in moral terms—is the territorial evidence of the collapse of "Islam and the West" on the historic premise of a national liberation that now stands for the world at large. Consider the fact that the rise of Black Lives Matter in the United States is singularly important to this universalization of the Palestinian cause. The murder of George Floyd and the guilty verdict of his murderer should change the way Americans viewed Palestinians under brutal Israeli occupation. If we remember how Black Lives Matter was launched by three African American women—Alicia Garza, Patrisse Cullors, and Opal Tometi—then we see how the fusion of race and gender (to which I have devoted two chapters in this book) revolutionized the Black struggle for justice and placed Palestinians' struggle for national liberation in an entirely different light. But, and this is equally crucial to keep in mind, the relationship is mutual. Palestine too has saved the Black Lives Matter movement from its potential provincialization and domestication inside the systemic corruption of American politics—where the election of a Barack Obama might seriously derail. The proposition that no one is free until African Americans are free is also true the other way around: no one is free unless Palestinians are free.

Within the larger global context, Gaza 2021 marks the epistemic and political exhaustion of both Islamism and Zionism as twin by-products of European colonialism. Under the smokescreen of this false opposition, what in effect is happening in Palestine is the coming together of the two eternal others of European white supremacy—its internal other of European Jews and its external other of non-European Muslims and their faith that was placed squarely opposite "the West." It is imperative to remember that the so-called "conflict" between Jews and Arabs is of a very recent colonial origin. The infamous statement of former US president Barack Obama that "the Middle East is going through a transformation that will play out for a generation, rooted in conflicts that date back millennia" is typical of the ahistorical assessments that manufactured hostility between Islam and Judaism, and perforce between Jews and Muslims. There is far more historical credence in the validity of a Judeo-Islamic heritage than in a "Judeo-Christian" one—with its history of pogroms leading to the Holocaust. Before and beyond the Zionist abuse of Judaism—identical to the Islamist abuse of Islam, colonial abuse of Christianity, fundamentalist abuse of Hinduism in India, or the nationalist abuse of Buddhism in Myanmar—there is an enduring and historically grounded proximity to the Judeo-Islamic heritage that started even before the legendary age of Andalusia. The spectacular sites of Judeo-Persian literary heritage or Judeo-Arabic philosophical lineage are today almost completely overshadowed by the radical contemporaneity of the "Israeli-Palestinian conflict." That heritage is decidedly blindsided by the presumed and false hostility between Jews and Arabs intended to sustain the supremacy of European settler colonialism—which is today chiefly sponsored by Christian evangelical Zionism.

The link between militant Islamism, triumphalist Zionism, and Christian imperialism in the context of European colonialism is the main frame of reference here. White supremacists like Steve Bannon (a strong advocate of Israel) use the term "Judeo-Christian tradition" as a subterfuge to fabricate a common religious foregrounding for anti-Muslim bigotry. These three complementary ideological fanaticisms are chiefly responsible for the sustained bifurcation manufactured today between Islam and Judaism to foreground "the Arab-Israeli conflict"—all of them handmade of European colonialism, all of them invested in denying and dismissing the legacies of the Judeo-Islamic tradition. Militant Islamism, fanatical Zionism, and Christian imperialism are the triangulated foregrounding of fear and fanaticism that has wreaked havoc in our world and systematically and consistently distorted the clarity of our historical visions. This triumphalist triangulation has degenerated the geopolitics of the entire region into a deadly sectarian politics that stands in opposition not to the other European proposition of "secularism" (which is Christianity in disguise) but to the inherent cosmopolitan worldliness that European colonial conquests have systematically destroyed or distorted around the world.

Fanatical Wahhabism in Saudi Arabia, militant Shi'ism in Iran, secular zeal of Kemalism in Turkey, and triumphalist Zionism in historic Palestine have all been the identical ideological by-products of European colonialism. In opposition to European colonialism, militant Islamism (both the Sunni and Shia versions of it), stripped Islamic moral imagination and intellectual history of their factual pluralistic and cosmopolitan character, reducing them to a singular site of political resistance to European colonialism—and thus turning the rich heritage of Islam precisely into the mirror image of their political nemesis. In the same vein, Zionism, extending the racist logic of European colonialism into the heart of the Arab and Muslim world, stripped Judaism of its equally worldly moral and prophetic imagination. Fanatical Islamism, settler colonial Zionism, and evangelical Christianity are chiefly responsible for this terrorizing state of affairs of pitting Jews against Muslims to keep triumphalist Christianity on top. The troubled spot of the "Israel-Palestinian conflict" is where the exposed delusion of "Islam and the West" continues to flex its atrophied muscles.

Retrieving a lost but evident cosmopolitan culture, Palestinians (Jews, Christians, and Muslims) are today the microcosm of a worldly resurrection of a reality long hidden under the smokescreen of colonial conquest. As Israelis and Palestinians, Jews and Arabs have been pitted against each other to sustain the ideological supremacy of colonial Christianity. They are fighting someone else's fight on their own broken backs, at the heavy toll of their own lives and their own bruised moral imagination. The future of a liberated Palestine in and of itself sustains the historical presence of Jews in their ancestral homeland—right next to their Christian and Muslim neighbors. This does not mean all Jews around the world must move to and live in Palestine. Like anyone else, Jews belong right where they are. American Jews are Americans, Iranian Jews are Iranians, Canadian Jews are Canadians—as German Jews were and remain Germans. In and of itself, the Palestinian cause brings the internal and external others of Europe together, defies the false binary of "Islam and the West," and liberates the world from a false and falsifying consciousness. Palestine is today the crucible of a rising cosmopolitanism where two alterities of "the West," Jews and Arabs, have come to meet and in the very fact of their evidence dismantle the overriding myth that has historically distorted the evident truth. In the coming together of the Jew and the Palestinian, two historically harmed and systemically maligned peoples, "Islam and the West" as the singular site of dividing the world to rule it better will have finally met its demise—and the whole of humanity is saved from the last vestiges of a "West" that never was.

"The War on Terror"

In February 2021, as the twentieth anniversary of the dramatic events of 9/11 was fast approaching, both the Trump and the Biden administrations concluded US negotiations with the Taliban in Doha, Qatar, for the cession of hostilities among all parties and the departure of American and NATO forces from Afghanistan. Late in August, as the United States and its allies were leaving Afghanistan, the Taliban staged a blitzkrieg, recapturing their homeland and, with the notable exception of the Panjshir Valley, getting full control of their country, ousting the puppet regime the US and its allies had installed in Kabul. The Taliban had returned, the United States and its partners had gone, the imperial narrative of "the War on Terror" had closed a chapter and turned a page to a new episode.

The events of 9/11 in 2001 marked the resurrection of American imperial wherewithal from the slumber of its Vietnam syndrome, where for a couple of decades the United States had been recalibrating its military apparatus to deal with a changing world. The dramatic failure of the Carter administration to rescue the American hostages in Iran in 1980 was perhaps the last iconic event that had put the military logic of the US empire under erasure. With the inauguration of the first term of the presidency of Ronald Reagan in 1981, that episode of post-Vietnam anxiety finally came to an end and the US military began flexing its atrophied muscles, initially in Latin America (Granada in 1983) and subsequently elsewhere in Asia and Africa. Massive military expenditure under Ronald Regan was ultimately put on stage by President George Herbert Walker Bush during the US invasion of Iraq in 1991. The subsequent decade under the Clinton administration redefined American military machinery and its global presence long before the events of 9/11 in 2001, such that the US invasion and occupation of Afghanistan in October 2001 and subsequently Iraq in March 2003 were rooted in the military logic of the US imperial imagination of the preceding decades since the Vietnam. But now this war machine had an ideological banner it called "War on Terror," and it had a potent propaganda pamphlet mapped out in deep-rooted Islamophobia.

As I have had multiple occasions to argue, the events of 9/11 were not the zenith but the nadir of the "Islam and the West" paradigm.

The staging of those acts of spectacular violence was entirely for the shocking effect, without any enduring political or even ideological significance. As a key by-product of "the West," the ideological force of Islamism had totally exhausted itself, as had that very "West" itself that had dialectically occasioned it. But the traumatic events and subsequent rise in the Islamophobic disposition of the "War on Terror" gave the phantom of "Islam and the West" a renewed lease on capturing the political imagination of an entire era, from 2001 to 2021. Although, as I have demonstrated in this book, the colonial pedigree of "Islam and the West" goes back much deeper than the events of 2001, the spectacular staging of a terrorizing event in the United States code-named "9/11" sustained the course of the binary illusion and gave it a fake sense of longevity. The US imperial machinery had now targeted a floating signifier and called the goose-chasing operation "War on Terror." With the departure of US and coalition forces from Afghanistan on the twentieth anniversary of the events of 9/11, the imperial narrative of "Islam and the West" is finally exhausted. Although the rhetoric of "War on Terror" continues the Islamophobic disposition of this ideology in order to sustain itself, the amorphous disposition of the US imperial machinery would no longer need to work through or rely on the "Islam and the West" prototype.

The exhaustion of the paradigm of "Islam and the West" is the consequence of an imperial condition that is no longer predicated on territorial conquest. The United States and its European and regional allies now dwell on the strategic distribution of a network of military bases around the globe. This "Empire of Bases," as it has been aptly termed, is no longer predicated on any fixed ideology. It is based on pure strategic calculations. The calculated exit from Afghanistan is the clear indication that it will suffice to keep only a few military bases in the region. Two decades after 9/11, the rhetoric of "War on Terror" may continue apace, but its Islamophobic disposition is now akin to anti-Semitism or Sinophobia. The amorphous capital has finally given birth to an amorphous empire, which is contingent neither on fixed territorial conquests nor on clear ideological articulations. Muslims in Saudi Arabia, Pakistan, the United Arab Emirates, Egypt, and the rest of the Arab and Muslim world are all integral to this "Empire of Bases," with their reactionary and counterrevolutionary claims to Islam entirely intact. Two decades after 9/11, the US forces are out of Afghanistan. "The War on Terror" may continue its parasitical life for a few more years or even decades, but Muslims as Muslims are today entirely liberated from the phantom fixation with the figment of their own colonized imagination they kept calling "the West." "The West" is wasted. Islam, and perforce Muslims, will now have to find a different touchstone to recast themselves upon a fragile world.

Today Muslims are liberated from Islamism as Jews are from Zionism. The imperial logic of "the West" had occasioned both Islamism and Zionism at one and the same time, where Muslims and Jews were trapped inside a false consciousness made up of their own ancestral faith and an ideological straitjacket that denied them freedom of their moral conscience. The final collapse of the "Islam and the West" binary spells out the emerging contours of a political emancipation that will wed the fate of liberated Muslims and Jews to the fragile future of our humanity at large.

Notes

Introduction

1. See Jamelle Bouie, "Stephen Miller's Sinister Syllabus," *New York Times*, 15 November 2019, available online here: https://www.nytimes.com/2019/11/15/opinion/stephen-miller-emails.html.

2. Ibid.

3. See the Southern Poverty Law Center's report on the racism of Stephen Miller, "Stephen Miller's Affinity for White Nationalism Revealed in Leaked Emails," available online here: https://www.splcenter.org/hatewatch/2019/11/12/stephen-millers-affinity-white-nationalism-revealed-leaked-emails.

4. See Hamid Dabashi, "Norway: Muslims and Metaphors," *Aljazeera*, 31 July 2011, available online here: https://www.aljazeera.com/indepth/opinion/2011/07/201173184110804329.html.

5. See Samuel Huntington, *The Clash of Civilizations and the Remaking of World Order* (New York: Simon and Schuster, 1996). For my critique of this argument, see Hamid Dabashi, "For the Last Time: Civilizations," *International Sociology* 16, no. 3 (September 2001): 361–68.

6. See the Southern Poverty Law Center's report on the racism of Stephen Miller, "Stephen Miller's Affinity for White Nationalism Revealed in Leaked Emails," op. cit.

7. See Neil Lazarus, "The Fetish of 'the West' in Postcolonial Theory," in Crystal Bartolovich and Neil Lazarus (eds.), *Marxism, Modernity, and Postcolonial Studies* (Cambridge: Cambridge University Press, 2002), 44.

8. Ibid., 60.

9. Karl Marx, *Capital: A Critique of Political Economy*, vol. 1, translated by Samuel Moore and Edward Aveling, edited by Frederick Engels (Moscow: Progress Publishers, 1887), available in the public domain online here: https://www .marxists.org/archive/marx/works/download/pdf/Capital-Volume-I.pdf.

10. See the introduction to my *Post-Orientalism: Knowledge and Power in Time of Terror* (London: Routledge, 2009) for even earlier traces of the critique of Orientalism.

11. I have worked through this idea of "doppelgänger" over the last two decades, most recently in my book *Reversing the Colonial Gaze: Persian Travelers Abroad* (Cambridge: Cambridge University Press, 2019), 177 and 238; and before that in my book *Iran: Rebirth of a Nation* (New York: Palgrave, 2016), 246; and before that in my essay "The End of the West and the Birth of the First Postcolonial Person," in Mojtaba Mahdavi and W. Andy Knight (eds.), *Towards the Dignity of Difference? Neither "End of History" Nor "Clash of Civilizations"* (Burlington, VT: Ashgate Publications, 2012), 397–406. I have developed this idea through the metaphor of "mirror" and "mirroring" at least since my essay of two decades ago, "For the Last Time: Civilizations," *International Sociology* 16, no. 3 (September 2001): 361–68. More recently this idea of "doppelgänger" as "mirrored oppositionalism" has also been addressed by Caroline Rooney in her excellent book *Creative Radicalism in the Middle East: Culture and the Arab Left after the Uprisings* (London: I. B. Tauris, 2020).

12. This is to gloss over the fact that the very idea of "world religion" is itself a recent colonial concoction. For an excellent critique of the idea of "world religion," see Tomoko Masuzawa, *The Invention of World Religions; or, How European Universalism Was Preserved in the Language of Pluralism* (Chicago: University of Chicago Press, 2005).

13. Sigmund Freud, *The Future of an Illusion*, Pelican Freud Library, vol. 12, translated from the German under the general editorship of James Strachey (London: Penguin Books, 1985), 212–13.

14. For a scholarly examination of this text, see Carmen Cardelle de Hartmann, "The Textual Transmission of the Mozarabic Chronicle of 754," *Early Medieval Europe* 8, no. 1 (1999): 13–29. Available online here: https://www.researchgate.net /publication/230321169_The_textual_transmission_of_the_Mozarabic_Chronicle_of _754. It is important to note that as late as 1999, Hartmann points out, "because of the difficulty it presents, the text was largely neglected by historians, until two recent editions, translations into Spanish and English and several studies have returned it to the central place it deserves as a source for the eighth century."

15. This issue has been recently addressed by the Italian historian Alessandro Barbero in a short and useful account where he summarizes all these developments in his essay "Battle of Poitiers and the Invention of Europeans," 8 March 2015, available online here: http://www.theglobaldispatches.com/articles/732-ac-the-battle-of-poitiers-and-the-invention-of-europeans.

16. Ibid.

17. Ibid.

18. Cited in ibid.

19. Cited in ibid.

20. Iskander Rehman, "The Sword and the Swastika: How a Medieval Warlord Became a Fascist Icon," 28 November 2016, available online here: https://warontherocks.com/2016/11/the-sword-and-the-swastika-how-a-medieval-warlord-became-a-fascist-icon/.

21. Ibid.

22. Ibid.

23. Ibid.

24. For more on the life and thoughts of Al-Ghazali, see Eric Ormsby *Ghazali: The Revival of Islam* (London: Oneworld Academic, 2012).

25. In July 2017 in Poland, Trump said: "As the Polish experience reminds us, the defense of the west ultimately rests not only on means but also on the will of its people to prevail. The fundamental question of our time is whether the west has the will to survive." See "Trump Says West Is at Risk, During Nationalistic Speech in Poland: US President's Speech in Warsaw Calls for Defense of 'Our Civilization' from Terrorism, Bureaucracy and Erosion of Traditions," *The Guardian*, 6 July 2017, available online here: https://www.theguardian.com/us-news/2017/jul/06/donald-trump-warn-future-west-in-doubt-warsaw-speech.

26. In his classical study of the *world system*, Immanuel Wallerstein has given a thorough theoretical basis for this view of our world dis/order. See his "The Rise and Future Demise of the World Capitalist System: Concepts for Comparative Analysis," *Comparative Studies in Society and History* 16, no. 4 (September 1974): 387–415.

27. See Kimberlé Crenshaw, "Demarginalizing the Intersection of Race and Sex: A Black Feminist Critique of Antidiscrimination Doctrine, Feminist Theory and Antiracist Politics," *University of Chicago Legal Forum*, vol. 1989, article 8 (1989): 140, available online here: http://chicagounbound.uchicago.edu/uclf/vol1989/iss1/8.

28. Freud, *The Future of an Illusion*, op. cit., 214.

Chapter 1. Islam in the World

1. Roger Hardy, "Islam and the West," BBC, 12 August 2002, available online here: http://news.bbc.co.uk/2/hi/in_depth/world/2002/islamic_world/2188307.stm.

2. In a fine new study, *Islam without Europe: Traditions of Reform in Eighteenth-Century Islamic Thought* (Chapel Hill: University of North Carolina Press, 2018), Ahmad S. Dallal has mapped out in exquisite details one particularly poignant moment in this history.

3. I have theorized this early period of the formation of Muhammad's charismatic authority in my *Authority in Islam: From the Rise of Muhammad to the Establishment of the Umayyads* (New Brunswick, NJ: Transactions Publishers, 1989). For the classical study of the life of Prophet Muhammad in this early period, see W. Montgomery Watt, *Muhammad at Mecca* (Oxford: Oxford University Press, 1953).

4. This period of the Prophet's career is covered in detail by W. Montgomery Watt in his classic work, *Muhammad at Medina* (Oxford: Oxford University Press, 1968).

5. I have traced the dynamic of this aspect of Islam in my book *Shi'ism: A Religion of Protest* (Cambridge, MA: Harvard University Press, 2011).

6. See my *Authority in Islam*, op. cit., chapters 1–2.

7. For more details, see ibid., chapter 3.

8. I have borrowed the idea of "charismatic authority" from Max Weber's sociology of authority. For one rendition of this theory, see Max Weber, *From Max Weber: Essays in Sociology*, translated, edited, and with an introduction by Hans Gerth and C. Wright Mills (Oxford: Oxford University Press, 1946), chapter 9, 245–52.

9. For Weber's theorization of this "routinization of charisma," see ibid., 248–50.

10. There are excellent new studies of pre-Islamic Arabic society. See, for example, Robert G. Hoyland, *Arabia and the Arabs: From the Bronze Age to the Coming of Islam* (London: Routledge, 2011).

11. For details, see my *Authority in Islam*, op. cit., chapter 2.

12. For a study of these "Satanic Verses," see Shahab Ahmed, *Before Orthodoxy: The Satanic Verses in Early Islam* (Cambridge, MA: Harvard University Press, 2017).

13. For an excellent study of the crisis of succession to Prophet Muhammad, see Wilfred Madelung, *The Succession to Muhammad: A Study of the Early Caliphate* (Cambridge: Cambridge University Press, 1996).

14. This is the central argument of my *Authority in Islam*. See its chapter 8 for details.

15. I have developed this theory in detail in my book *Truth and Narrative: The Untimely Thoughts of 'Ayn al-Qudat al-Hamadhani* (London: Routledge, 1999).

16. For more details on Arabic and Persian literary humanism (*adab*), see George Makdisi, *The Rise of Humanism in Classical Islam and the Christian West* (Edinburgh: Edinburgh University Press, 1990), and Hamid Dabashi, *The World of Persian Literary Humanism* (Cambridge, MA: Harvard University Press, 2012).

17. Examples of such mystifying conceptions of a pure and perfect Islam abound, but by far the most prolific proponent of it has been Seyyed Hossein Nasr, who has a constitutionally flawed, ahistorical, propagandist, and proselytizing conception of Islam. Particularly since the events of 9/11, Nasr has been promoting himself as a bona fide guru for this New Age compatible conception of Islam. See his *The Heart of Islam: Enduring Values for Humanity* (New York: HarperCollins, 2004).

18. I am borrowing these two terms from Emmanuel Levinas's seminal work, *Totality and Infinity: An Essay on Exteriority* (Pittsburgh, PA: Duquesne University Press, 1969).

19. Karl Marx, *Critique of Hegel's Philosophy of Right* (1844), edited by Joseph O'Malley, translated by Annette Jolin and Joseph O'Malley (Cambridge: Cambridge University Press, 1970), available online here: https:// www.marxists .org/archive /marx /works /1843 /critique -hpr/.

Chapter 2. "The West"

1. See Catherine Shoichet, "What Historians Heard When Trump Warned of a 'Foreign Virus,'" CNN, 12 March 2020, available online here: https://www.cnn .com/2020/03/12/us/disease-outbreaks-xenophobia-history/.

2. Georg Wilhelm Friedrich Hegel, *The Philosophy of History*, with preface by Charles Hegel, translated by J. Sibree (Kitchener, ON: Batoche Books, 2001), available online here: http://libcom.org/files/Philosophy_of_History.pdf.

3. A major source documenting this crucial transition is Peter Gay's monumental work, *The Bourgeois Experience: Victoria to Freud*, vol. 1, *Education of the Senses* (New York: Oxford University Press, 1984).

4. For an authoritative biography of Kant, see Manfred Kuehn, *Kant: A Biography* (Cambridge: Cambridge University Press, 2002).

5. See Immanuel Kant, *Observations on the Feeling of the Beautiful and Sublime*, translated by John T. Goldthwait (Berkeley: University of California Press, 1960), 109–10.

6. For a critical assessment of Kwame Anthony Appiah's ideas of identity, see Nkiru Nzegwu, "Questions of Identity and Inheritance: A Critical Review of Kwame Anthony Appiah's '*In My Father's House*,'" *Hypatia* 11, no. 1, "The Family and Feminist Theory" (Winter 1996): 175–201.

7. In his 1952 Reith Lectures, *The World and the West* (London: Oxford University Press, 1953), Arnold Toynbee sought to give equal footing to non-Western civilizations, as he called them, by way of de-centering "the West" as a narrative device. Philip D. Curtin, some half a century later, used precisely the same title for almost the same purpose, *The World and the West: The European Challenge and the Overseas Response in the Age of Empire* (Cambridge: Cambridge University Press, 2000). Both ended up consolidating even further the unexamined assumption of "the West" as a conceptual category.

8. William McNeill, in his *The Rise of the West* (Chicago: University of Chicago Press, 1963), takes the European site of the Industrial Revolution completely for granted and has no global conception of the rise of a middle-class bourgeoisie on a global scale, which was universally contingent on this revolution.

9. Marx, *Critique of Hegel's Philosophy of Right*, op. cit.

10. Ibid.

11. See Antonio Gramsci, *Selections from the Prison Notebooks*, edited and translated by Quintin Hoare and Geoffrey Nowell Smith (New York: International Publishers, 1971), 210.

12. See Veronica Stracqualursi, "Congress' Asian Pacific American Caucus Chair: It's Dangerous for Trump to Call Coronavirus 'the Chinese Virus,'" CNN, 21 March 2020, available online here: https://www.cnn.com/2020/03/21/politics /judy-chu-coronavirus-trump-china/index.html.

Chapter 3. The West and the Rest

1. See Whitney Abernathy, "Religion, Sexuality, Power: The French in Morocco 1900–1914," *Journal of Western Society and French History* 41 (2013), available online here: https://quod.lib.umich.edu/w/wsfh/0642292.0041.011/--religion-sexuality -power-the-french-in-morocco-1900-1914?rgn=main;view=fulltext.

2. I have explored the idea of this invention in a short essay, "The Invention of the White People," *Aljazeera*, 28 August 2017, available online here: https://www .aljazeera.com/opinions/2017/8/28/the-invention-of-the-white-people. The pioneering study in this field is by Theodore W. Allen, *The Invention of the White Race* (New York: Verso, 2012).

3. For a sustained argument of this point, see Walter D. Mignolo, *The Darker Side of Western Modernity: Global Futures, Decolonial Options* (Chapel Hill, NC: Duke University Press, 2011).

4. See Rifa'a al-Tahtawi, *An Imam in Paris: Account of a Stay in France by an Egyptian Cleric (1826–1831)*, translated with an introduction by Daniel L. Newman (London: Saqi, 2004).

5. See Nikki R. Keddie, *An Islamic Response to Imperialism* (Berkeley: University of California Press, 1983).

6. For an excellent overview of all these Muslim thinkers, see the edited volume John J. Donohue and John L. Esposito (eds.), *Islam in Transition: Muslim Perspectives*, 2nd ed. (Oxford: Oxford University Press, 2006).

7. For more on Abduh, see Mark Sedgwick, *Muhammad Abduh*, Makers of the Muslim World (London: Oneworld Academic, 2014).

8. For more on Amir Shakib-Arsalan, see William L. Cleveland, *Islam against the West: Shakib Arslan and the Campaign for Islamic Nationalism* (Austin: University of Texas Press, 2011).

9. For more on his thoughts, see William L. Cleveland, *The Making of an Arab Nationalist: Ottomanism and Arabism in the Life and Thought of Sati' Al-Husri*, Princeton Studies on the Near East (Princeton, NJ: Princeton University Press, 1971).

10. For a study of his thoughts, see J. M. S. Baljon, *The Reforms and Religious Ideas of Sir Sayyid Ahmad Khan* (Lahore: S. M. Ashraf, 1964).

11. For more on Mawdudi's ideas, see S. V. Reza Nasr, *Mawdudi and the Making of Islamic Revivalism* (Oxford: Oxford University Press, 1996).

12. See S. Abid Husain, *The Destiny of Indian Muslims* (Bombay: Asia Publishing House, 1965).

13. For more details see M. C. Ricklefs, *A History of Modern Indonesia since c. 1300*, 2nd ed. (London: Macmillan, 1991).

14. See Taufik Abdullah, *Schools and Politics: The Kaum Muda Movement in West Sumatra (1927–1933)* (Sheffield, UK: Equinox Publishing, 2009).

15. Bernard Lewis, "What Went Wrong?" *Atlantic*, January 2002, available online here: https://www.theatlantic.com/magazine/archive/2002/01/what-went-wrong/302387/.

16. See Bartolomé de Las Casas, *A Short Account of the Destruction of the Indies* (London: Penguin Classics, 1992).

17. Max Weber's *Protestant Ethic and the Spirit of Capitalism* (London: Penguin Classics, 2002) exposes the thematic transmutation of Puritan ethics into the colonizing spirit of capitalism.

18. As Theodor Adorno and Max Horkheimer articulate it in their classic study *Dialectic of Enlightenment* (Stanford, CA: Stanford University Press, 2002).

19. Karl Marx, *Wage-Labor and Capital* (New York: International Publishers, 1933), 30.

20. Ibid., 30.

21. Ibid., 32.

22. Ibid.

Chapter 4. What's in a Name?

1. For a video of this interview see: https://aalbc.com/authors/author.php ?author_name=Malcolm+X.

2. See Peter Gay, *The Cultivation of Hatred* (Oxford: Oxford University Press, 1993). The full five volumes of *The Bourgeois Experience* are: *The Education of the Senses* (1984), *The Tender Passion* (1986), *The Cultivation of Hatred* (1993), *The Naked Heart* (1995), *Pleasure Wars* (1998).

3. See Steven Marcus, *The Other Victorians: A Study of Sexuality and Pornography in Mid-Nineteenth-Century England* (New York: Basic Books, 1966).

4. Gay, *The Cultivation of Hatred*, op. cit., 68–94.

5. Ibid., 85.

6. Ibid., 86.

7. I have given a detailed account of this argument in my *Shi'ism: A Religion of Protest* (Cambridge, MA: Harvard University Press, 2012).

8. A representative sample of Soroush's writings is edited and translated with a critical introduction by Mahmoud Sadri and Ahmad Sadri in *Reason, Freedom, and Democracy in Islam: Essential Writings of Abdolkarim Soroush* (Oxford: Oxford University Press, 2002).

9. Abdolkarim Soroush, *Qabz-o Bast-e Teoric-e Shari'at/Theoretical Contraction and Expansion of Religious Knowledge* (Tehran: Sirat Publications, 1984), 180–81.

10. For a detailed study of Osama bin Laden's life and adventures see Michael Scheuer, *Osama bin Laden* (Oxford: Oxford University Press, 2012).

11. Giorgio Agamben, "On the Limits of Violence," *Diacritics* 39, no. 4 (Winter 2009): 103–11. The original Italian appeared in *Nuovi argomenti* in the Winter of 1970.

12. See Samuel P. Huntington, "The Clash of Civilizations?" *Foreign Affairs* (Summer 1993), available online here: https://www.foreignaffairs.com/articles /united-states/1993-06-01/clash-civilizations.

13. See Alan Bloom, *Closing of the American Mind: How Higher Education Has Failed Democracy and Impoverished the Souls of Today's Students* (New York: Simon and Schuster, 1987).

14. See Francis Fukuyama, "The End of History?," *The National Interest* 16 (Summer 1989): 3–18.

15. See Harold Bloom, *The Western Canon: The Books and School of the Ages* (New York: Riverhead Books, 1995).

16. See Jacques Barzun, *From Dawn to Decadence: 1500 to the Present; 500 Years of Western Cultural Life* (New York: HarperCollins, 2001), ix.

17. Long before the rise of Donald Trump and his xenophobic zeal in the 2010s, there were widely popular books like Peter Brimelow's *Alien Nation: Common Sense about America's Immigration Disaster* (New York: Harper Perennial, 1996) spreading fear and anxiety about the new immigrants.

18. See Juan Cole's review of Bernard Lewis's *What Went Wrong: Western Impact and Middle Eastern Response*, 20 May 2018, available on Cole's *Informed Comment* website: https://www.juancole.com/2018/05/bernard-western-response.html.

19. E. M. Cioran, *The Temptation to Exist* (Chicago: University of Chicago Press, 1998), 53–54.

Chapter 5. The Monologue of Civilizations

1. The late Edward Said had criticized the US military occupying forces' having recruited Feldman for a task for which he was so patently ill-prepared. For more, see Karim Fahim's essay from the *Village Voice* back in 2004, available online here: https://www.villagevoice.com/2004/06/22/have-a-nice-country/.

2. See Hamid Dabashi, "For the Last Time: Civilizations," *International Sociology* 16, no. 3 (September 2001): 361–68.

3. The most cogent argument in this transmutation is offered by Michael Hardt and Antonio Negri in their seminal text *Empire* (Cambridge, MA: Harvard University Press, 2001).

4. Marx, *Capital: A Critique of Political Economy*, op. cit.

5. See Hamid Dabashi, *The Shahnameh: The Persian Epic as World Literature* (New York: Columbia University Press, 2019).

6. For a collection of his writings on "World History," see Hans Adler and Ernest A. Menze (eds.), *Johann Gottfried Herder on World History: An Anthology*, translated by Ernest A. Menze and Michael Palma (London: Routledge, 1996).

7. See Raymond Grew, "Expanding Worlds of World History," *Journal of Modern History* 78, no. 4 (December 2006): 882.

8. Ibid.

9. For an electronic version of this seminal work of Walter Benjamin, see here: https://www.sfu.ca/~andrewf/CONCEPT2.html.

10. Ibid.

11. Ibid.

12. See Ranajit Guha, *History at the Limit of World-History* (New York: Columbia University Press, 2003).

Chapter 6. Gendering the Difference

1. For a portrait of Ibtihaj Muhamad's achievements, see Sopan Deb, "Ibtihaj Muhammad: The Olympic Fencer Is Charting Her Own Path," *New York Times*, 24 July 2018, available online here: https://www.nytimes.com/2018/07/24/books/ibtihaj-muhammad-fencing-hijab-olympics.html.

2. See Chandra Talpade Mohanty, "Under Western Eyes: Feminist Scholarship and Colonial Discourses," *Boundary 2* 12, no. 3 (Spring–Autumn 1984): 333–58. The essay was subsequently expanded into a volume: *Feminism without Borders Decolonizing Theory, Practicing Solidarity* (Durham, NC: Duke University Press, 2003). Equally important in this rich and engaging field are the pathbreaking works of Leila Ahmed in her *Women and Gender in Islam: Historical Roots of a Modern Debate* (1992), Fatima Mernissi's *The Veil and the Male Elite: A Feminist Interpretation of Women's Rights in Islam* (1992), Lata Mani's *Contentious Traditions: The Debate on Sati in Colonial India* (1998), Saba Mahmood's *Politics of Piety: The Islamic Revival and the Feminist Subject* (2011), Lila Abu-Lughod's *Do Muslim Women Need Saving?* (2013), and Marnia Lazreg's *Islamic Feminism and the Discourse of Post-Liberation: The Cultural Turn in Algeria* (2020), among others. Common in all this critical body of scholarship is a fiercely contested constitution of Muslim women within the generic disposition of "Islam and the West."

3. Mohanty, "Under Western Eyes: Feminist Scholarship and Colonial Discourses," op. cit., 344. For a cogent critique of Mohanty's own fetishization of "the West" in immaterial terms, see Lazarus, "The Fetish of 'the West' in Postcolonial Theory," op. cit., 59–60. That legitimate criticism, however, does not diminish Mohanty's critique of gender politics I cite here.

4. See Kimberlé Williams Crenshaw, "Mapping the Margins: Intersectionality, Identity Politics, and Violence against Women of Color," in Martha Albertson Fineman and Rixanne Mykitiuk (eds.), *The Public Nature of Private Violence* (New York: Routledge, 1994), 93–118. For a cogent critique of the limitations of Kimberlé Crenshaw and other theorists of "intersectionality," see David McNally's

essay "Intersections and Dialectics: Critical Reconstructions in Social Reproduction Theory," in Tithi Bhattacharya (ed.), *Social Reproduction Theory* (London:
Pluto, 2017), 94–111.

5. For a selection of my essays on Shirin Neshat, see Hamid Keshmirshekan
(ed.), *Contemporary Art, World Cinema, and Visual Culture: Essays by Hamid
Dabashi* (London: Anthem Press, 2019).

6. For an English translation of the Persian original, see Shahrnush Parsipur,
Women without Men, translated from Persian by Kamran Talattof and Jocelyne
Sharlet, afterword by Persis Karim (New York: The Feminist Press, 2004).

7. Gayatri Chakravorty Spivak, "Feminism and Deconstruction, Again: Nego-
tiating with Unacknowledged Masculinism," in Teresa Brennan (ed.), *Between
Feminism and Psychoanalysis* (London: Routledge, 1989), 206.

8. Judith Butler, *Gender Trouble: Feminism and the Subversion of Identity* (London: Routledge, 1990), 1–2.

9. Michel Foucault, "Afterword: The Subject and Power," in Hubert L. Drey-
fus and Paul Rabinow (eds.), *Michel Foucault: Beyond Structuralism and Hermeneutics* (Chicago: University of Chicago Press, 1982), 208.

10. See Gayatri Spivak, "Can the Subaltern Speak," in Cary Nelson and Law-
rence Grossberg (eds.), *Marxism and the Interpretation of Culture* (London: Macmillan, 1988). Spivak used the phrase specifically about Hindu women and the
practice of Sati. More specifically on Muslim women, see Lila Abu-Lughod, *Do
Muslim Women Need Saving?* (Cambridge, MA: Harvard University Press, 2013).

11. There are countless printed and online copies of Sojourner Truth's "Ain't I
a Woman" speech. Here is one such link: https://www.nps.gov/articles/sojourner
-truth.htm. For the original version of the speech in the *Anti-Slavery Bugle*, 21 June
1851, p. 160, see the facsimile at the US Library of Congress available online here:
https://chroniclingamerica.loc.gov/lccn/sn83035487/1851-06-21/ed-1/seq-4/.

12. For detailed biographies of Nur Jahan, see Ruby Lal, *Empress: The Astonishing Reign of Nur Jahan* (New York: W. W. Norton, 2018), and Findly Ellison
Banks, *Nur Jahan: Empress of Mughal India* (Delhi: Oxford University Press,
1993).

13. See Mary Wortley Montagu, *Life on the Golden Horn* (London: Penguin,
2007).

14. For an English translation of this memoir, see Taj al-Saltaneh, *Crowning Anguish: Memoirs of a Persian Princess from Harem to Modernity*, translated by
Anna Vanzan (Washington, DC: Mage Publishers, 2003). The title and subtitle of
the English translation are entirely concocted from the Orientalist fantasies of
the publisher and have nothing to the with the original.

15. These two treatises have been critically edited and published in the United States by Hasan Javadi (ed.), *Ruyaru'i-e Zan-o Mard dar Asr-e Qajar: Do Resaleh Ta'dib al-Niswan wa Ma'ayeb al-Rejal* [*The Confrontation between Men and Women in the Qajar Period: The Two Treatises of Failings of Men and Edification of Women*] (Chicago: Kanun Pazhuhesh-e Tarikh-e Zanan-e Iran, 1992).

16. For a full discussion of Marziyeh Meshkini's *The Day I Became a Woman*, see my *Masters and Masterpieces of Iranian Cinema* (Washington, DC: Mage Publishers, 2007), 369–92.

Chapter 7. De-racing Civilizations

1. The *New York Times* has documented a whole list of Representative Steve King's racist remarks. See Trip Gabriel, "A Timeline of Steve King's Racist Remarks and Divisive Actions," *New York Times*, 15 January 2019, available online here: https://www.nytimes.com/2019/01/15/us/politics/steve-king-offensive -quotes.html. The essay points out: "While some Republicans suggested the Iowa congressman's views were new to them, Mr. King has a long and documented history of denigrating racial minorities."

2. See David Perry and Matthew Gabriele, "Steve King Says He Was Just Defending 'Western Civilization.' That's Racist, Too," *Washington Post*, 15 January 2002, available online here: https://www.washingtonpost.com/outlook/2019/01 /15/steve-king-says-he-was-just-defending-western-civilization-thats-racist-too/.

3. Ibid.

4. See "'Western Civilization' Means Classics . . . and White Supremacy," *Pharos*, 25 January 2019, available online here: http://pages.vassar.edu/pharos /2019/01/25/western-civilization-means-classics-and-white-supremacy/. See also "White Nationalism/Racism and Western Civilization Narratives," 9 December 2016, available online here: https://networks.h-net.org/node/20292/discussions /156355/white-nationalismracism-and-western-civilization-narratives.

5. See Gregory Hood, "Western Civilization Is White Civilization," American Renaissance, 21 January 2019, available online here: https://www.amren.com /commentary/2019/01/western-civilization-is-white-civilization/.

6. See Glenn Fleishman, "A Racist Message Buried for Thousands of Years in the Future," *Atlantic*, 24 October 2018, available online here: https://www .theatlantic.com/science/archive/2018/10/crypt-of-civilization-racism/573598/.

7. Ibid.

8. See Larry Buchanan, Quoctrung Bui, and Jugal K. Patel, "Black Lives Matter May Be the Largest Movement in U.S. History," *New York Times*, 3 July 2020,

available online here: https://www.nytimes.com/interactive/2020/07/03/us /george-floyd-protests-crowd-size.html.

9. I get these citations from the official page of Columbia University on Core Curriculum. See here: https://www.college.columbia.edu/core/timeline.

10. For more on this period at Columbia, see the excellent collection of essays by the participant observers on Columbia's campus, Paul Cronin (ed.), *A Time to Stir: Columbia '68* (New York: Columbia University Press, 2018).

11. There are some detailed studies of this period on US campuses. See, for example, Kenneth J. Heineman, *Campus Wars: The Peace Movement at American State Universities in the Vietnam Era* (New York: New York University Press, 1992).

12. David Denby's *Great Books* (New York: Simon and Schuster, 1997) catered precisely to these alumnae interests. Denby was a Columbia College graduate who had come back to take a couple of these courses later in his life and wrote a nostalgic book about the texts he had read. The aging alumnae loved the book.

13. See Walter Benjamin, "Thesis on the Philosophy of History," in his *Illuminations*, translated by Harry Zohn, edited with an introduction by Hannah Arendt (New York: Schocken Books, 1968), 253–64 (see URL p. 304, n. 9).

14. See Hisham Aidi, "Did Coltrane Say 'Allah Supreme?,'" *Aljazeera*, 9 December 2014, available online here: https://www.aljazeera.com/indepth /opinion/2014/12/did-coltrane-say-allah-supreme-201412810939759431.html.

15. Ibid.

16. Ibid.

17. Ibid.

18. Toni Morrison, *Song of Solomon* (New York: New American Library, 1977), 328. For a discussion of such African Muslim references, see Nada Elia, "'Kum Buba Yali Kum Buba Tambe, Ameen, Ameen, Ameen': Did Some Flying Africans Bow to Allah?," *Callaloo* 26, no. 1 (Winter 2003): 182–202, available online here: https://muse.jhu.edu/article/39829. See also Nada Elia, *Trances, Dances and Vociferations: Agency and Resistance in Africana Women's Narratives* (London: Routledge, 2000).

19. See Elia, "'Kum Buba Yali Kum Buba Tambe, Ameen, Ameen, Ameen,'" op. cit., 183.

20. Ibid., 194–95.

21. Ibid.

22. There are numerous fine studies of the history of Islam in the United States, among them Kambiz Ghaneabassiri, *A History of Islam in America: From the New World to the New World Order* (Cambridge: Cambridge University Press, 2010).

23. See Nadia Marzouki, *Islam: An American Religion* (New York: Columbia University Press, 2017).

24. See Amir Hussain, *Muslims and the Making of America* (Waco, TX: Baylor University Press, 2016).

25. Sylviane A. Diouf, *Servants of Allah: African Muslims Enslaved in the Americas* (New York: New York University Press, 2013).

Chapter 8. Nations beyond Borders

1. Walter Benjamin, "Unpacking My Library: A Talk about Book Collecting," in Walter Benjamin, *Illuminations: Essays and Reflections*, translated by Harry Zohn, edited and with an introduction by Hannah Arendt, preface by Leon Wieseltier (New York: Schocken Books, 1968), 60.

2. Ibid., 67.

3. I have fully explored this fact in the case of one crucial Muslim country in my *Iran without Borders: Towards a Critique of the Postcolonial Nation* (New York: Verso, 2016).

4. See "Trump Says West Is at Risk, during Nationalistic Speech in Poland," *Guardian*, 6 July 2017, available online here: https://www.theguardian.com/us-news/2017/jul/06/donald-trump-warn-future-west-in-doubt-warsaw-speech.

5. I have discussed this systematic abuse in my recent book, *The Shahnameh: The Persian Epic as World Literature* (New York: Columbia University Press, 2019).

6. I have discussed this text in detail in my *Reversing the Colonial Gaze: Persian Travelers Abroad* (Cambridge: Cambridge University Press, 2020).

7. I have explored this process of canonization in detail in my book *The World of Persian Literary Humanism* (Cambridge, MA: Harvard University Press, 2012).

8. For a detailed account of Goldziher's fascination with Islamic intellectual history, see my chapter on him in my *Post-Orientalism: Knowledge and Power in Time of Terror* (New Brunswick, NJ: Transactions Publishers, 2008), 17–122.

Conclusion

1. For more on this crucial turn to decoloniality, see Walter Mignolo and Catherine E. Walsh, *On Decoloniality: Concepts, Analytics, Praxis* (Durham, NC: Duke University Press, 2018), and Achille Mbembe, *Out of the Dark Night: Essays on Decolonization* (New York: Columbia University Press, 2021).

2. For a detailed discussion of this "Orientalism in Reverse" proposition, see Gilbert Achcar, "Orientalism in Reverse: Post-1979 Trends in French

Orientalism," in his *Marxism, Orientalism, Cosmopolitanism* (Chicago: Haymarket Books, 2013). For a far more serious Marxist critique of Edward Said's *Orientalism*, see Aijaz Ahmad, "Orientalism and After: Ambivalence and Metropolitan Location in the Work of Edward Said," in *Theory: Class, Nations, Literature* (London: Verso, 1992), 159–220.

3. I have detailed this central significance of Rosa Luxemburg in "Rosa Luxemburg: The Unsung Hero of Postcolonial Theory," *Aljazeera*, 12 May 2018, available online here: https://www.aljazeera.com/opinions/2018/5/12/rosa-luxemburg-the-unsung-hero-of-postcolonial-theory.

4. I have explored the full implication of that proverbial phrase of Fanon in my *Europe and Its Shadows: Coloniality after Empire* (London: Pluto, 2019).

5. See my *Post-Orientalism: Knowledge and Power in Time of Terror* (New Brunswick, NJ: Transactions Publishers, 2008), 17–122.

6. W. E. B. Du Bois, *The Souls of Black Folk* (New York: Tribeca Books, 2011), 3.

7. Marx, *Critique of Hegel's Philosophy of Right*, op. cit.

Index

Alexander the Great (336–323 BC), 22, 23–24, 247–48, 250

Ali, Mohammed (1769–1849; viceroy of Egypt, 1805–1848), 110

Aligarth Muslim University, 114

Almohad (1121–1269), 27

Almoravids (1040–1147), 27

A Love Supreme (1964), 223–24

Al-e Ahmad, Jalal, 258

al-Qaeda, 148–53

American Islamophobia: Understanding the Roots and Rise of Fear (2018), 3–4

Americanism, 157

Anatolia, 25

Anderson, Martin, 155

Anglo-Muhammadan Oriental College, 113

Another Cosmopolitanism (2008), 92

Ansar, 64

Anthony, Kwame, 256

Anthropology and Colonial Encounter (1973), 14

anti-Muslim violence: rise of and historical context, 1–5. *See also* Islamophobia

anti-Semitism, 39, 221, 294

Appiah, Anthony Kwame, 92

Aquinas, Thomas (1225–1274), 44–45

The Arabic Role in Medieval Literary History: A Forgotten Heritage (1990), 237

Arabic Thought and the Western World (1964), 239

Arab-Israeli conflict: Gaza and Israel, 2021 conflict between, 283–91; influence on Edward Said, 48, 246, 267; Israel, creation of state, 105–6, 111–12; Osama bin-Laden and, 150–51

Arab-Israeli War (1967), 111–12

Arab nationalism: colonizing the Muslim mind, 109–16; Edward Said and, 50, 250, 267–68

Arabs: conflagration with Muslims and politics of racialized domination, 241–47; influence of Arab-Israeli conflict on Said's insights, 246, 267–68; key historical landmarks, 25, 26, 136–37; oligarchic patrimonialism, 67–68; the world after Muhammad, 67–73

The Arabs in History (1950, 2002), 239

Arab Spring (2010s), 178–79

The Arab Spring: The End of Postcolonialism (2012), 10

Archcar, Gilbert, 273

Arjana, Sophia Rose, 271–72

Arkoun, Mohammed, 171

Arnold, Matthew (1822–1888), 254–55

Assad, Talal, 14

Assyrian Empire (1200–612 BC), 22

Astarabadi, Bibi Khanom (1858–1921), 51, 206–7

Atlantic (magazine), 119–20, 212

attributes (sifat), 146–47

Australia, 38

Averroes (1126–1198), 44–45

Ayn, Tahereh Qorrat al- (circa 1814–1852), 205

Azm, Sadik jalal al-, 273

Babylon, key historical landmarks, 22, 23

Babylonian Captivity (586–539 BC), 22

Babylonian Empire (612–539 BC), 22

Baghdad: Al-Ghazali in, 43; British colonialism, 111; *Greek Thought, Arabic Culture: The Graeco-Arabic Translation Movement in Baghdad and Early 'Abbasid Society* (1998), 238; key historical landmarks, 24,

capitalist modernity (*continued*) invention of the West and, 81–85, 172–73; Islam and globalized capital, 141–44; logic and lunacy of capital, 158–62; making of an amorphous empire, 176–81; national cultures, 84–85; Orientalism and Christian missionaries, 120–24; Orientalism as a distancing discourse, 124–29; prolonged Orientalism and rise in New Age mysticism, 163–68; the West as an illusion, 29–30, 279–80

Carroll, Lewis, 265

charismatic authority, 65–66

charismatic character, 65

charismatic paradox: defined, 66–67; the world after Muhammad, 67–73

Chateaubriand, François-René de, 34

Chechnya, 142

Chejne, Anwar, 237

Chopra, Deepak, 166

Christianity: as colonizing force, 98; Crusades, misremembering of, 43–46; as depicted in, *Bataille de Poitiers en Octobre 732* (1837), 30–37, 31*fig*; divide between "Eastern" and "Western" Europe, 238; Europe, premodern power configuration, 84; French Christianity, 101–2; influences of Persia on European self-understanding, 249–50; Kant, de-Christianizing of colonized subjects, 90–91; key historical landmarks, 24–26, 136–37; Mediterranean trade routes, cultural interaction and, 45–46, 82; Orientalism and Christian missionaries, 120–24; in Palestine, 284; secular Christianity, 101–4; in the service of Empire, 30; the West as another term for

Christendom, 39, 136, 182–84, 213, 279–80

Cioran, E. M., 168–69

civilization: de-racing civilization, overview of, 210–14; dialogue among cultures, possibility of, 173–76; dismantling the myth of civilizational divides, 270–74; Enlightenment standards for, 83; Kant and making "the Western" subject universal, 86–91; labor as "other civilizations," 126; logic and lunacy of capital, 158–62; mutation of the West from militant to iconic, 153–58; national cultures, 84–85; Orientalism as a distancing discourse, 124–29; prolonged Orientalism and rise in New Age mysticism, 163–68; rejection of civilizational thinking, 177–81; undoing of "Western civilization," 214–22, 216*fig*; universal civilizations, 84–85; the West as subterfuge for, 39; Western Christianity as penultimate stage, 136

Civilization: The West and the Rest (2012), 11, 41, 271

clash of civilizations, 174–75; Dante's *Divine Comedy*, 41–42; ghosts of terrors past, 5–16; overview of, 4–5; paths through ahistorical confusion, 46–53

The Clash of Civilizations and the Remaking of the World Order (1998), 16

"The Clash of Civilizations?" (1993), 153–54, 161

class: feminism without borders, 192–96, 200, 202; intersectionality of race, class, and gender, 48, 52, 56–53, 186, 191–92, 201–8, 222, 261;

Karl Marx on false consciousness, 77, 280; Kimberlé Crenshaw on intersectionality, 52–53; new class of middle-class bourgeoisie, emergence of, 8, 81, 84, 96–97

Closing of the American Mind: How Higher Education has Failed Democracy and Impoverished the Souls of Today's Students (1987), 154, 156, 271

Cohn, Bernard, 15

Cole, Juan, 165

collective trauma, 221

Collins, Jane L., 161

colonialism: as center of the Islam vs the West binary, 243; Christianity as a colonizing force, 98; colonial modernity and Islam as an abstraction, 73–77, 241–42; decolonization, need for, 269–74; gender across colonial boundaries and borders, overview of, 189–92; Industrial Revolution as a global development, 93–97; Islam as site of ideological resistance, 61–63, 82–83, 104–6; Kant and making "the Western" subject universal, 88–91; key historical events, 111, 136–37; logic and lunacy of capital, 158–62; Morocco, French occupation of, 101–2; national cultures and, 85; Orientalism as a colonial project, 8–9, 83–84; Palestinian and Israeli conflict 2021, 284–91; paths through ahistorical confusion, 46–53; postcolonial studies, 160–62, 273; prolonged Orientalism and rise in New Age mysticism, 163–68; religion as secular, 102; religion in the service of, 30; reorienting history, reimagining geography, and liberating the postcolonial subject,

274–82; Socialist movements, 107–9; United States as modern imperial power, 6–8. *See also* capitalist modernity; coloniality; imperialism

Colonialism and its Forms of Knowledge: The British in India (1996), 15

coloniality: colonizing the Muslim mind, 109–16; condition of, overview, 101–4; as interlocutor of Islam, 104–6; Orientalism and Christian missionaries, 120–24; Orientalism as a distancing discourse, 124–29; recasting the global politics of space, 107–9; rentier intellectuals, role in fabricated hostility of Islam and the West, 116–20; rentier intellectuals, role of, 116–20. *See also* colonialism

Coltrane, John, 223–24, 230

Columbia University, core curriculum, 216–22

Columbus, Christopher, 121

commodity fetishism. *See* fetishized abstraction, commodity, or ideology

Constantinople, 25, 136–37

Constituting Americans: Cultural Anxiety and Narrative Form (1995), 161–62

Contesting Islamophobia (2019), 4

Corbin, Henry (1903–1978), 258, 274–75

Cosmopolitanism: Ethics in the World of Strangers (2007), 92

COVID-19 pandemic, 5, 78–79, 100

Creasy, Edward Sheperd, 34

creative conflict, Islam after Muhammad, 68–73

Crenshaw, Kimberlé, 52–53, 195–96

The Crisis of Islam: Holy War and Unholy Terror (2003), 164

Dietrich, Albert, 237
Diouf, Sylviane A., 229
DisForming the American Canon: African-Arabic Slave Narratives and the Vernacular (1993), 161
dividing practices, 200–201
doctrinally polyfocal, Islam as, 71–73
"Don't Forget the Ladies" (1776), 202
double-consciousness, 277–78
Douglass, Frederick, 210
Dozy, Rheinhart, 236
D'Souza, Dinesh, 116, 155
dual consciousness, 134, 277–78
Du Bois, W.E.B., 134, 277, 281
Dussel, Enrique, 15

Early Middle Ages (476–1000), 24–25
Early Orientalism: Imagined Islam and the Notion of Sublime Power (2012), 15
East, the. *See* Orientalism
Eastern Orthodoxy, key historical landmarks, 24–26
educational politics: Columbia University, core curriculum, 216–22; undoing of "Western civilization," 214–22, 216*fig*
Egypt: Ali Abd al-Raziq (1888–1966), 111–12; al-Tahtawi (1801–1873), 110; Arab Spring, Tahrir Square, 178–79; colonizing the Muslim mind, 109–16; European interest in ancient cultures, 250, 259; Inji Aflatoun (1924–1989), 207–8; Islamism, rise of, 142–43, 152; key historical landmarks, 23, 111; Maimonides, 45–46, 243; Muhammad Abduh (1849–1905), 110–11, 143; US military and, 6, 294
Elia, Nada, 226–27

Emerson, Ralph Waldo (1803–1882), 233, 252
The Emperor Is Naked: On the Inevitable Demise of the Nation-State (2020), 10
Empire (2000), 172–73
End of History (1989), 271
The End of History and the Last Man (1993), 16
"The End of History?" (1989), 156
En Islam iranien (1971–1973), 275
Enlightenment: civilization, standard for, 83; democracy in Islamic world, failures of, 108–9; divide between "Eastern" and "Western" Europe, 237–38; influences of Persia on European self-understanding, 250–51, 252; interplay of cultures during, 177–78; invention of the West and, 81, 83–85; modernity and the globalized bourgeoisie, 96–97; Orientalism and Christian missionaries, 122–23; Orientalism as a distancing discourse, 127–29; poststructuralist critique of, 159–62
epistemically polyvocal, Islam as, 71–73
Essays on the Closing of the American Mind (1989), 154
essence (dhat), 146–47
Euphemius, 26
Eurocentric feminism, 193–96
Europe: as creation of the Third World, Frantz Fanon on, 274; as depicted in, *Bataille de Poitiers en Octobre 732* (1837), 30–37, 31*fig*; divide between "Eastern" and "Western" Europe, 237–38; Industrial Revolution as a global development, 93–97; influences of Persia on European self-understanding,

of, 101–2; slave trade, 227. *See also* colonialism

French Revolution, 81, 179, 182

Freud, Sigmund, 28–30, 37, 53–54, 91, 273, 279

Friedman, Thomas, 116

From Dawn to Decadence: 1500 to the Present; 500 Years of Western Cultural Life (2000), 158

From the Cape to Cairo, (Udo Keppler), 216*fig*

Fukuyama, Francis, 4, 16, 136, 155, 156, 243, 271

The Future of an Illusion (1927), 37

Gabriele, Matthew, 211

Garza, Alicia, 288

Gauguin, Paul, 259

Gay, Peter, 134–35

Gaza as Metaphor (2016), 288

Geller, Pamela, 3, 5

gender: across colonial boundaries and borders, overview of, 189–92; Columbia University, core curriculum, 218; *The Day I Became a Woman* (2000), 208–9; dialogical construction of woman as a human being, 196–201; Ibtihaj Muhammad, 189–90; intersectionality of race, class, and gender, 201–8; intersectionality of race and gender, 52–53, 195–96

Gender Trouble: Feminism and the Subversion of Identity (1990), 199–200

genocide: European Jewish genocide, 159; Native Americans, 162; Orientalism and Christian missionaries, 122–24

geography: colonialism and the geography of conquest, 95–97; "Islam and the West" as an imaginative geography, 20, 38, 40, 44–45, 79, 241, 247, 257, 259–60; liberation geography, 178–79; map of memory, 21–28; Muslim scientific achievements, 72; reimagining of, 274–82

Ghazali, Abu Hamid Mohammad al- (1058–1111), 43–46

Ghaznavids (977–1186), 27, 242–43

Ghazoul, Ferial, 171

Gibbon, Edward, 33–34

Gifford, Paul, 9

globalization. *See* capitalist modernity; globalized capital

globalized bourgeoisie, Enlightenment modernity and, 96–97

globalized capital: as center of the Islam *vs.* the West binary, 12–13; circulatory dispositions of labor and capital, 239–40; clash of civilizations, overview of, 7–16; Industrial Revolution as a global development, 93–97; invention of the West and, 81–85, 172–73; Islam and globalization, 141–44; making of an amorphous empire, 176–81; Orientalism as a distancing discourse, 124–29. *See also* capitalist modernity

global politics of space, 107–9

Goethe, Johann Wolfgang von, 83, 251–52

Goldziher, Ignaz (1850–1921), 258, 275

Golf for Enlightenment: The Seven Lessons for the Game of Life (2003), 166

Gottschalk, Peter, 3

Gramsci, Antonio, 14, 99, 258

Great Britain, colonial occupations by, 111, 113, 115, 267. *See also* colonialism

28–30; the West as an illusion, 80, 83–84, 273–74, 279–80

immigration: Islamophobia and, 5; multiculturalism, 161–62; US as epicenter of globalized capital, 222, 247; US demographic shifts, 161, 176; Western civilization and immigrants from Europe, 215–16, 217–18; white supremacy and, 1–2

imperialism: globalization and "Western Imperialism," 95–96, 160–61; Industrial Revolution as a global development, 94–97; in the interest of capital, 94–95, 178; Islam and ideologic resistance to imperialism, 104–8, 142, 152, 168; key historical landmarks, 27–28, 75–76; religion as tool for, 289–90; of United States, 6–7. *See also* colonialism

Imposters in the Temple: American Intellectuals Are Destroying Our Universities and Cheating Our Students of Their Future (1992), 155

India, 105–6, 113–14

Indonesia, 115, 116, 143

Industrial Revolution: as a global development, 93–97; inventing "the West" and, 46–47, 81, 241

Indus Valley, 23

intersectionality: of race, class, and gender, 52–53, 195–96, 201–8. *See also* class; race; women

Inventing Eastern Europe (1994), 237–38

The Invention of Africa (1988), 15

Iqbal, Muhammad (1875–1938), 143, 252

Iran: American hostage crisis (1980), 292; Bibi Khanom Astarabadi (1858–1921), 206–7; Constitutional Revolution (1906–1911), 256, 257;

Ferdowsi (940–1020), 247–48, 254–55; Forough Farrokhzad (1934–1967), 207; Islamic Republic, creation of, 106; Islamic Revolution and the end of Islamism, 138–41, 142; Jamal al-Din al-Afghani (1838–1897), 270–71; Nur Jahan (1577–1645), 50–51, 204; rise and demise of Islamic ideology, 143, 144–53; war with Iraq (1980–1988), 139; women's rights movement in, 206–7. *See also* Persian Empire

Iraq: Abd al-Rahman al-Bazzaz (1913–1977), 112–13; beneficiaries of imperialism, 94; invasion of Kuwait, 148; Islamism, rise of, 112–13, 142, 152; key historical landmarks, 111; Nazik al-Mala'ikah (1922–2007), 207; revolution (1958), 111; US occupation of, 171; US wars with, 34, 118–19, 174, 292; US war with, as ideological war, 5–6, 175–76; war with Iran (1980–1988), 139

ISIS, 142, 152, 179, 262

Islam: as an illusion, 28–30; arts, culture, and science contributions of, 72–73; Black Muslim liberation theology in America, 228–32; charismatic paradox, 66–67; clash of civilization with the West, overview of, 4–16, 82–83; coloniality as interlocutor of Islam, 104–6; colonial modernity, Islam as an abstraction, 73–77; colonizing the Muslim mind, 109–16; conflagration of Arabs with Muslims and politics of racialized domination, 241–47; contemporary cultural formations and the undoing of Islam and the West binary, 222–28; crisis of succession, 68–69; Crusades, misremembering of,

Islam (*continued*)
43–46; as culturally polylocal religion, 70–71; Dar al-Islam *vs.* Dar al-Harb (Abode of Peace *vs.* Abode of War), 107–9; decolonized history, importance of, 269–74; as depicted in *Bataille de Poitiers en Octobre 732* (1837), 30–37, 31*fig*; dialogical thinking within Islamic world, 184–86; as doctrinally polyfocal, epistemically polyvocal, and culturally polylocal, 71–73; as fetishized commodity, 10–16, 75–77; Islamism, the end of, 138–41; jazz music and, 223–25; key historical landmarks, 21–28, 136–37; as a lived experience, overview of, 59–63, 281–82; Mediterranean trade routes, cultural interaction and, 45–46, 82; Muslims in history, 63–67; Orientalism and Christian missionaries, 120–24; path to post-Islamist and post-Western world, 246–47, 261–63; the power of ideology and the ideology of power, 16–21; as religion of protest, 63–65, 168; rentier intellectuals, role in fabricated hostility of Islam and the West, 116–20; reorienting history, reimagining geography, and liberating the postcolonial subject, 274–82; rise and demise of Islamic ideology, 144–53; Shi'ism as religion of protest, 140–41; as site of colonial resistance, 61–63, 82–83, 104–6; in Spain, 235–40; as synonymous with terrorism, 3–5; and the West, the twain collide and collapse, 168–69; the world after Muhammad, 67–73; Zionism, response to, 105–6. *See also* Islamism / Islamist movements; Muslims

Islam: An American Religion (2017), 229
Islam and the Medieval West: Aspects of Intercultural Relations (1980), 237
Islam and the West (1993), 164
Islam and the West: A Conversation with Jacques Derrida (2008), 271
Islam and the West: The Making of an Image (1993), 236
Islamic civilization, invention of, 83–84
Islamic Da`wah in the West: Muslim Missionary Activity and the Dynamics of Conversion to Islam (1992), 236
Islamic law (Shari'ah), 69–70, 82, 113
Islamic Liberation Theology (2008), 228–29
Islamic mysticism (Tasawwuf), 70, 75, 113
Islamic philosophy (Falsafah), 69–70
Islamic Republic, creation of, 106, 139–41, 145, 147, 287
Islamic Spain 1250–1500 (1992), 236
Islam in European Thought (1991), 15
Islam in European Thought (1992), 237
Islam in Liberalism (2015), 272
Islamism / Islamist movements: colonizing the Muslim mind, 106, 109–16; Dar al-Islam *vs.* Dar al-Harb (Abode of Peace *vs.* Abode of War), 107–9; dialogical thinking within Islamic world, 184–86; as distancing discourse, 128–29; globalization and Islam, 141–44; goal of an Islamic state, 17; historical view of, 20; as ideology of domination *vs.* resistance, 106; "Islam" and "the West," collision and collapse of, 168–69, 232, 261–63, 293–94; Islamic ideology, from militant to

iconic, 153–58; Islamic ideology, rise and demise of, 5–6, 18–19, 61, 75, 106, 107–9, 134, 138–41, 144–53, 157; rentier intellectuals, role in fabricated hostility of Islam and the West, 116–20; Shi'ism as religion of protest, 140–41; Zionism, links to, 287–91, 294

Islamophobia: dismantling of the false binary of Islam and the West, 20–21, 179–80, 273, 281; Hamas as a false synechdoche for all of Palestine, 286–87; rise of and historical context, 1–5; use of *Bataille de Poitiers en Octobre 732* (1837), 33–37; war on terror and, 292–94; xenophobia, recent rise of, 39

Islamophobia and the Politics of Empire (2012), 3–4

Islamophobia: Making Muslims the Enemy (2007), 3–4

Israel: Arab-Israeli conflict, influence on Edward Said, 48, 246, 267; Arab-Israeli War (1967), 111–12; creation of state of, 105–6, 111–12; Gaza military strikes in 2021, 283–91; key historical landmarks, 23; occupation of Palestine by, 118; Osama bin Laden views on, 150–51; as part of "the West," 38; Zionism and militant Islamism, link between, 289–91

Italy, colonial occupations by, 111

Jacobs, Thornwell, 212

Jahan, Nur (1577–1645), 50–51, 204

Jama'at-i Islami, 114

Jamia Millia Islamia University, 114

Jan-Mohamed, Abdul R., 9

Java, 115

Java wars (1825–1830), 115

jazz music, Islam and, 223–25

Jerusalem: British occupation of (1917), 111; change in direction of Muslim prayer, 68; Israeli actions toward Palestinian families in, 284–85; lived experiences of Muslims and non-Muslims, 82; Muslim conquest of (638), 136; Osama bin Laden references to, 150, 151

Jihad: The Trail of Political Islam (2002), 17

Jones, William (1746–1794), 251

Jordan, US military and, 6

Journey to an Illusion: The West Indian in Britain (1966), 256

Judaism: Holocaust, 159, 220–21; Israel, creation of state, 105–6, 111–12; Jews in Palestine, 284; key historical landmarks, 25–26; Mediterranean trade routes, cultural interaction and, 45–46, 82

Judy, Ronald A. T., 161

Ka'bah, 151

Kant, Immanuel (1724–1804), 78, 83, 86–91, 97, 161

Kashmiris, 108

Katznelson, Ira, 219

Kaum Muda (The Young Group), 115

Kaviraj, Sudipta, 181

Kelmar, Ivan, 15

Kenya, 148

Kepel, Gilles, 17, 20, 243

Keppler, Udo, 216*fig*

Khan, Genghis, 27

Kharijite Islam, 68–69

Khatami, Mohammad, 139, 174–75

Khatib, Ahmad (1855–1916), 115–16, 143

Khobar Military Complex, 148

Khomeini, Ayatollah, 138–39

Khorasan, 24–25, 27, 43

Makiya, Kanaan, 119
Mala'ikah, Nazik al- (1922–2007), 207
Malaysia, 115, 116, 143
Malcolm X, 52, 133, 214, 228–32
Malcolm X (1992, film), 218
Manheim, Karl, 14
Manichean Aesthetics: The Politics of Literature in Colonial Africa (1983), 9
Manichean dualism, 9, 18, 36, 41, 59, 81, 91, 194–95, 247
"Mapping the Margins: Intersectionality, Identity Politics, and Violence against Women of Color" (1994), 195–96
Maqasid al-Falasifah (The Aims of the Philosophers), 44
Marable, Manning, 219
Marcus, Steven, 134, 254
Martel, Charles (ca. 688–741), 26, 32, 34
Marx, Karl: on capitalism, 91, 125, 126, 127; on commodity fetishism, 12–14; on fetishism, 180–81; on religion, 76–77, 98
Marzouki, Nadia, 229
Massad, Joseph, 272
Massignon, Louis (1883–1962), 258, 275
Matar, Dina, 288
Matisse, Henri, 259
Mawdudi, Abu al-Ala al- (1903–1979), 113–14
McNeill, William, 93, 238
Mead, George Herbert, 14
Mecca: Osama bin Laden references to, 150–51; Prophet Muhammad and, 64–67, 68
Medina: Osama bin Laden references to, 150–51; Prophet Muhammad in, 64–67, 68

Mediterranean basin: invention of the West and, 82–85, 243, 248; trade routes, 45–46, 82
The Mediterranean and the Mediterranean World in the Age of Philip II (1949), 45
Menocal, María Rosa, 171, 237
Meshkini, Marzieh, 208–9
Mesopotamia, 23
The Metaphysics of Morals (1797), 88
Meyer, Eugene A., 239
Middle East, key historical landmarks, 21–28, 136–37
Mignolo, Walter, 92, 256
migration: Islam and globalization, 141–44; Islamophobia, rise of, 4–5; US demographic shifts, 161; Western civilization and immigrants from Europe, 215–16, 217–18; white supremacy and xenophobia, 2–5, 39, 56
militant Islamism. *See* Islamism / Islamist movements
Miller, Stephen, 1–3, 5
modern, defined, 96
modernity: coloniality as interlocutor of Islam, 104–6; colonial modernity and Islam as an abstraction, 73–77. *See also* capitalist modernity
Mohammed, Charlemagne and the Origins of Europe: Archaeology and the Pirenne Thesis (1983), 237
Mohanty, Chandra Talpade, 192–93, 200
Mongol Empire (1206–1368), 27
Montague, Mary Wortley (1689–1762), 51, 205–6
Montesquieu, 250
Morey, Peter, 4
Morier, James, 256–60
Morocco, 101–2, 184–86

Morrison, Toni, 225-28, 230
Mozarabic Chronicle, 33
Mozart, Wolfgang Amadeus, 254
Mudimbe, Y. V., 15
Mughal Empire (1526-1857), 27, 50-51, 242-43
Muhajirun, 64
Muhammad, Ibtihaj, 189-90
Muhammadan Anglo-Oriental Education Conference, 113
Muhammadiya, 115
Mulk, Khwajah Nezam al- (1018-1092), 204
multiculturalism, 161-62, 176
Musaddeq, Muhammad (1881-1967), 138
The Muslim Discovery of Europe (2001), 164
Muslims: colonizing the Muslim mind, 109-16; conflagration of Arabs with Muslims and politics of racialized domination, 241-47; dialogical thinking within Islamic world, 184-86; double-consciousness and, 277-78; feminism and the imagined "Muslim woman," 202-8; in history, 63-67; Islam as a lived experience, overview of, 59-63, 281-82; Islamophobia and, 3-5. *See also* Islam
Muslims and the Making of America (2016), 229
Muslims in the Western Imagination (2015), 271-72
mysticism, 70, 113; contemporary cultural formations and the undoing of Islam and the West binary, 223-28; influences of Persia on European self-understanding, 258; prolonged Orientalism and rise in New Age mysticism, 163-68; Rumi,

modern appeal of, 178; Sufism, birth of, 75

Nairobi, Kenya, 148
Nasr, Seyyed Hossein, 166
national cultures, 81, 84-85, 126, 128, 129, 159
National Identities and Post-Americanism Narratives (1994), 162
The National Interest, 156
nationalism: colonizing the Muslim mind, 109-16; Islamic Revolution and the end of Islamism, 138-41; Orientalism as a distancing discourse, 127-29; as resistance to colonialism, 107-9; secularism and Islam, 114-15
nations beyond borders, 233-35; Islam in Spain, Orientalist scholarship and, 235-40; from Orientalism to Persophilia, 240-47
Negri, Antonio, 172-73
neo-Nazis, 35-36, 39, 41
neo-Orientalism, as a colonial project, 8-9
Neshat, Shirin, 196-201
New Age mysticism, rise in, 163-68
New York Times, 1-2
New Zealand, 38
Nietzsche, Friedrich, 14, 89, 91, 253, 259
9/11 terror attacks, 5, 20; dialogue among cultures, possibility of, 173-76; Osama bin Laden, 147-53; rentier intellectuals, role in fabricated hostility of Islam and the West, 116-20. *See also* war on terrorism
nomocentricism, 62, 69-70, 113
Nubia, 23

The Occidental Quarterly, 35
Okihiro, Gary, 220

O'Malley, Robert, 219
Omar, Mullah, 151–52
Omar Khayyam, 254
"On the Concept of History" (1940), 182–83
Oriental despotism, 15
Orientalism, 5, 14–15; Christian missionaries and, 120–24; as a colonial project, 8–9, 85; Dar al-Islam vs. Dar al-Harb (Abode of Peace vs. Abode of War), 107–9; as a distancing discourse, 124–29; historical blindspots of, 265–70; as ideology of domination vs. resistance, 106; Islamic civilization, invention of, 83–84; Orientalism in reverse, 273; paths through ahistorical confusion, 46–53; prolonged Orientalism and rise in New Age mysticism, 163–68; reorienting history, reimagining geography, and liberating the postcolonial subject, 274–82
Orientalism (1978), 9, 14. See also Said, Edward
Orientalism in Crisis (1963), 14
Oriental Renaissance (1950), 14, 47, 244
The Other Victorians: A Study of Sexuality and Pornography in Mid-Nineteenth- Century England (1966), 134, 254
Ottoman Empire (1299-1922), 25–28, 76; divide between "Eastern" and "Western" Europe, 237–38; non-Arab Muslim empires, 242–43
Our Country (1885), 135

Pahlavi, Mohammed Reza, 138–39
Pakistan, 106, 114; India partition along Hindu-Muslim divide, 105–6, 114; Osama bin Laden and, 148; Taliban and, 142; US military and, 6

Palacios, Miguel Asín (1871-1944), 42
Palestine: Edward Said, defense of, 50, 160, 267; Islamism, rise of, 140, 142; Israel, creation of state, 105–6; Israeli military strikes in 2021, 283–91; key historical landmarks, 23; Socialist movements and, 108
Pan-Islamism, 252
parapublic sphere, 48, 53, 239–40, 245–46
Parsipur, Shahrnush, 196
Pease, Donald E., 162
Perry, David, 211
Persian Empire: influence on European self-understanding, 247–56; invention of the West and, 79–80; key historical landmarks, 21–24; non-Arab Muslim empires, 242–43
Persian Letters (1721), 250
The Persians (472 BC), 22, 240–41, 249, 256
Persian Wars (490-480 BC), 23
Persophilia: Henry Corbin and, 258; James Morier and, 256–60; from Orientalism to Persophilia, 240–47
Persophilia: Persian Culture on the Global Scene (2015), 15, 47–48, 240, 244–47, 276–77
Philosophical and Political History of the Two Indies (1770), 122
philosophy: colonizing the Muslim mind, 113–16; Kant and making "the Western" subject universal, 86–87; philosophy of history, geography of conquest, 91–97. See also individual philosopher names
Philosophy of History (1837), 91–97
Picasso, Pablo, 54–55, 55fig
Pipes, Daniel, 165
Pizan, Christine de, 202
Pope Urban II, 137

postcolonial theory, 273; decolonized history, importance of, 269–74; Edward Said and, 268, 273; Guha's critique of Helgelian historiography, 183–84; intersectionality and, 53, 56, 194, 207–8; Marxist historiography and, 15, 273; positivist historiography and critiques of modernity, 159–60; reorienting history, reimagining geography, and liberating the postcolonial subject, 274–82; resubjection of the postcolonial person, 92; Rosa Luxemburg and, 273; "The Fetish of 'the West' in Postcolonial Theory," Neil Lazarus, 9–10, 11; thematic mutation of Islam as subject, 61–62, 155

Poston, Larry, 236

Profscam: Professors and the Demise of Higher Education (1988), 154

Prolegomena to Any Future Metaphysic That Shall Lay Claim to Being a Science (1783), 87

prophetic paraphrastic, 69–70

Prophet Muhammad (570–632), 64–67; as charismatic character, 65–66; charismatic paradox, 66–67; key historical landmarks, 24, 25–26; the world after Muhammad, 67–73

Protestant Reformation, invention of the West and, 81

Punic War (264–202 BC), 23–24

Qabz-o Bast-e Teoric-e Shari'at (Theoretical contraction and expansion of religious knowledge), 146

"Question Concerning Technology" (1957), 159

Qur'an: colonizing the Muslim mind, 109–16; Edward Gibbon on fear of Islam, 33–34; narrative variations in, 72–73; Prophet Muhammad as charismatic authority, 65–66; Soroush on religious knowledge, 145–46

Qutb, Sayyid (1906–1966), 143

race, 52; Black Muslim liberation theology in America, 228–32; conflagration of Arabs with Muslims and politics of racialized domination, 241–47; contemporary cultural formations and the undoing of Islam and the West binary, 222–28; deracing civilizations, overview of, 210–14; Immanuel Kant, racism of, 88–89; intersectionality of race, class, and gender, 52–53, 195–96, 201–8; multiculturalism, 161, 162; Orientalism and Christian missionaries, 120–24; postmodern critiques of Enlightenment, 161–62; racism in the Victorian era, 134–35; skin color, dangerous delusions about, 103–4; undoing of "Western civilization," 214–22, 216*fig*

Raynal, Abbé Guillaume Thomas François (1713–1796), 122

reactionary violence, 152–53

Reading "National Geographic" (1993), 161

Rehman, Iskander, 34–35, 36

religion: divide between "Eastern" and "Western" Europe, 238; Europe, premodern power configuration, 84; as false consciousness, 37, 279–80; French Christianity, 101–2; fundamentalism as distancing discourse, 128–29; historical cultural contexts and, 42; influences of Persia on European self-understanding, 249–50; Karl Marx

on, 76–77, 98, 279–80; Mediterranean trade routes, cultural interaction and, 45–46, 82; non-Arab
Muslim empires, 242–43; Orientalism and Christian missionaries,
120–24; religious suffering, 76–77;
rise and demise of Islamic ideology, 144–53; secular Christianity,
101–4; Shi'ism as religion of protest, 140–41; the West as another
term for Christendom, 39, 136, 182–
84, 213. *See also* Christianity; Islam;
Judaism
*Religion within the Limits of Reason
Alone* (1793), 87–88
rentier intellectuals, role in fabricated
hostility of Islam and the West,
116–20
*Reversing the Colonial Gaze: Persian
Travelers Abroad* (2020), 276–77
Rida, Rashid (1865–1935), 110–11, 143
*The Rise and Fall of Paradise: When
Arabs and Jews Built a Kingdom in
Spain* (1990), 236
The Rise of Eurocentrism (1992), 236
The Rise of the West (1964), 238
Rodinson, Maxime, 14–15
Rohingyas, 108
Roman Catholic Church, key histori-
cal landmarks, 24–26
Roman Empire: influences of Persia
on European self-understanding,
249–50; invention of the West and,
80; key historical landmarks, 23–24
Romanticism: Battle of Pointiers, cel-
ebration of, 34; influences of Persia
on European self-understanding,
245, 251–53
Roosevelt, Theodore, 34
Roy, Olivier, 243
ruling classes, ideologies of, 97–100

ruling class hegemony, 99–100
Rumi (1207–1273), 178, 252
Rupp, George, 219
Rushdie, Salman, 116, 139

Sack of Constantinople (1204), 25
Sa'di (circa 1210–1292), 252
Safavid Empire (1501–1736), 27,
242–43
Said, Edward: Arab-centric stance of,
250, 267–68; death of, 170; historical blind spots of, 118, 127, 266–68,
272–73, 275–76; influence of Arab-
Israeli conflict on Said's insights,
50, 246, 253; on knowledge produc-
tion as colonial project, 137, 159,
160–61; Orientalism and, 9, 19, 47,
48–49, 91; Orientalism as discourse
of alienation, 123, 125; on "The
Orient" as a politically motivated
construct, 244; on "the West" as a
myth, 11–12, 13
Saltaneh, Taj al- (1884–1936), 206
Samanids (819–999), 27
Sampaio, Jorge, 173
Sassanid Empire (224–651), 76, 79–80
Saudi Arabia: Osama bin Laden, 148–
49, 152; US military and, 6, 294;
Wahhabism in, 290
Scheler, Max, 14
Schiller, Friedrich, 32
Schwab, Raymond, 14, 47, 48–49,
244
scientific advancements, in Islam,
72–73
Second Siege of Constantinople, 25
secular Christianity, 101–4
secularism, contrast with Islam and,
114–15
Seleucid Empire, 24, 25
Seljuk Empire, 204

Van Ess, J., 237
Varlik, Nükhet, 79
Victorian age, 134–35, 254
A Vindication of the Rights of Woman
(1792), 51, 202
violence, reactionary, 152–53
visual violence, 149–53

Wahhabism, 108
Wahid, Abdurahman, 143
Wald, Priscilla, 161–62
*The War against the Intellect: Episodes
in the Decline of Discourse* (1989),
154
war on terrorism, 5, 167, 174; Afghanistan, US 2021 withdrawal from,
291–94; ghosts of terrors past, 5–16;
rentier intellectuals, role in fabricated hostility of Islam and the
West, 116–20
Washington Post, 211
Watt, W. Montgomery, 236
Weber, Max, 83, 159
West, Allen, 34
West, the: as an illusion, 28–30, 103–4;
clash of civilizations with Islam,
overview of, 4–16; coloniality as
interlocutor of Islam, 104–6; colonizing the Muslim mind, 109–16;
decolonized history, importance
of, 269–74; defining of, 38–39; as
depicted in, *Bataille de Poitiers en
Octobre 732* (1837), 30–37, 31*fig*;
as fetishized commodity, 10–16;
Industrial Revolution as a global
development, 93–97; invention of
the West, 81–85, 172–73; and Islam,
the collision and collapse, 168–69;
Kant and making "the Western"
subject universal, 86–91; key historical landmarks, 21–28, 79–81,

136–37; making of an amorphous
empire, 176–81; Mediterranean
trade routes, cultural interaction
and, 45–46; mutation of the West
from militant to iconic, 153–58;
national cultures, 84–85; Orientalism and Christian missionaries,
120–24; Orientalism as a distancing discourse, 124–29; path to post-
Islamist and post-Western world,
246–47, 261–63; philosophy of history, geography of conquest, 91–97;
the power of ideology and the ideology of power, 16–21; recasting
the global politics of space, 107–9;
as recent conceptual invention, 8;
rentier intellectuals, role in fabricated hostility of Islam and the
West, 116–20; reorienting history,
reimagining geography, and liberating the postcolonial subject, 274–82;
ruling ideologies, ruling classes,
97–100; as subterfuge for Christendom, 39, 136, 182–84, 213, 279–80;
as subterfuge for civilization, 39; the
world in world history, 181–84
West and the Rest binary: Columbia
University, core curriculum, 216–22;
racism in the Victorian era, 135–36;
rejection of civilizational thinking,
177–79. *See also* West, the
The Western Canon (1994), 157
Western civilization: contemporary
cultural formations and the undoing of Islam and the West binary,
222–28; as euphemism for white
supremacy, 210–14; mutation of
the West from militant to iconic,
153–58; undoing of "Western civilization," 214–22, 216*fig*. *See also*
West, The

Western Imperialism, 94–97
*Western Views of Islam in the Middle
Ages* (1962), 236
*What Went Wrong? The Clash between
Islam and Modernity in the Middle
East* (2002), 16–17, 119–20, 271
*What Went Wrong: Western Impact and
Middle Eastern Response* (2001), 164
Whitehouse, David, 237
white nationalism, 1–5, 39, 211. *See also*
nationalism; white supremacy
white supremacy: de-racing civili-
zations, overview of, 210–14; as
emblem of "the West," 29, 211;
European white supremacy and the
Israeli-Palestinian conflict, 289;
Islamophobia and, 3–5; racism in
the United States, 214; recent rise
of, 39; skin color, delusions about,
103–4, 281; undoing of "Western
civilization," 56, 214–22, 216*fig*; use
of *Bataille de Poitiers en Octobre 732*
(1837), 34–37; W.E.B. Du Bois on
dual consciousness, 134, 277–78
Witica (Witiza), 26
Wolff, Larry, 237–38
Wollstonecraft, Mary, 51, 202
women: *The Day I Became a Woman*
(2000), 208–9; dialogical construction of woman as a human being,
196–201; Eurocentric feminism,
193–96; feminism and the imagined "Muslim woman," 202–8;
feminism without borders, 192–96;
gender across colonial boundaries and borders, overview of, 189–
92; Ibtihaj Muhammad, 189–90;

intersectionality of race and gender, overview of, 52–53; Montagu,
Mary Wortley (1689–1762), 51;
Muhammadiya, women's rights
and, 115; multiculturalism, 161,
162; Nur Jahan (1577–1645), 50–51;
Tahereh Qorrat al-Ayn (1814–1852),
51; Taj al-Saltaneh (1883–1936),
51; in the transnational public
sphere, 50–52. *See also* feminism;
intersectionality
Women without Men (2009), 196–201
*The World and the West: The European
Challenge and the Overseas Response
in the Age of Empire* (2002), 237
world in world history, 181–84
World Trade Center attacks,
148–49
Wretched of the Earth (1961), 267

xenophobia: COVID-19 and anti-
Asian sentiment, 100; recent rise
of, 39, 79, 179
Xenophon (ca. 430–354 BC), 21–22,
249, 256
Xerxes I, 23

Yaqin, Amina, 4
Yathrib (*Madinat al-Nabi*, or City of
the Prophet), 64
Yemen, 112, 148

Zakariya, Fareed, 116
Zarathustra, 253
Zionism, 105–6, 111–12; Palestinian
and Israeli conflict 2021, 284–91
Zoroaster, 253

Founded in 1893,
UNIVERSITY OF CALIFORNIA PRESS
publishes bold, progressive books and journals
on topics in the arts, humanities, social sciences,
and natural sciences—with a focus on social
justice issues—that inspire thought and action
among readers worldwide.

The UC PRESS FOUNDATION
raises funds to uphold the press's vital role
as an independent, nonprofit publisher, and
receives philanthropic support from a wide
range of individuals and institutions—and from
committed readers like you. To learn more, visit
ucpress.edu/supportus.